BIG AND LITTLE HISTORIES

This book introduces students to ethics in historiography through an exploration of how historians in different times and places have explained how history *ought* to be written and how those views relate to different understandings of ethics.

No two histories are the same. The book argues that this is a good thing because the differences between histories are largely a matter of ethics. Looking to histories made across the world and from ancient times until today, readers are introduced to a wide variety of approaches to the ethics of history, including well-known ethical approaches, such as the virtue ethics of universal historians, and utilitarian approaches to collective biography writing while also discovering new and emerging ideas in the ethics of history. Through these approaches, readers are encouraged to challenge their ideas about whether humans are separate from other living and non-living things and whether machines and animals can write histories. The book looks to the fundamental questions posed about the nature of history making by Indigenous history makers and asks whether the ethics at play in the global variety of histories might be better appreciated in professional codes of conduct and approaches to research ethics management.

Opening up the topic of ethics to show how historians might have viewed ethics differently in the past, the book requires no background in ethics or history theory and is open to all of those with an interest in how we think about good histories.

Marnie Hughes-Warrington is Deputy Vice-Chancellor Research and Enterprise at the University of South Australia and Visitor at the School of History, Australian National University, Australia. She is the author of several historiography texts, including *Fifty Key Thinkers on History* (three editions), *History Goes to the Movies* (2007) and *History as Wonder* (2018).

Anne Martin is Director of the Tjabal Indigenous Higher Education Centre at the Australian National University, Australia. She is an Aboriginal rights activist and educator who is dedicated to changing the future for our next generation of leaders.

What does it mean to do history "ethically"? Marnie Hughes-Warrington's book examines this question from a variety of different vantage points, ingeniously linking the continued effort of approaching our pasts morally to the scale and scope by which we comprehend and represent those pasts. Whether it be from the perspective of microhistory, Big history, and everything in between, Hughes-Warrington deploys an assortment of examples from antiquity to 9/11. She thereby raises important issues that have bearing not only on how we engage ethically and empathetically with the world as it was but also with the world as it is and may yet become.

Daniel Woolf, *Queen's University, Canada*

In eminently readable prose, Marnie Hughes-Warrington and Anne Martin take us on a magisterial tour of how narrating the past sheds light on the choices that face us in the present. There's no cookie-cutter way to write the past. Every single choice entails the denial of others. Yet together, the kaleidoscopic range of historical writing offers a vital guide to the never-ending work of leading the good life. *Big and Little Histories* is an indispensable guide in this process.

Sam Wineburg, *Stanford University, USA*

This is an astonishingly agile and stimulating book. It scales heights and depths and zooms in and out, scoping histories from the micro level of minutes to the macro of millennia, as it explores the proposition that Aristotle's modelling of ethics as practical, inexact and plural can help us think productively about histories as much as ethics and about the interactions between them. The book is a history and an exposition of a range of ethical theories – addressing virtue, utilitarian, deontological, cosmopolitan ethics, infinite, entanglement ethics and much more. Equally, it is an exploration of varieties of historiography, including microhistory, children's histories, global histories, collective biographies, and indigenous histories. It is also a sustained reflection on the ethical implications of the form of history telling – exploring circular narrative structures, first and second-personal histories, universal philosophical histories, reflexive histories and much else besides. It does all this with admirable clarity and lightness of touch. The book communicates an infectious curiosity about the rich complexities of human and animal pasts - ranging over slice histories of moments, didactic thumb bibles, Big Histories of 13.8 billion years, snowball hurling, oxygen holocausts, and swarm histories written by algorithms. Its chapters enact their arguments, scale-shifting themselves and anchoring insights in particular moments and in grand narrative arcs. It is both highly readable and cries out to be read and re-read. It will be enjoyed with great profit by students of history and students of philosophy and is an argument by example for closer dialogue between the two.

Arthur Chapman, Associate Professor in History Education, *UCL Institute of Education, UK*

Big and Little Histories is stimulating reading that imaginatively integrates the theories and problems of ethics with the histories of different sizes and shapes across the globe. This is an important book, because it not only argues that ethics is foundational for the writing of history, but also explains how ethics as individual responsibility is relevant and present in this practice.

Jouni-Matti Kuukkanen, *University of Oulu, Finland*

BIG AND LITTLE HISTORIES

Sizing Up Ethics in Historiography

Marnie Hughes-Warrington, with Anne Martin

LONDON AND NEW YORK

First published 2022
by Routledge
2 Park Square, Milton Park, Abingdon, Oxon OX14 4RN

and by Routledge
605 Third Avenue, New York, NY 10158

Routledge is an imprint of the Taylor & Francis Group, an informa business

© 2022 Marnie Hughes-Warrington, with Anne Martin

The right of Marnie Hughes-Warrington, with Anne Martin to be identified as authors of this work has been asserted by them in accordance with sections 77 and 78 of the Copyright, Designs and Patents Act 1988.

The Open Access version of this book, available at www.taylorfrancis. com, has been made available under a Creative Commons Attribution-Non Commercial-No Derivatives 4.0 license.

Trademark notice: Product or corporate names may be trademarks or registered trademarks, and are used only for identification and explanation without intent to infringe.

British Library Cataloguing-in-Publication Data
A catalogue record for this book is available from the British Library

Library of Congress Cataloging-in-Publication Data
A catalog record has been requested for this book

ISBN: 978-0-367-02354-6 (hbk)
ISBN: 978-0-367-02355-3 (pbk)
ISBN: 978-0-429-39999-2 (ebk)

DOI: 10.4324/9780429399992

Typeset in Bembo
by SPi Technologies India Pvt Ltd (Straive)

For Bruce and Ari, loved across all scales

CONTENTS

Acknowledgements	*ix*
Advisory for Aboriginal and Torres Strait Islander readers	*xi*
1 Good histories	1
2 Universal histories and virtue ethics	11
3 Collective biographies and utilitarian ethics	29
4 Philosophical world histories and deontological ethics	47
5 Little world histories and sentiment ethics	65
6 Global histories and cosmopolitan ethics	85
7 Microhistories and social contract ethics	102
8 Slice histories and infinite ethics	118
9 Big histories and information ethics	136
10 Non-human histories and entanglement ethics	154

viii Contents

11 Indigenous histories and place ethics *with Anne Martin*   174

12 One angel? Scaling the ethics of history   184

Bibliography   *188*
Index   *205*

ACKNOWLEDGEMENTS

From Marnie Hughes-Warrington:

You can walk past a door multiple times and not notice it. When you do see it, you wonder where it will lead you. I want to thank everyone who encouraged me to ask why no two histories are the same size and to seek the answer by knocking on doors around the world. Those doors were generously opened by many scholars, and I am profoundly grateful for their intellectual hospitality.

Frank Bongiorno played a key role in encouraging me to step from wonder to ethics in historiography. His support and conviviality, along with that of Chris Wallace, Ann McGrath and other colleagues in the Australian National University School of History, continue to inspire. Peter Harrison, Charlotte Rose-Millar, Ethan Kleinberg, Mark Donnelly, Jouni-Matti Kuukkanen, Arthur Chapman, Anna Clark, Tamson Pietsch, Kristyn Harman, Paul Kiem and colleagues generously hosted seminars and discussions on the ideas in this book—some when my ideas were very nascent—at the Institute for Advanced Studies in the Humanities at the University of Queensland, Wesleyan College, St Mary's University Twickenham, the Centre for Philosophical Studies at Oulu University, University College London, the Australian Centre for Public History at the University of Technology Sydney, the University of Tasmania and the History Teacher's Association of New South Wales. I am also grateful for those who read and commented on sections of the book, including Tyson Retz at Stavanger University, Norway. Merry Wiesner-Hanks and David Christian were thought-provoking interlocutors at the World History Association Conference in San Juan, Puerto Rico, in 2019. The 2019 humanities forum at Rhodes House in Oxford provided a great opportunity to test some of the questions in the conclusion. I am also grateful to the Institute for Advanced Study, Princeton, at which the proposal for this book took shape, and to Roland Wenzelheumer and colleagues at Ludwig Maximilians Universität München, whose generous offer of a research fellowship made it possible to complete the work for Chapter 9.

x Acknowledgements

My thanks to David Lloyd, the Deans Research Group, the Research and Enterprise team and colleagues at the University of South Australia, who encouraged me to write and provided me with the opportunity to do so. The staff at the New South Wales State Library, Macquarie University Library, New York Public Library, British Library, University of Texas miniature book collection and University of South Australia library also made a huge difference through the provision of access to materials from around the world. Aunty Anne Martin and many Ngunnawal, Ngambri and Kaurna Elders have been generous teachers, and I am grateful for the opportunity to continue to learn from them.

Finally, as always, I want to thank the Hughes and the Warrington families for encouraging me—in so many ways, every day—to see ethics as my own making. Finally, B and A, this one is for you, as always. When I write, I say I love you.

From Anne Martin:

As I gaze from my window and take in the beauty of the Arafura Sea on the edge of Larrakeyah country, I remember precious time spent with Marnie here not so long ago. We walked on country and shared stories and learnt so much from each other. From the first moment I sat in a lecture theatre and listened to Marnie speak, I was mesmerised. Here was somebody who did not just tell a story but took you on a journey which was passionate and vibrant, and you not only listened to but felt the words she spoke. The deep respect and understanding that Marnie has of our culture, the oldest living culture in the world, has forged something more than a friendship—to me Marnie, Bruce and Ari are family. I am forever grateful that Marnie knocked on my door and sought some answers, as in asking these questions, she opened my mind to so much that had been locked away for many decades. We walked side by side on a journey that has enriched my life.

ADVISORY FOR ABORIGINAL AND TORRES STRAIT ISLANDER READERS

Aboriginal and Torres Strait Islander readers are advised that this book may contain the names, words and ideas of people who have died.

1

GOOD HISTORIES

KAURNA COUNTRY, ADELAIDE, AUSTRALIA. No two histories are the same size. Some are so tiny that you can nestle them in your hand, their translucent pages fluttering with your breath. Others range over many volumes, challenging the strength of your grip with the combined weight of their leather covers, rag paper pages and glassine illustration protectors. Some hold us enthralled with split-second events in tiny places, others stretch our thoughts by accounting for changes over billions of years across the universe.

It is strange that there is no set size or scale for a history. After all, we have precise and often globally agreed on ways of measuring all kinds of things. There are committees and inspectors to check kilograms and the green of traffic lights, for instance. Not so for histories. This book argues that ethics helps to explain why histories vary in size and scale and that the variety of histories across time and space is good.

This seems like a banal statement. Why, after all, would people make histories unless they thought they were good? Moreover, surely hate histories aren't good. Between any simple statement and split-second riposte, though, lies a vast field of assumptions. These can be difficult to get into focus and to hold in view. They are like doors that you walk past every day without noticing, until one day you do. An unexpected door was opened for me when a flood destroyed the library collection that I used every day for over five years. I realised that I missed the weight and feel of each of the history books that I had read there and that if I thought hard enough about it, I could even remember how big and heavy they were. Just as the floodwaters had punched their way through the collection, it hit me that the size and the scale of histories matters and that they ought not be taken for granted.

With my handheld memories in stock, I journeyed out across libraries and the world to find histories again and to understand why no two are the same. It was only when a global pandemic circumscribed that journey to a suburban house in Adelaide—Kaurna Country to the local Aboriginal people—that I began to

DOI: 10.4324/9780429399992-1

2 Good histories

understand why. Our interactions with a world of bountiful and bounded scales shape us, and us it. Those interactions form part of the ancient expectation that the ethics of history is of our own making, always. What 'our' means in ethics is not universally agreed upon. This is not a bad thing. The variety of histories now, and across time, is a sign of the ethical health of history making.

Introductory texts have much to say about making good histories. Our field is blessed with a bountiful number of these texts, and they offer similar lines of sensible advice. In the preface to the fifth edition of *The Pursuit of History* (2010), for example, John Tosh acknowledges that the discipline of history is a minefield.[1] Disagreement runs through its seams. Nevertheless, he ventures in, characterising history makers as responsible: responsible for thinking about the past, for evading the service of ideology and for presenting ideas and arguments that are relevant to the present.[2] Addressing history students in *The Essential Guide to Writing History Essays* (2020), Kate Antonova also speaks of responsibility. By this she means the student's responsibility of self-regulation, of managing time, staying focused, acknowledging mistakes and asking for help. But it is also the responsibility of the history student to think critically about cause and effect, understand diversity empathetically, process and analyse information and not take historical sources at face value.[3] Antoon de Baets goes even further, signalling in *Responsible History* (2009) that historians have a duty worldwide to protect the right of people to memory and history and to protect those who make histories.[4]

Responsibility is a matter of ethics. Ethics is the study of how we should act. It explores what is good, as well as what is fair and just, to give just a few examples. I can add a few more terms and note that some people see them as synonymous, and some people treat them very differently. We will gain a sense of that variety throughout this book. For the moment, we should note that when people write about the responsibility of history makers, they are writing about the ethics of history.

We can be responsible in different ways. We can be responsible to and for ourselves, to and for others. We can be responsible as individuals and as groups. When people write about the responsibility of history makers and the ethics of history, they tend to have individuals in mind. The constitutions and codes of conduct of organisations like the American Historical Association, the Royal Historical Association, the International Committee of Historical Sciences and the Australian Historical Association foreground the relationship between individual historians and their subjects. They speak, rightly, of informed consent with the living and of the just treatment of those with different backgrounds to the historian. Their views feed into ethics approval processes in which historical subjects are treated as autonomous, independent agents who are asked for informed consent or as vulnerable subjects around whom protections are built.

So too theorists as varied in approach as George Kitson Clark, Arthur Child, E. P. Thompson, David Carr and Rudolf Makkreel and Adrian Oldfield have sought to understand how and why historians as individuals judge the actions of individuals and groups and whether ethical judgements apply only to intentional acts.[5]

Scaling the ethics of history

There is more to the ethics of history than individual responsibility. In order to explain this idea, I would like to switch disciplines for just a moment, from history to health. In writing about the ethics of health, Onora O'Neill opens up an intriguing line of thinking. Public health responsibilities within and beyond states, she observes, are not necessarily the same as those of individual health practitioners towards their patients.[6] Public health promotes the wellbeing of groups—not just individuals—with epidemiology tracking and predicting how those groups are faring. Whereas a health practitioner prioritises informed consent, a public health body may argue for compulsory and uniform measures across a group, as with the measures in a number of states to manage the spread of the novel coronavirus COVID-19. Does history have something akin to public health and epidemiology? Not strictly, if evidence of compulsory or uniform measures like legislation for social distancing, use of seatbelts or plain packaging for cigarettes is required. Yet there is also a sense in which good history making is not entirely a matter of individual decision, as the books and codes of conduct I mentioned earlier show. Groups of people have a view about what counts as good history. If we look across the trends and patterns of those views, can we discern what—if anything—drives them?

Thomas V. Cohen is not unusual in insisting that the history 'discipline, perforce, disciplines' on the basis of financial and moral capital. History, he argues,

> upholds standards of performance, squelching shoddy work and nudging scholars to do their best. Whether a discipline, in doing all this, stifles or encourages eccentric ideas and novel methods that deserve a hearing much depends on its habits, and its openness to nonconformist members and procedures. A discipline channels capital, both the cash it conveys, cascading from granting agencies outside it, and the less tangible moral capital that lodges inside, in the form of prestige, recognition, and esteem. This moral capital dwells in the rankings of its journals, congresses, invited lectures, and awards and in the charisma of host institutions.[7]

For many readers, these words will spark a twinge of recognition and perhaps even disappointment and anger. Yet this notion of history as a discipline is not ultimately convincing. Neither the jurisdiction of history nor the activities of history makers are effectively agreed upon. Insisting that histories are made by those with doctorates, or members of professional organisations or people who know multiple languages, to take just a few examples, does not stop people from making histories. Indeed, a history made without fulfilling any of these requirements can be a bestseller or even critically acclaimed. History making has never been a tightly bounded or policed activity, as its own history shows. If financial and moral capital are the drivers of good history making, it would be hard to argue that history making is hermetically sealed off from other decisions about what is good in other disciplines and everyday life.

4 Good histories

Take the example of Richard J. Evans' expert testimony in the case of *David Irving v. Penguin Books and Deborah Lipstadt*.[8] Evans' contribution proved a powerful counter to those who wish to minimise or deny the Holocaust. It should not escape our attention, though, that Evans was asked for expert advice within a court of law and that he did not hand down the formal judgement. In Cohen's terms, this is an example of moral capital being disciplined by law. There are many other examples that spring to mind, as with political decisions to review or to introduce particular history curriculums or to build museums or memorials to commemorate particular events or phenomena. Yet neither law nor formal politics account for the variety of histories made, in the same way that I argued earlier that professional bodies are not in the sole driving seat of determining what history is.

Hayden White provides another explanation in the idea of history as narrative.[9] He asks us to appreciate that narrative and genre conventions are powerful shapers of the content of the form of history. This makes a lot of sense: his accounting for particular histories as tragedies or romances rings true with the literary devices that history makers use.[10] Yet White never saw narrative as fully explaining why histories take a variety of forms: he saw it as diagnostic of ideology and that ideology, in turn, was diagnostic of ethics. As he argued in his classic text *Metahistory*,

> In my view, there are no extra-ideological grounds on which to arbitrate among the conflicting conceptions of the historical process and of historical knowledge appealed to by the different ideologies. For, since these conceptions have their origins in ethical considerations, the assumption of a given epistemological position by which to judge their cognitive adequacy would itself represent only another ethical choice.[11]

Ethics shapes ideology, ideology shapes narrative. This is a powerful and intriguing claim. White speaks of the ethical moment when the history maker selects materials. In the act of selection, the world goes from *as is* to *as it ought* to be understood in the hands of the history maker.[12] White thereby sharpens and refines our focus on the history maker's responsibility, as with Tosh and Antonova. But what is the nature of that responsibility and of that ethics? Where does it come from?

The answer to this question does not rest with White or with any thinker from our times. Much of our global understanding of the ethics of history as the individual responsibility of the history maker has its roots in the writings of Plato and, more importantly, Aristotle. This is not to suggest that history makers acknowledge Aristotle as a progenitor or that they have followed what he said about ethics either knowingly or strictly. My argument, is, rather, that he thought about ethics in ways that have had a profound impact on history making. More specifically, I hold that the variety of histories stems in no small part from Aristotle's account of ethics as our practical and inexact efforts to do good and to live well, as *ethos*.

My argument: the ethics of history is effort, *Ethos*

In my last book, I highlighted the role of metaphysics—the branch of philosophy which aims to make sense of how the world hangs together—in the history of histories. I noted that history and philosophy give shape to one another and that the idea of wonder has in some ways fuelled that mutual relationship. This is an idea I credited back to Aristotle.[13] But I also observed that our attempts to make sense of the world are often accounts of how it *ought* to be, rather than how it was or is. I let that view stand, without fully explaining it. What I did not account for was the variety of those explanations of how the world ought to be. This book brings the ethics of history to the foreground, whilst acknowledging that the sense making activity of metaphysics still matters. They belong together, but each deserves substantive attention.

Moreover, Aristotle's role in the ethics of history deserves substantive attention. Aristotle did not invent ethics, and he arguably did not invent metaphysics either. He certainly did not invent philosophy. Nor could it be argued that philosophy worldwide, or history making worldwide, are simple variations on his work. He did, though, say two things about the nature of ethics which have played a shaping role in history making and which are underappreciated. In combination, they help to explain why histories come in different sizes and scales. Their application has resulted in a variety of views of the ethics of history and of history making.

Aristotle viewed ethics as practical and inexact. These two ideas play a critical role in this book and form the basis of my argument that individual histories, and the wider body of histories over time and space, are expressions of *ethos*, the effort of ethics.

Like Plato (428–4 to 348/7 BCE) before him, Aristotle characterised ethics as practical. A practical endeavour is not the study of something for its own sake or pleasure, it should help us to live well (*Eudemian Ethics*, 1241a; *Nicomachean Ethics*, 1139a26–8; 1149b29–32). This is still our expectation of ethics: ethics helps us in everyday life, particularly when we face tough questions about what we ought to do. When we think about what we ought to do, we can look to other people and other sources of information for guidance. This long-standing treatment of ethics as practical helps to explain why people look to literature, to the law and to history, to name just a few examples, for guidance on what they ought to do and how they ought to live. It explains why some people think of history as philosophy teaching by example or history as a source of lessons that we either heed or ignore. It is a view of the purpose of history making that has been present since ancient times and which is found in various forms of history making across the world.

Aristotle also saw ethics as inexact. This, as Brad Inwood and Raphael Woolf have noted, is one of the most striking and underappreciated features of Aristotle's ethics. Inwood and Woolf see this as part reflection of the audience Aristotle sought to address in his ethical works: those experienced in politics rather than those experienced in philosophy.[14] But it also chimes true when we consider Aristotle's

6 Good histories

further claim that there is no simple relationship between good acts and a good life. Aristotle cites the examples of wealth fuelling misery and of courage costing you your life (*Nicomachean Ethics*, 1094b1; 1106a–b28; 1106a36–b7). Yet whilst Aristotle identified a number of virtues that he saw as key to living a good life—and characterised each in words and chart form as the mean between vices—he did not see living them as a simple matter. To put it in everyday terms, ethics is not a matter of a checklist or a tick box activity that we can follow without thinking or without taking responsibility.

Aristotle had more to say about the inexact nature of ethics that is important for our purposes. He noted that we can have different expectations about exactness and precision in different endeavours and that the exactness of ethics is more like that of a carpenter than of a mathematician. Consequently, navigation to any virtue will be an imprecise act, like navigating out of a dark tunnel by veering from one side to another. He explains the first point in *Nicomachean Ethics* 1904b:

> Now our treatment of this science will be adequate, if it achieves that amount of precision which belongs to its subject matter. The same exactness must not be expected in all departments of philosophy alike, any more than in all the products of the arts and crafts.... We must therefore be content if, in dealing with subjects and starting from premises thus uncertain, we succeed in presenting a broad outline of the truth: when our subjects and our premises are mere generalities, it is enough if we arrive at generally valid conclusions. Accordingly we may ask the student also to accept the various views we put forward in the same spirit; for it is the mark of an educated mind to expect that amount of exactness in each kind which the nature of the particular subject admits. It is equally unreasonable to accept merely probable conclusions from a mathematician and to demand strict demonstration from an orator.

Earlier on, in 1098a, he explains the second point by comparing the right angles of the carpenter and the mathematician:

> We must not look for equal exactness in all departments of study, but only such as belongs to the subject matter of each, and in such a degree as is appropriate to the particular line of enquiry. A carpenter and a geometrician both try to find a right angle, but in different ways; the former is content with that approximation to it which satisfies the purpose of his work; the latter, being a student of truth, seeks to find its essence or essential attributes. We should therefore proceed in the same manner in other subjects also, and not allow side issues to outbalance the main task in hand.
>
> (See also *Eudemian Ethics*, 1142a)

The third and subsequent point concerning the inexactness of navigating to any virtuous mean follows in 1109b:

> This much then is clear, that it is the middle disposition in each department of conduct that is to be praised, but that each should lean sometimes to the side of excess and sometimes to that of deficiency, since this is the easiest way of hitting the mean and the right course.

It is worth letting what Aristotle has to say sink in. The level of precision we need in ethics is not the same as for other kinds of philosophy. This is not a deficit, but appropriate for thinking about everyday problems which can have multiple, conflicting answers.

Now instead of thinking of the previous excerpts with the example of a carpenter, what if we substituted in a history maker and replayed the line of argument? We would read that we should not expect a history maker to use the same levels of precision as a mathematician. Indeed, expecting them to do so might get in the way of them being able to engage with the task at hand. That task is to select and to connect information to account for the world as it ought to be understood, as theorists like White have suggested. That history maker is responsible for that selection and connection of information, as writers like Tosh and Antonova remind us. That history maker, we learn further, cares about 'right angles' but turns out slightly different work every time, as the maker of craft or art. We expect individual history makers and groups of history makers to produce work that is different. Those differences are not the sign of deficient work but reflect the effort of ethics.

Aristotle's ethics helps us to see is that history is not an endeavour to be got precisely right, once. We should expect there to be histories, plural, and we expect there to be ethics, plural. We will have to look over time and space to see those histories. The ethics of history is thus historical and global. Conversely, we should be worried about claims that a history is definitive or the last word. In Aristotle's terms, this denotes a backing away from the responsibility of thinking through ethical problems now and into the future. We expect history makers to keep exploring topics, even if they have been much explored in the past. Furious agreement can be the territory of history's dark angels or hate histories. Another way of putting this is to say that history making is an unending effort to do good, which Aristotle described as *ethos*. He saw ethics as an unending activity in which we grapple with what we ought to do.

As this book will show, the history of history making is shaped in no small part by *ethos*, the effort of ethics. It is not just seen in the ways in which historians treat other individuals. It is seen in acts of selection and connection that include and exclude humans, living and non-living entities. It is seen in the choice of tiny and enormous spatio-temporal scales. It is seen in speeding through and skipping events, and in dwelling on micro-moments. Intriguingly, it is also seen in scale switching, when history makers slip seamlessly from talking about individuals to groups and back again or use little histories like blocks to build up a big account of how the world ought to be understood. And it is seen over time and across the globe. This ethics of history cannot be described as a simple act of tipping in or taking out evidence, or of folding and smoothing out a narrative. This is because the dynamic shifts in the sizes and scales of histories over time and across the world have ushered

8 Good histories

in repeated challenges to the idea of ethics as being concerned with humans or even living entities, let alone treating those entities as autonomous or even distinctive. Practically, too, history makers have repeatedly challenged the idea of codes for the conduct of responsible research as addressing human, adult history makers.

These challenges and their driver—the underlying expectation that ethics is of our own making and inexact—ensure that history making is never at rest and never effectively agreed upon. They keep the ethics of history historical and open to change in the future. Asking whether machines can make histories and whether there was a bacterial 'holocaust' billions of years ago are not destabilising, destructive questions but signs of the ethical health of history making. When you see a collection of histories and none of them are the same, you are not seeing a replication crisis. You are seeing ethics at work. You see good histories.

My journey in this book: the ethics of history is practical

The ethics of history is a much bigger topic than has been credited in the past. We can find ethics at play in most of the choices made by history makers. It is not possible for me to cover all of the contours of *ethos* in this book.

This book argues for a bigger view of the ethics of history via a selection of histories across time and space. In one way, it might be thought of as an introductory ethics text in the manner of Peter Singer's *Practical Ethics*, which stressed its practicality through a range of examples.[15] Unlike *Practical Ethics*, however, this book is not an argument for a single—utilitarian—view of ethics. Rather, it is an argument for us to appreciate the generative nature of Aristotle's theory of ethics. If you present ethics, as Aristotle did, as a practical and inexact effort, you can expect that lots of different ethical questions, answers, actions and artefacts will result over time and space. This is thus a book which shows that a variety of approaches to history making have been, and continue to be, connected to a variety of ethical theories.

Virtue ethics is included, as you might expect of an ethics text, as well as utilitarianism. But this is not the simple story of how history makers adopt and use ethical theories invented by philosophers. The effort of history making means that the ethics of history will not be a simple recital. Rather, I show that various ways of thinking about ethics can be transformed and challenged through the leaps, skips and scale switches of history makers. It is also a story about history making in the broad, from women's collective biographies through to Indigenous histories, African novels to photographs and from big histories to microhistories. These histories encourage us to consider views of ethics that are often not well captured, or even seen, in philosophical discussions. To that end, the ethics of history may contribute to new understandings of ethics.

Finally, this is also a practical ethics in that it involves me. In the local Aboriginal language Kaurna, the question 'Niina marni' means not only 'How are you going?' but also 'Where are you going?' This book documents some of my journey with *ethos* across forms of history making and across place. It shows how everyday experiences have encouraged me to think about the ethics of history, reinforcing the practical nature of the ethics of history.

Chapter 2 connects our daily encounters with extremes back to the moderating moves of virtue ethicists and ancient universal historians in the Hellenistic and Islamic worlds. Chapter 3 explores whether the little goods we do can be aggregated into larger ones in the manner of an industrial production line through a look at utilitarian ethics and modern women's collective biographies. Discerning ethical rules in everyday life, and through the nesting of little histories within bigger ones, is the focus of Chapter 4, which looks to philosophical world histories and deontological ethics. Chapter 5 looks at how the ambiguous limits of 'you' and 'our' in little world histories made for children can open up a universe of sensed universal ethical connections.

Chapter 6, written in the aftermath of Hurricane Maria on Puerto Rico, acknowledges the fences, boundaries and structures that complicate attempts at cosmopolitan ethics and global history making. Chapter 7 looks to strange encounters in the present and the past of microhistories to ask whether our ethical structures have to turn on human relationships. Chapter 8 stretches the boundaries of human relational ethics by asking why it is hard to write histories of mass murder and genocide at scale, whereas Chapter 9 makes the case for lifting history and ethics up to consider the flourishing of all living and non-living entities. This opens the way for us to consider histories made by artificial agents. Chapter 10 teases that idea apart via an exploration of the idea that non-human entities may make history for us, and we them, in a universe of entanglements. This is a world in which histories can be made, for example, using ant colony optimisation algorithms. This paves the way for chapter eleven—made with Aunty Anne Martin—which explores how Aboriginal and Indigenous thinkers view place, time and ethics as one.

I hope that the examples canvassed in this book will encourage you to see that history making is not separate from our daily lives. It is also not separate from the places where we live and interact with others. It took a flood and a journey across the world for me to begin to understand the depth, complexity and timeliness of Australian Aboriginal ethical views of country. Aunty Anne Martin played a pivotal role in helping my understanding to grow. My journey in understanding the ethics of country is not finished, and nor is my journey with the ethics of history and history theory. The effort of *ethos* continues for me, as it does for history making around the world. As I hope this book will show, the ethics of history is unending.

Notes

1 John Tosh, *The Pursuit of History*, 5/e, London: Pearson, 2010, p. ix.
2 John Tosh, *The Pursuit of History*, pp. 9, 37, 51.
3 Kate Pickering Antonova, *The Essential Guide to Writing History Essays*, Oxford: Oxford University Press, 2020, pp. 10, 47, 103, 155.
4 Antoon de Baets, *Responsible History*, Oxford: Berghahn, 2009.
5 See for example, Brian Fay (ed), *History and Theory: History and Ethics Theme Issue*, 2004, vol. 43(4) for contributions by Frank Ankersmit, Antoon de Baets, Michael Bentley, James Cracraft, Elizabeth Deeds Ermath, Jonathan Gorman, Keith Jenkins, Jörn Rüsen and Richard T. Vann. See also David Carr and Rudolf Makreel (eds), *The Ethics of History*,

10 Good histories

Evanston, IL: Northwestern University Press, 2004; Adrian Oldfield, 'Moral Judgements in History', *History and Theory*, 1981, vol. 20(3), pp. 260–77; E. P. Thompson, 'The Moral Economy of the English Crowd in the Eighteenth Century', *Past and Present*, 1971, no. 50, pp. 76–136; George Kitson Clark, *The Critical Historian*, London: Routledge, 1967; and Arthur Child, 'Moral Judgement in History', *Ethics*, 1951, vol. 61(4), pp. 297–308.

6 Onora O'Neill, *Justice across Boundaries: Whose Obligations?*, Cambridge: Cambridge University Press, 2016.

7 Thomas V. Cohen, *Roman Tales: A Reader's Guide to the Art of Microhistory*, Abingdon: Routledge, 2019.

8 See the judgement of Charles Gray, *Irving v. Penguin Books Limited, Deborah E. Lipstadt*, EWHC QB 115 (11 April 2000), online at: https://www.bailii.org/ew/cases/EWHC/QB/2000/115.html; and Richard J. Evans, *Lying about Hitler: History, the Holocaust, and the David Irving Trial*, New York: Basic Books, 2001.

9 Hayden White, *The Content of the Form: Narrative Discourse and Historical Representation*, Baltimore, MD: Johns Hopkins University Press, 1990.

10 Hayden White, *Metahistory: The Historical Imagination in Nineteenth-Century Europe*, Baltimore, MD: Johns Hopkins University Press, 1975.

11 Hayden White, *Metahistory*, p. 26.

12 Hayden White, *Metahistory*, p. 27.

13 Marnie Hughes-Warrington, *History as Wonder: Beginning with Historiography*, Abingdon: Routledge, 2019.

14 Brad Inwood and Raphael Woolf, 'Introduction,' *Eudemian Ethics*, Cambridge: Cambridge University Press, 2013, pp. xxii.

15 Peter Singer, *Practical Ethics*, 3/e, Cambridge: Cambridge University Press, 2011.

Primary texts

Aristotle, *Eudemian Ethics*, Cambridge: Cambridge University Press, 2013.

Aristotle, *Nicomachean Ethics*, 2/e, Cambridge: Cambridge University, 2014.

Australian Historical Association Code of Ethics https://www.theaha.org.au/about-the-aha/aha-code-of-ethics/ <accessed 15 April 2020>.

International Committee of Historical Sciences Constitution http://www.cish.org/index.php/en/presentation/constitution/ <accessed 20 April 2020>.

Royal Historical Society Statement on Ethics https://royalhistsoc.org/rhs-statement-ethics/ <accessed 15 April 2020>.

2

UNIVERSAL HISTORIES AND VIRTUE ETHICS

Elias Lönnrot | Herodotus | Diodorus Siculus | Paulus Orosius | Rashīd al-Dīn Ṭabīb | Atâ-Malek Juvayni | Aristotle

OULU, FINLAND. It is broad daylight at 9 p.m. Our talk is of the left-wing, right-wing vision of history promoted by the Finns Party, *Perussuomalaiset*. I can't make sense of it. Grasping, I reach back to Eric Hobsbawm's description of our times as an 'Age of Extremes' and his warnings about the harm that historians can do with ordinary words.[1] Histories, he wrote in 1997, 'can turn into bomb factories like the workshops in which the [Irish Republican Army] has learned to transform chemical fertiliser into an explosive'.[2] In the 20 years following his warning, passenger planes and trucks became weapons, and the number of histories and history makers burgeoned with large thanks to the internet and social media. Yet for all of Hobsbawm's foresight, I do not think he counted on the Finns Party's take on history, or others like it. If you have a left-wing, right-wing account of history, does that mean the cancellation of extremes and a potentially peaceful future? Or does it mean a state of tension, an unstable touchpaper ready to ignite?

The Finns have a past to explain the coexistence of extremes, and they call it *The Kalevala*. *The Kalevala* is a collection of stories and songs from Finland, Sápmi and Karelia which Elias Lönnrot crafted into a poetic epic in the mid-nineteenth century. As an epic, it meets the expectation—articulated as far back as Aristotle's *Poetics*—of a tragic story form. Its characters navigate multiple reversals of fortune (*Poetics*, 1450a). Much of what drives those reversals are the choices of its characters. Sometimes they decide to act in ways that you and I might see as good, and sometimes they act in ways that we would seek to avoid. Over the course of the epic, we build up a picture of each individual's character—their ethical qualities as virtues or vices—and we may judge them to be better or worse than ourselves (*Poetics*, 1448a). Sometimes these judgements are easy to make, but most of the time, they are hard because the characters are neither persistently good nor bad. They even veer one way and the other, moving between extremes.

DOI: 10.4324/9780429399992-2

12 Universal histories and virtue ethics

This focus on character makes *The Kalevala*, in part, a useful introduction to character-based, or virtue-based ethics, which is the focus of this chapter. Yet it is also a magical work. The world it describes is wrought from the fragments of eggs, and prosperity and poverty flow from the location of fragments of the mysterious object called the sampo. What joins or breaks apart these fragments—and other parts of the world—is words. Words spoken or sung by the characters diminish rivals, resurrect the dead and summon entities that are 'neither big nor small' to find things for them (9:288; 9:296; 20:20). Words keep the world of *The Kalevala* connected and in motion. It is never firmly or stably a place of virtue or vice, veering in the manner of its characters.

History makers have also long been interested in character and virtue, reversals of fortune and extremes. Their works, this book argues, are no less magical. They, too, construct worlds from fragments, transforming evidence into history through the power of words, images, movements and sounds. They have done so at least as far back as the first universal histories, which lived in spoken, sung and drawn forms long before they were written down. Universal history writing took flight in the sixth century BCE in the wake of imperial and military campaigns, the advent of standardised systems of chronology and the spread of monotheistic religions, such as Christianity and Islam. Writers followed no single template, and, consequently, their works varied widely in scope, form and purpose. Eusebius of Caesarea (c. 263–339 CE), St. Augustine of Hippo (354–430 CE) and Bishop Otto of Freising (c. 1111–58 CE), for example, narrated the history of God's work in the world through a seven-age framework which had been adapted from Jewish works like Josephus ben Matthias' *Jewish Antiquities* (93 CE). Islamic writers like Abu Ja'far al-Tabari (c. 839–923 CE) also saw universal history as structured through successive ages, but the number of ages in their works was more often three than seven. Furthermore, they derived their status as universal histories in part because of their construction out of *isnāds*: unbroken chains of transmission. For many writers across the Islamic world, universal history thus entailed both chronological and historiographical continuity.

Chronologically arranged universal histories were also produced in China, as with Sima Guang's (1019–86 CE) *Zi Zhi Tong Jian* (*Comprehensive Mirror to Aid in Government*) demonstrates, but thematically and chronologically histories were more common. The first four official histories, the *Shiji* (*Records of the Grand Historian*) begun by Sima Tan (d. c. 110 BCE) and completed by Sima Qian (145–80 BCE), the *Hanshu* (*History of the Former Han Dynasty*) by Ban Gu (32–92 CE), the *Sanguozhi* (*History of the Three Kingdoms*) by Chen Shou (d. 297 CE) and the *Hou Han shu* (*History of the Later Han*) by Fan Ye (398–445 CE) established a four-part division of histories into imperial annals (*benji*), tables of government office events (*biao*), treatises on features of the natural and human-made world (*shu*) and biographies or memoirs (*juan* or *liezhaun*). Though modified, this structure was employed in official histories right up to *Qingshi gao* (*Draft History of the Qing Dynasty*, 1928).

Even if European, Islamic and Chinese universal histories were written in a strictly chronological style, they were still more or less connected, unified or explained by a kind of phenomenon, idea, concept or truth. A very simple hypothetical example

Universal histories and virtue ethics **13**

might be a history of the known world as explained by our relationship with sugar, or cats. Yet my examples—which I will explore further in the world histories of objects and organisms in Chapter 8—do not square with the history of universal histories. Rather, they tend to have been seen by their makers as unified by human or divine attributes and, more particularly, human qualities taken to be good or bad, or in or out of alignment with fortune or the divine. Universal histories were thus ethical statements about how the world ought to be, as well as how it had been.

The first written universal history that we know about was Hecateus of Miletus' *Perigesis* ('Journey Around the World'), which survives only as a description in Herodotus' (c.484–25 BCE) *The Histories*. Herodotus saw Hecateus' account as inaccurate, and he set himself the task of describing the world more reasonably and in a few words (2.4.36). Describing the world in a few words requires selection. Herodotus' interest—and basis for selection—is signalled in the opening of *The Histories*. He does not want the 'great and marvellous' deeds from the past to be forgotten (*The Histories*, 1.1.0).

Herodotus' opening words suggest a focus on actions and character, much like that of the younger work *The Kalevala*. Would this have made *The Histories* an epic? Aristotle did not think so. He saw history and epic poetry as distinct. As he explains in *Poetics*,

> The writings of Herodotus could be put into verse and yet would still be a kind of history, whether written in metre or not. The real difference is this, that one tells what happened and the other what might happen. For this reason poetry is something more scientific and serious than history, because poetry tends to give general truths while history gives particular facts. By a 'general truth' I mean the sort of thing that a certain type of man will do or say either probably or necessarily.
>
> (1451b)

What we see here is the assumption that history deals with what happened, and epic poetry deals with what might happen. This distinction follows from Aristotle's claim that history deals with particular facts and poetry with general truths.

At first sight, this seems a reasonable division. Yet I do not believe that Aristotle was right in this case. History makers are interested in what is good in a general sense. Moreover, this has been a long-held interest, and it has generated a range of innovative claims about ethics. In this chapter, I will begin to unfold this claim by showing how Herodotus and a range of universal history makers from the ancient and medieval world helped to make virtue ethics historical in nature. Herodotus, Diodorus Siculus (90–30 BCE), Paulus Orosius (375–420 CE), Atâ-Malek Juvayni (1226–83 CE) and Rashīd al-Dīn Ṭabīb (1247–1318 CE) used spatio-temporal scales dynamically in their works in part because of their assumptions about virtue ethics. They established a tradition of scale shifting that persists in history making today—an ethical blueprint, if you like, that has remained out of focus for too long. It is time to bring that blueprint into view so that we can better understand the nature of ethics in history making today.

14 Universal histories and virtue ethics

Dynamic virtue ethics

It is important to begin by saying a little about the nature of virtue ethics. Virtue ethicists focus on people's actions. They consider how people act in specific times and places but also how they act over the course of their lives. They do so in order to help us to understand how to live a good life. The first major virtue ethicists that we know about, Plato and Aristotle, thought that living a good life was the key to happiness and wellbeing, or eudaimonia (εὐδαιμονία; Plato, *Euthydemus* 282a1; Aristotle, Nicomachean *Ethics*, 1094a; and *Eudemian Ethics* 1214a). Living the good life, Plato and Aristotle argued, resulted from exercising virtues—ethical dispositions or skills—rationally. They both named specific virtues in their works, and their lists overlapped in part. Plato's *Republic* included an extended exploration by Socrates of how his companions understood the virtues of justice, courage, piety and wisdom (*Republic*, 427e–434c). Aristotle shared an interest with Plato in courage and temperance as major virtues, but he also devoted considerable discussion to the traits of what he called liberality, magnificence, ambition, good temper, truthfulness, wit, friendliness, modesty and proper indignation.

Aristotle also explained the nature of the virtues in ways that turned out to be influential in history making. I want to focus on two ideas that he promoted. First, Aristotle thought of the virtues as developing through habit or *ethos* (ἦθος). This means that we are neither born virtuous, nor virtuous without effort. Living the good life and experiencing happiness and wellbeing takes time. We need to look across our own lives, and those of others—at history, in short—to see whether virtuous behaviour is evident. Moreover, we need to look across time because Aristotle thought that *ethos* involved steering between vices to reach a virtuous mean or middle way. (*Eudemian Ethics*, 1220b; *Nicomachean Ethics* 1104a, 1108b). This is why some people call virtue ethics 'goldilocks' ethics because the virtues are 'just right'. Aristotle did not see steering to the virtues as finely tuned. He saw us as prone to oversteer between vices in developing the virtues, but he also did not see this as a problem. Indeed, he thought of our clumsy attempts at practising ethics as the best way to attain the virtues. As he writes in *Nicomachean Ethics*,

> This much then is clear, that it is the middle disposition in each department of conduct that is to be praised, but that should lean sometimes to the side of excess and sometimes to that of deficiency, since this is the easiest way of hitting the mean and the right course.
>
> (*Nicomachean Ethics* 1109b)

Ethics is lived and not just thought, and living ethics is not a precise or fine-tuned activity. As a consequence, if we look at one action at one point in time, we might not get a good read on our own or another person's character. We may need to cast the net wider, to scale our view in order to gain a sense of character. This will also not be a fine-grained appraisal because Aristotle reminds us that there is no one way to steer to the virtues, and we may not exhibit the same virtues as one another. A sick person, for example, may see health as good, a poor person wealth as good. Yet it is also possible to be healthy or wealthy and to be unhappy. It may be good for an athlete to eat large amounts of food, for example, but not a person who exercises very little. You have to live the virtues and not just think about them (1103b; *Eudemian Ethics* 1152a). This makes it helpful to look at a range of peoples' actions. You can do so at a point in time, but you can also do so over time, in histories.

The second idea Aristotle promoted is that virtues might be seen in groups of people, as well as individuals. Consider these passages in *Nicomachean Ethics*:

> For even though it be the case that the Good is the same for the individual and the state, nevertheless, the good of the state is manifestly a greater and more perfect good, both to attain and to preserve. To secure the good of one person only is better than nothing; but to secure the good of a nation or a state is a nobler and more divine achievement.
>
> (1094b)

And,

> It is clear that we should consider it more desirable when even the smallest of other good things were combined with it, since this addition would result in a larger total of the good, and of two goods the greater is always the more desirable.
>
> (1097b)

We can see that this is not just an argument that *ethos* applies to groups as well as to individuals. It is also suggested that the good attained by groups is greater and more perfect than that by individuals on account of combination or addition. This means that I might do well to consider my actions or those of others in a group over time.

Aristotle's two ideas point us in the direction of seeing virtue ethics in action over time and space. More than that, they encourage scaling: to see the practice of ethics—*ethos*—over big spans of time and space. For these reasons, I think of virtue ethics as well-tuned to history making.

Herodotus and pre-Socratic ethics

I am not the first person to see the connection between the virtues and larger-scale writings. Credit for that belongs to a range of ancient writers. As Charles Kahn observed, pre-Socratic Greek prose writers presented inquiries (ἱστορίη or historiē) in the manner applied to the past by Herodotus.[3] These inquiries explored topics such as cosmology and geography, but they also made observations that can be read as ethical statements. There were a few soundings of the idea that opposites must be navigated in life, as with this fragment from Heraclitus (c.535–c.475 BCE): 'It is not better for humans to get all they want. It is sickness that makes health pleasant and good; hunger, plenty; weariness, rest'.[4] Sound thinking about these interconnections in a universe in which some things persist through flux was in Heraclitus' view the greatest virtue.[5]

16 Universal histories and virtue ethics

Soundings about ethics can also be found in universal histories, like Herodotus' *The Histories*. Indeed, commentators like Lisa Hau have described ancient universal histories as ethically saturated. As she argues, 'Wherever we look, we find historiographers referring to the didactic usefulness of their works and readers of historiography expecting to learn something from them'.[6] She has backed this claim up with a careful study of the virtues and vices that interested a range of history makers. More can be said, though, about how these works describe individuals and groups as leaning one way or another in developing *ethos*. This encourages us to think about the form as well as the contents of works like *The Histories* and more particularly Herodotus' shifts in time and space.

Herodotus was born in Halicarnassus in the Persian Empire, and *The Histories* was an account of the Greco-Persian Wars between 499 and 449 BCE. Herodotus has long been acknowledged for his writing style, as well as his understanding of his world. Ingrid Beck, Henry Immerwahr, Irene de Jong and Rosalind Thomas, for example, have all argued that Herodotus was a skilful ring writer like the epic poet Homer.[7] This argument has merit, for there are a number of places in *The Histories* where we can see what we might call an A-B-A sequence. A good way to explain this is through the use of an example like the sequence 6.121.1–123.1 in which I have used A and B to signal his shifts:

> [A] It is a wonder to me—indeed, I do not accept the story—that the Alcmaeonidae ever showed that shield by arrangement with the Persians or that they were willing to subject the Athenians to the barbarians and Hippias, inasmuch as they can be clearly seen to be at least as much haters of despots as Callias or even more. Callias was the son of Phaenippus and father of Hipponicus, and he was the only one of all the Athenians who dared to buy at public auction the goods of the despot Pisistratus when he was expelled from Athens, and in other ways he showed the bitterest enmity to the despot.
> [B] Everyone should remember Callias on many grounds. First, as I said before, he was a man who had a chief share in freeing his country; and second for his wins at Olympia, where he won the horse race, ridden, and was second with the four-horse chariot, and for his earlier victories at the Pythian games. He made a great show before all the Greeks for his immense spending. And then again, what a man he proved himself to be in the matter of his three daughters! For when they were all ripe for marriage, he gave them the most magnificent present: their free-will choice of any man in Athens that each of them wanted!
> [A] The Alcmaeonidae were certainly no less against despots than this man. As I said, it is a wonder to me, and I do not admit the charge, that they showed that shield as a signal.

Ring sequences can be used for many reasons. In epic poems like Homer's *Iliad* or *The Kalevala*, for example, repeated phrases and arguments might have been used as a memory aid for those saying or singing the story. 'It is a wonder to me', for example, might function as a memory prompt, as well as a statement of distancing. But the example also opens up a relatively complex picture of Callias II (500–432 BCE) in few words. Section A details his stance against despots. This is counterbalanced by the claim in B that he was profligate. In the return to A, his stance against despots is again noted, but it is tempered by the statement that he was not isolated in his stance. Indeed, we see the suggestion that a group—the Alcmaeonidae—of narrative rings can make an ethical point and, indeed, a nuanced or even complex one.

Herodotus' use of ring structures might be thought of as contributing to *ethos*: re-stating for the development of ethical appreciation and understanding. He did not, however, use ring structures all the time. Arguably just as pervasive was his use of variant or conflicting explanations of events or things. F. J. Groten has noted that there are over 120 examples of this throughout *The Histories*.[8] They range from slightly different accounts of the same thing through to contrasting explanations. Most of the time, Herodotus resolved the variants he presented, and we might think of these cases as supporting his claims to methodological rigour. On other occasions, though, he did not. In some of these cases, Herodotus tells us that he could not confirm what happened because the evidence was not definitive. This is seen in the example of him withholding judgement about whether the Spartan prince Dorieus (d. 510 BCE) assisted the Sybarites in battle (5.44.1–45.2). In other parts of the text, he withheld judgement because differing views of good and justice were at stake. Consider his account of when the Pelasgians were driven from Attica to Lemnos by the Athenians:

> When the Pelasgians were driven out of Attica by the Athenians, whether justly or unjustly I cannot say, beyond what is told; namely, that Hecataeus the son of Hegesandrus declares in his history that the act was unjust; for when the Athenians saw the land under Hymettus, formerly theirs, which they had given to the Pelasgians as a dwelling-place in reward for the wall that had once been built around the acropolis—when the Athenians saw how well this place was tilled which previously had been bad and worthless, they were envious and coveted the land, and so drove the Pelasgians out on this and no other pretext. But the Athenians themselves say that their reason for expelling the Pelasgians was just. The Pelasgians set out from their settlement at the foot of Hymettus and wronged the Athenians in this way: Neither the Athenians nor any other Hellenes had servants yet at that time, and their sons and daughters used to go to the Nine Wells for water; and whenever they came, the Pelasgians maltreated them out of mere arrogance and pride. And this was not enough for them; finally they were caught in the act of planning to attack Athens.
>
> (6.137.1–138.1)

Herodotus cannot tell us what is just or unjust in this case. All we can see are claims and counterclaims of envy and covetousness, and arrogance and pride. As with *The Kalevala*, we come to appreciate in Herodotus' *Histories* that we sometimes encounter extremes that cannot be reconciled in a moment. What we can do is look over a longer course of time to see whether the character of groups becomes clearer.

18 Universal histories and virtue ethics

Variants and rings highlight contrasts in and across time. Conversely, they can highlight connections. Herodotus assumes, for example, that the same virtues and vices demonstrated by individuals can also be demonstrated by groups. Individuals can be profligate; groups can be profligate. Variants and rings can, therefore, also highlight contrasts at different group or spatial scales. Callias II stands against despots; the Alcmaeonidae stand against despots. Can you see the magic he has wrought here? He shifts spatio-temporal scales. Herodotus writes about individuals, then groups and then individuals, all the time emphasising the virtues and vices at play in the contrasts and continuations of the past.

We might not think of this as particularly novel but imagine a world in which histories do not shift scales. Consider the hypothetical example of a history that looks to the actions of one person at one point every year. This hypothetical is feasible, and it is even possible that a history like this has been made. It is not, however, a requirement that all history makers do this. History makers shift scales frequently and often fluidly. Indeed, they do this so routinely now that it is hard to bring it into focus. This means in practical terms that large-scale histories can also include small-scale events and phenomena, and small-scale histories can also include large-scale events and phenomena. A world history may include an account of one moment in an individual's life; a microhistory may include an account of long-range environmental changes on a global scale. Histories are mixed in the way that the characters of individuals and groups are mixed. Anyone who sees bigger and smaller histories as opposites or as extremes has likely not accounted for this point.

Herodotus wanted the actions and character of individuals and groups to be remembered. He shifted spatio-temporal scales and contrasted people and things in order to do that. He did so practically: he did not present a theory of ethics in the manner of Aristotle, and the pre-Socratic philosophers rarely rate a mention in his inquiry. Yet Herodotus' world is more than the details of its wars and virtues and vices; it is one of contrasts and flux, like that of Heraclitus.[9]

Universal histories and *ethos*

While the traces of pre-Socratic ethics are like fine lacework in Herodotus' *The Histories*, it is much easier to discern the imprint of Plato's—and often more significantly Aristotle's—thoughts on virtue ethics in universal histories after the fourth century BCE. This is not simply the case for the Christian world; it is also the case for histories made from the Near East through to the Middle East from at least the ninth to the twelfth century CE.

Diodorus Siculus (90–30 BCE) provides a good starting point to look at virtue ethics in history making. This may seem a surprising choice, for he has been little celebrated as a history maker. Diodorus' *Library of History* has been regarded variously as a clumsy summary of earlier histories or as an expression of blunt-force moralising. Lisa Hau, for example, has described Diodorus' repeated description of Olympias' (375–16 BCE) inhuman treatment of Eurydice (19.11.4–7), as lacking in subtlety and even innovation. The reader, she argues, has not so much been guided to a moral reading as been forcefully dragged into it. The narrator does not seem to trust his reader to arrive at the obvious conclusion on his own, and so the message has been made abundantly clear.[10]

Diodorus' failure is that of not letting his audience navigate their way to the virtues. If we consider Aristotle's idea of practising ethics in *ethos*, though, there is cause to consider Diodorus' approach anew. Repetition, in this light, might be seen as part of the development of the habit of ethics.

Diodorus, like Herodotus, wanted to ensure that the actions of people in the past were not forgotten. Building on that idea, he noted that the study of history is helpful because we can look to the failures and hurts of other people without experiencing them ourselves (1.3–4; 10.11.12; 11.45.46). This is a really interesting claim that deserves a closer look. At work is the idea that we can learn from the *ethos* or ethical practise of others and that perhaps—stretching the point further—this might help us to attain the virtuous mean with less pain and failure than those in the past. We may think of this as a pretty routine point given that we are used to hearing sayings such as George Santayana's (1863–1952) '[t]hose who cannot remember the past are condemned to repeat it'.[11] There is no guarantee, however, that reading about someone else's actions will lead to virtuous conduct. Nor is there a guarantee that presenting an account of actions by multiple people over time will lead to virtuous conduct. So why did Diodorus write at world scale, narrating the history of the world from its beginning to the fall of Troy (books 1 to 6), from Troy to the death of Alexander (356–23 BCE) (books 7 to 17) and from the death of Alexander to around 60 BCE (books 18 to 40)?

In answering this question, we must remember that Diodorus' *Library of History* is above all else a history of the virtues and that he saw the virtues as persisting more clearly over time than other traces of the past:

> Time which withers all else, preserves for these virtues and immortality, and the further it may advance itself in age, the fresher the youth it imparts to them.
>
> (10.12.12; see also 14.1.1)

Diodorus did not explain why the virtues persist over time. The simplest explanation we might offer for this is that he believed in a stable set of virtues—like Plato and Aristotle—and that these contrasted with the flux of historical particulars. As with Plato and Aristotle, for instance, he was interested in the virtues of courage and temperance, and he repeatedly provided examples of both (4.28.3; 4.73.6; 11.74.4; 16.4; 16.9; 16.12; 20.22.6; 31.44; 36.10.1; and 1.68.5; 3.61.4; 4.45.3–5; 11.44.4–5:14.2.1, respectively). As might also be expected of a Christian writer, though, he also placed stress on the virtue of piety (4.8.5; 8.15.1–5; 35.9).

To Diodorus' interest in the virtues over time we can add an interest in the virtues in time. As with Aristotle, he saw the same virtues as present in both individuals and groups (1.60; 1.68.5; 1.44.4–5; 11.67.2; 14.45.1; 11.70.3–4; 33.18.1; and

20 Universal histories and virtue ethics

37.5–6). This enabled him to account for the history of individuals and groups and to switch between them. Both this scale switching and his long-range tracking of the virtues might be thought of as delivering on Aristotle's 'bigger is better' view of ethics, which I introduced earlier in the chapter. He also thought, though, that smaller-scale histories might not do justice to the complex lives of people. As he explains in 12.1.1, people demonstrate a mixture of good and evil acts:

> A man may justly feel perplexed when he stops to consider the inconsistency that is to be found in the life of mankind; for no thing which we consider to be good is ever found to have been given to human beings unadulterated; nor is there any evil in an absolute form without some admixture of advantage.
>
> (See also 20.30.1)

This reinforces the connection of actions to character and the need to acknowledge that a person's character will never be simply good or evil. People will act in ways that appear inconsistent, perhaps they will even veer between the extremes of the vices. They may also engage in actions over the short scale, which display a range of vices as well as virtues. A larger view over time allows us to moderate and to make an appraisal of the character of individuals, as well as groups. This means also being prepared to look at a person acting in the same ways repeatedly. The result is not forceful moralising that deprives us of the work of ethical judgement but an invitation for us to weigh up character over time and to also reflect on our own character over time.

Diodorus also looked to larger-scale history making as an exercise in moderation. He argued repeatedly for due proportion and stuck to his word by dividing books into two even length parts, even if that meant ending a book section abruptly. Seen in one way, Diodorus is a blunt-force moraliser; seen in another way, he is a practitioner of *ethos* and navigation to the virtuous mean. We first see this intent at the conclusion of his account of the flooding of the Nile in book one:

> We shall rest content with what has been said, in order that we may not overstep the principle of brevity which we resolved upon at the beginning. And since we have divided this Book into two parts because of its length, inasmuch as we are aiming at due proportion in our account, at this point we shall close the first portion of our history.
>
> (1.41.10)

Here he tells us that the book will be literally divided into two, and the size of the two parts matched out of respect for the principle of brevity (1.1.42.1; see also 1.1.98.10). This proportionate sizing of history entailed skipping over events and actions that he took to be without virtue (see, for example, 2.22.2 and 4.30.6). On other occasions, he stopped short in describing events, telling his readers that he did not want books to be disproportionate or longer than intended. This is seen in his abrupt endings for books 2 to 4, 13, 14 and 19. His aim was to avoid being like Timaeus (350–260 BCE), whom, he tells us, bestowed, it is true, the greatest attention upon the precision of his chronology and had due regard for the breadth of knowledge gained through experience, but he is criticised with good reason for his untimely and lengthy censures.

(5.1.1)

Proportion also comes into play within books, with a good example provided after his discussion on the heroic deeds of the children of the mythological Argonaut, Nestor. We 'shall be satisfied with what has been said', he tells us, 'since we are aiming at due proportion in our account' (4.68.3; see also 11.5.12; 11.19.20). Having satisfied his aim of accounting for a person's virtues and vices, he stops.

Diodorus' navigation to a history making mean was echoed by later Christian writers such as Eusebius (265–339 CE). Eusebius glossed over the history of early martyrs in his *Ecclesiastical History*, he tells us, out of 'regard to the due proportions of the book'.[12] In Paulus Orosius' *Seven Books of History against the Pagans* (hereafter *Histories*) we see an even more fine-grained reflection of Aristotle's views on attaining the virtuous mean. Sometimes you have to fly forward in time via leaps and bounds, Orosius tells us, in order to move through the 'thick forest' of history (1.12.1). Orosius' description preceded his decision to skip over 1,000 years of Assyrian history in favour of Greek and Roman events. After all, he tells us, the millennium in question was almost entirely defined by wars waged by or against the Assyrians. Later in *The Histories*, he passes over long stretches of Roman, Sicilian and Lacedaemonian history for a similar reason (2.12.1; 2.14.2; and 3.2.10). Moreover, he often reminds us that space is tight in *The Histories*; far too tight, for example, to recount the labyrinthine twists of Roman seditions (5.17.3) or events that ought to be well known to us such as the fall of Troy (1.17.2).

Orosius leapt repeatedly in his case for a Christian world history told through the misfortunes of non-believers (7.43.20). This was not without justification. As he notes at the opening of book three of *The Histories*, you have to think very carefully about what to include and what to leave out of your writing:

> The very breadth of the material about which I am complaining puts me in narrow straits and I am bound all the tighter by this anxiety—namely that if, in my eagerness to be concise, I omit some event or other, it will be thought I did not know about it or that it did not happen at that time. But, on the other hand, if I gird my loins to speak about everything, not expatiating at length, but just using concise summaries, I would make my work obscure with the result that most people will think that what I have said appears to say nothing at all.
>
> (3.preface.2)

The logic at play in this explanation would not be out of place in a history made today. We gain the sense of the history maker treading a fine line between too much and too little detail. Orosius wanted to ensure that his 'small book with a

22 Universal histories and virtue ethics

scant number of words' clearly conveyed the unified message that while the present appears fraught, the lives of unbelievers in the distant past were 'all the more horribly wretched' (2.18.4; 1.preface.13). We might not agree with his argument, but at least he had one, and he wanted to write in a way that would make it clear to his readers.

If you read on in the same passage from book three, though, Aristotle's acknowledgement of virtue ethics as an imprecise activity comes to the fore. Conciseness and exhaustiveness are 'vices', Orosius tells us, and he will 'indulge in both of them' so that they 'might be mitigated by one another' (3.preface.3). Navigation by vices probably does not strike us as an ethical approach to making history, and swinging from one extreme to the other in the hope that they will be tempered seems like poor methodology. Yet that is the way of virtue ethics: it presumes that we will develop the virtues over time through action. We do not demonstrate them from birth, and we can fail to demonstrate them consistently. Echoing this, Orosius gives us a glimpse of history making as being akin to habit development. We may start with clumsy moves, navigating to what is good in a manner to navigating out of a tunnel by bumping into the walls. Moreover, he intimates that this navigation will not be easy. We cannot take for granted that we will strike a finely tuned balance in history making or that we will maintain it.

Dawla: turning on the virtues in history making in the Islamic World

Orosius' take on history making as ethical development is not unusual. Leaps, bumps and shifts across spatial and temporal scales can be found in different forms of history making across the globe. The ethical views that drive those shifts are open to variation, as this book will show. It is important to acknowledge, however, that Aristotle's view of ethics as *ethos*—the development of the habit of acting virtuously via imprecise means—helped to set this dynamic play of scales in motion. Dynamic 'virtue shifts' between individuals and groups, for instance, are a feature of histories made across the Islamic world from the ninth and the twelfth centuries CE. The rich development of this approach followed waves of translation, adaption and response to the writings of Aristotle and to a lesser extent Plato. Writers like Al-Kindī (c.801–73), Al-Farabi (c.872–951), Ibn Sīnā (Avicenna, c.980–1037) and Ibn Rushd (Averroes, 1126–98) promoted the attainment of the virtuous mean as aligned with the divine. Moreover, they did not see people as naturally virtuous or as able to maintain the virtues over time. In common with history makers, they held to the idea of individuals—and more commonly—groups cycling through virtues and vices. The driver of these cycles was the presence or absence of moderation. Desert life was associated with moderation, urban life with excess and thus the vices. Scott Savran has described this association to be so common as to be stock:

> Historians made use of stock imagery and rhetorical themes contained within an 'Arab versus '*ajam* [non-speaker of Arabic]' literary discourse contrasting stereotypical notions of Persian grandeur and hierarchy with conceptualisations of

the Arabs' Bedouin existence circulated among intellectuals living in urban environments that, were needless to say, far removed from desert nomads.[13]

This use of stock imagery and rhetorical devices, as well as in chains of transmission—isnāds—has led some commentators to describe history making in the Islamic world as conservative in approach and thought.[14] We ought to acknowledge in response that some of these features likely made oral transmission easier, as with the handing down of the songs that came to be included in *The Kalevala*. Yet Savran also acknowledges that history makers across the Islamic world showed varying levels of attention to detail in their accounts of the cycles of virtues and vices.[15]

There are multiple reasons why history makers vary the level of detail in their works. Orosius, we recall, informed us that it resulted from his clumsy attempts to achieve moderation in description. He veered between the vices of profligacy and parsimony. Orosius thus saw history making as an exercise in navigation to the mean, with a proportionate level of detail being the mean in that case. What he perhaps failed to understand, though, was that more than one virtue might be at play in history making. Silence and speaking, for example, might also be seen as virtues in different contexts, as the Ilkhanite (1236–1335 CE) Iranian historian Rashīd al-Dīn Ṭabīb's *Jamiʿ al-tawāñkh*, or *Compendium of Chronicles*, shows us. Rashīd al-Dīn's account of the known world as told through the rise of the Mongols is organised by a clever framework. The reign of each of 15 Mongol rulers is presented through five sections or *qism* which cover the history of a ruler's reign, his family, the lands of his reign, significant battles, and anecdotes and evidence of his character. This multi-stranded structure supported Rashīd al-Dīn's argument that the Mongol empire was strong by virtue of being like a quiver of arrows. Each ruler could display good character through a lifetime of virtuous acts, and in combination, the character of these rulers was unbreakable (1.4.2; 2.2.2; 2.2.9). Technically, too, it provided a blueprint which could be used to describe rulers to come through Rashīd al-Dīn's endowment of a scriptorium.[16]

Rashīd al-Dīn's inclusion of parallel histories in his *Compendium* set up the same opportunity for the presentation of variant claims—and thus oblique judgement—seen in Herodotus and another very well documented case from ancient China, Sima Qian's (c. 110 BCE) *Shi Ji*.[17] Rashīd al-Dīn, like Herodotus and Sima Qian, also offered histories of varying lengths and levels of detail. Just over half of the surviving *Compendium*, for example, is dedicated to the discussion of the reigns of Genghis (1162–1227 CE) and Ghazan (1271–1304 CE), and within these accounts, most detail is included in anecdotes that highlight Genghis' virtues: his concern for order and propriety, honour, respect, sobriety, care for family and piety (2.2.1–2.2.2; on Ghazan, see 2.2.17). The 48 anecdotes about the reign of Genghis' third son Ögedei (1185–1241 CE) are similarly generous, highlighting his virtues of mercy, justice and generosity (2.2.4). A contrast follows with the brief anecdotes for his successor—Güyük—showing him as succumbing to the vices of debauchery, sacrilege and liberality (2.2.8), and the section on character is missing for Genghis' conspiring first son Jochi (1182–1227 CE) altogether.

24 Universal histories and virtue ethics

The presence or absence of virtues explains the varying lengths of Rashīd al-Dīn's *qism*. By focusing on the virtues, he saw himself as providing affirmation of the divine:

> In order for divine wisdom to make manifest traces of its power, it necessarily brings into being a strange and marvellous thing in every age of the world of generation and corruption, and the locus of that thing is a peerless, noble person favoured by the divine gaze and protected by divine mercy so that this thing may cause those of insight to learn a lesson and those of the world to witness His perfect power and so that by rendering thanks for God's infinite bounties they may continue forever and that they may know for certain that the continuum of the creation of beings, in general and in particular, is tied to the will of the creator.
>
> (2.1.1)

In the virtuous acts of people, we see the imprint of God, and the description of the virtues is therefore a contribution to the pious contemplation and recognition of God.

The example of Rashīd al-Dīn's *Compendium* shows us how the length of a history could signal affirmation of the virtues and the divine. Speaking or writing celebrated the good, the right, the just. Silence condemned those who lived contra to God's wisdom. But there were also more dynamic markers of an interest in the virtues, as is seen in the case of *dawla*, which Savran translates as 'turn'. *Dawla* was used to refer to a shift in a cycle between the virtues and vices, most often as a consequence of the drift from desert to urban living. *Dawla* might be demonstrated through the life of an individual or a group. As history makers of the Islamic world—like those of the Hellenistic world—assumed that individuals and groups displayed the same virtues, it could also be displayed through both. This provided the opportunity to scale switch in histories, leaping from individuals to groups and back again. It was like zooming in and out via the use of the virtues—or vices—as a lens.

Savran provides an interesting case of *dawla* as virtue and vice scale shifting in al-Tha'alibi's (961–1038 CE) *Kitab Ghurar akhbar muluk al-Furs wasiyarihim*. In book one, we learn of the Sasanian ruler Shapur II's (309–79 CE) encounter with an old woman in the desert:

> The swords of Shapur had not yet been quenched by the blood of the Arabs and he was not yet finished devouring them when an eloquent old woman stood in his way and shouted out to him. Now it was the custom of kings to stop when someone shouted out to him. So he stopped for her. She said to him, 'Oh King, if you have come seeking vengeance, then surely you have achieved it and then some! Indeed, you have spread death amongst the Arab tribes. But know that there will be revenge for this, even it takes some time.'

So Shapur commanded to stop killing the Arabs.... Shapur did what he did out of fear of the Arabs. For he had heard from the wind blowing from the direction of the Arabs of the latter's rise and the ground that he never rose again.

(1.3)

In this excerpt, we see *dawla* epitomised in the woman from the desert and the wind. They signal the rise of the Arabs to Sharpur. This turn resulted from his campaigns against the Arabs (325 CE–), in which he killed and brutally injured many, and destroyed their water supplies. A larger-scale example can be seen in al-Tabari's (839–923 CE) *History of the Prophet and Kings*, where we see the turn of power from the Iranians to the Arabs and then to the Hashimites and their Khurusan allies under Marwan II (691–750 CE). As he writes,

O people of Khurasan, this land used to belong to your forefathers. They were granted victory over their enemies because of their justice and good behaviour, until they changed and acted tyrannically. So God became angry with them and took away their power, empowering over them the lowliest nation to share the earth with them. They took their country, slept with their women and enslaved their children. Yet they governed with justice, fulfilled their contracts, and aided the oppressed. But they too changed their ways, ruled oppressively and brought fear to the pious members of the Prophet's family. So now God has empowered you over them so that He may take revenge on them through you[18].

The trigger for the change, as with al-Tha'alibi's history, was the shift from just to oppressive behaviour. What this example shows us is that *dawla* made it possible for universal history makers to mix what we would call biography, civilisational and world history together. They did not persistently write on one scale.

Al-Tabari's invocation of God raises a question about whether the fate of individuals was in their hands alone. This was an issue that the Persian history maker Atâ-Malek Juvayni grappled with in his history of the Mongol Empire, the *Tañkh-I Jahān-gushā* or *History of the World Conquerer*. Juvayni's history documented Helugu Khan's Mongol Ilkhanid conquest of Persia, and he lamented both the turmoil and losses of his times. He also saw it as providing an opportunity for his audience to study horrifying acts in safety and to avoid them in favour of virtuous acts. He did not, though, see individuals as being entirely in control of the turns of history, as he explains in the opening passages of his work:

When the phoenix of prosperity wishes to make the roof of one man its abode, and the owl of misfortune to haunt the threshold of another, though their stations be widely different, the one in the zenith of good fortune and the other in the nadir of abasement, yet neither scarcity of equipment nor feebleness of condition prevents the fortunate man from attaining his goal...

and neither abundance of gear nor excess of accoutrement can save the unfortunate one from losing even that which he hath…. For if craft, and might, and wealth, could accomplish ought, then would power and empire never have passed from the houses of former kings to another; but when the time of the decline of their fortunes was arrived, neither craft, nor perseverance, nor counsel could aid them…. And of this there is still clearer proof and plainer evidence in the instance of the Mongol people, when one considers in what circumstances and position they found themselves before they beat the drum of the greatness of [Genghis] Khan and his posterity.

(1.1)

Juvayni acknowledged both the ability of individuals to steer their own course and the hand of God in the turn or *dawla* of history. How he united the two was via the suggestion that the actions and character of individuals were limited by the larger context in which they lived. Thus, while an individual may work to cultivate the virtues, their success may be undone if the group of which they are a part experiences misfortune on account of their collective vices. This suggests that the big outweighs the small, as we recall Aristotle suggesting early on in this chapter.

Back to Oulu

Juvayni's account of the intersection of individual and group actions and character highlights the potential complexity of virtue ethics in history making. Without too much thought, for example, we might wonder how big a group needs to be before its actions outweigh those of other groups, as with the actions of an extended family versus a village. So too we might wonder what the virtuous mean might be for different groups and individuals. We saw this, for example, in the suggestion above that writing in moderation might conflict with the idea of speaking or remaining silent to express judgement about the actions of others. These points take us to one of the key criticisms of virtue ethics: that it does not provide us with specific guidance about what we ought to do. Virtues can make opposing demands of us as individuals and as members of various groups. Sometimes we may be able to work our way through these varying and even conflicting demands, but other problems may seem irreconcilable. This is ahead of us even acknowledging that there might not be a stable, certain or justified group of virtues.

This is a part of the history of histories that it is important for us to acknowledge. The intersection of virtue ethics and the critical inquiry of *historia* opened up a variety of options—including conflicting ones—for accounting for the past. In response, history makers presented variants and conflicting ideas in their works, and they indicated different options for the craft of history. In doing so, they drew upon evidence and a variety of rhetorical techniques. As this chapter has shown, they also ranged over spatio-temporal scales. There never was a singular size, scale or approach to history making, for good ethical reason. Even a universal history, which we may assume from this chapter was an attempt to capture the character of individuals and groups over time, was not made to an agreed template. Universal histories were short, and they were long. They made use of ring narratives and *qism*. They switched scales in varying ways, and they emphasised different virtues. It is easy for us to forget that.

It can also be easy to forget that even the first written histories placed a high demand on their audiences. Each, on its own, was an invitation for its audience to consider in safety how they might navigate to the virtues. In combination, they offered multiple and even conflicting navigational guides. This was even the case when history makers were roughly in agreement about a set of virtues. The expectation, in line with Aristotle's arguments, was that ethics is of our making.

The Kalevala offers that same expectation. For its magic, like that of the first written histories, was to have wrought a world from fragments but to have done so in a way that it never made singular, clear, stable sense. Its magic was to provide its maker, Lönnrot, with the opportunity to develop the habit of ethics by studying the actions and character of individuals and groups and for its audience to have that opportunity in their own way. This is the way that we can also think of the extremes of the Finns Party. It is tempting, as with many news outlets, to present extreme views with the expectation that we will navigate to a reasonable, moderate middle. This is not good ethical thinking, and it ought not be an expectation of history making. This is because views exist in time and space and may vary over each. We cannot expect a debate at a point in time to do our thinking for us. Virtue ethics requires effort—*ethos*—over time. It also requires us to navigate a world in which neither the virtues nor the vices are fixed because the good life will vary for all of us. This is what makes virtue ethics a heavy rational burden. As the next chapter will show, the makers of biographical catalogues introduced notions of additive value to bring more definition to Aristotle's idea of bigger goods in virtue ethics. The magic of history making as the ethical effort of *ethos*, however, had already taken root, and it remains with us today.

Notes

1 Eric Hobsbawm, *The Age of Extremes: The Short Twentieth Century, 1914–1991*, London: Abacus, 1995.

2 Eric Hobsbawm, 'Inside and Outside History,' in *On History*, London: Wiedenfeld and Nicholson, 1997, p. 5.

3 Charles Kahn, *The Art and Thought of Heraclitus*, Cambridge: Cambridge University Press, 1979, p. 96.

4 Heracleitus, *On the Universe*, trans W. H. S. Jones, Harvard: Harvard University Press, 1989, B110–111.

5 Heracleitus, *On the Universe*, B112.

6 Lisa Irene Hau, *Moral History from Herodotus to Diodorus Siculus*, Edinburgh: Edinburgh University Press, 2016, p. 2.

7 Ingrid Beck, *Die Ringkomposition bei Herodot und ihre Bedeutung für die Beweistechnik*, Hildesheim: Georg Olms, 1971; Henry R. Immerwahr, *Form and Thought in Herodotus*, Cleveland: Western Reserve University Press for the American Philological Association, 1966; Irene D. F. de Jong, 'Narrative Unity and Units', in *Companion to Herodotus*, eds E. J. Bakker, Irene J. F. de Jong and Hans van Wees, Leiden: Brill, 2002, pp. 245–66;

28 Universal histories and virtue ethics

and Rosalind Thomas, *Herodotus in Context: Ethnography, Science and the Art of Persuasion*, Oxford: Oxford University Press, 2000.

8 F. J. Groten Jnr, 'Herodotus' Use of Variant Versions', *Phoenix*, 1963, vol. 17(2), pp. 79–87.

9 Elliot Bartky, 'Aristotle and the Politics of Herodotus's "History"', *The Review of Politics*, 2002, vol. 62(3), pp. 445–68.

10 Lisa Irene Hau, *Moral History from Herodotus to Diodorus Siculus*, p. 85.

11 George Santayana, *The Life of Reason: Reason in Common Sense*, New York: Scribner's, 1905, p. 284.

12 Eusebius, *Ecclesiastical History*, trans K. Lake and J.E.L. Oulton, Cambridge, MA: Harvard University Press, 2 vols, 1926–32, 8.6.

13 Scott Savran, *Arabs and Iranians in the Islamic Conquest Narrative: Memory and Identity Construction in Islamic Historiography, 750–1050*, Abingdon: Routledge, 2018, p. 202.

14 Chase Robinson, *Islamic Historiography*, Cambridge: Cambridge University Press, 2002, pp. 85–6.

15 Scott Savran, *Arabs and Iranians in the Islamic Conquest Narrative*, p. 7.

16 Nourane Ben Azzouna, 'Rashīd al-Dīn Faḍl Allāh al-Hamadhānī's Manuscript Production Project in Tabriz Reconsidered', in *Politics, Patronage and the Transmission of Knowledge in 13th–15th Century Tabriz*, Leiden: Brill, pp. 187–200.

17 See, for example, Grant Hardy, *Worlds of Bronze and Bamboo: Sima Qian's Conquest of History*, New York: Columbia University Press, 1999.

18 Al Tabari, as quoted in Scott Savran, *Arabs and Iranians in the Islamic Conquest Narrative*, p. 74

Primary texts

Aristotle, *Eudemian Ethics*, trans B. Inwood and R. Woolf, Cambridge: Cambridge University Press, 2013.

Aristotle, *Nicomachean Ethics*, trans R. Crisp, Cambridge: Cambridge University Press, 2012.

Herodotus, *The Histories*, trans. A. D. Godley, London: Heinemann, 4 vols, 1921–4.

Atâ-Malek Juvayni, *Genghis Khan: The History of the World Conqueror*, trans J. A. Boyle, Manchester: Manchester University Press, 1998.

Elias Lönnrot, *The Kalevala*, trans K. Bosley, Oxford: Oxford University Press, 1989.

Orosius, *Seven Books of History against the Pagans*, trans A. T. Fear, Liverpool: Liverpool University Press, 2010.

Plato, *Euthydemus*, ed. E. H. Gifford, Cambridge: Cambridge University Press, 2013.

Plato, *Gorgias, Menexenus, Protagoras*, ed. M. Schofield, trans T. Griffith, Cambridge: Cambridge University Press, 2009.

Plato, *The Republic*, trans G. Griffith, Cambridge: Cambridge University Press, 2010.

Diodorus Siculus, *The Library of History*, trans C. H. Oldfather, C. L. Sherman, C. B. Welles, R. M. Geer and F. R. Walton, Cambridge, MA: Harvard University Press, 12 vols, 1933–67.

Rashīd al-Dīn Ṭabīb, *Compendium of Chronicles: A History of the Mongols*, trans W. M. Thackston, Cambridge, MA: Harvard University Department of Near Eastern Languages and Civilizations, 1998, 2 vols.

3

COLLECTIVE BIOGRAPHIES AND UTILITARIAN ETHICS

Liu Xiang | Fan Ye | Mary Hays | Lucy Aikin | Sarah Strickney Ellis | Mary Cowden Clarke | Jeremy Bentham | John Stuart Mill

MIDDLETOWN, CONNECTICUT, UNITED STATES of AMERICA. It is 3 a.m. I am wide awake with jet lag and trying to figure out where I am. The Middletown Inn, my gracious hosts have told me, has had multiple past lives. For over 200 years, it has been remodelled and even picked up and rotated on its foundations. All of these renovations and purposes were made possible by the same collection of hand-fashioned bricks. None of them are perfect: thumbprints, chips and stones all reveal individual stories. Yet they also combine in a structure which seems singular and strong. At its height, the bricks protected an armoury in a town that was the epicentre of gun manufacturing in the USA from the war of 1812 to the Civil War (1861–5). Not far away, Oliver Bidwell established the first factory for pistols. Each was made by hand, and their imperfections could deliver results as dangerous to their owners as to their targets. Simeon North also manufactured pistols by hand nearby, but his factory transitioned to precision milling and therefore achieved mass production.[1]

Machined pistol barrels are one of the examples used by Simon Winchester in *Exactly* (2019) to celebrate the role of accuracy and precision in the birth of modernity.[2] Accurate and precise mass production made it possible for you and me to have mobile phones and for me to use a computer to write this book. Winchester could have also celebrated machine-made bricks, but he did not. Bricks, like machined components, are so handy that it is tempting to look at them when we explain other things, like histories. For at the same time that Bidwell and North established their pistol factories, large-scale collections of biographies were created by many women authors and used in classrooms, homes and religious lessons around the world. It is tempting to dismiss these works as mass productions lacking creativity, as aggregations of biographical 'bricks' if you like. We might also wonder if they are dangerous in fostering a conformity of thought about ethics. The massive works of writers like Mary Hays (1759–1843), were not, however, the result of precise or even factory composition.

DOI: 10.4324/9780429399992-3

30 Collective biographies and utilitarian ethics

This is because, in my view, history making has never industrialised, even though the number of histories made in recent years has expanded dramatically. This is not to say that history making is entirely artisanal, with unique works turned out by hand. A history may, for instance, use standard forms of referencing or be mass printed or distributed via global digital networks. Yet even a mass distributed history is a hand-crafted statement about how we ought to act. No two histories are precisely the same and for good reason. They are human, all too human. This will become apparent when we think about how collective biographies contribute to our understandings of the ethics of history, and to our wider understanding of the nature and purpose of what is called utilitarian ethics.

The key idea in this chapter, as with the last, is *ethos*: the idea that we have to work at being ethical—and more specifically, virtuous—over the course of our lives. Knowing that we are neither born virtuous nor are always virtuous, we can look to others around us, and to those in the past, for guidance. In the previous chapter, we saw universal history makers pick this idea up, as well as Aristotle's argument in the *Eudemian Ethics* and *Nicomachean Ethics* that navigation to the virtues is not a finely tuned process. I suggested that it was akin to feeling your way out of a tunnel by bumping into the sides. This provides some explanation as to why history makers are interested in looking at extreme acts *over time*—vices, for example—including extremes displayed by single individuals or groups. I also introduced a second idea from Aristotle's ethics: that big goods are better than little ones. In explaining his idea, Aristotle specifies that the good of the state is better than that of the individual. This encouraged universal history makers to look *over space*, to write at scale about groups, as well as about individuals. They, therefore, looked across time and space in making history.

I also suggested that universal history makers moved across space and time dynamically. One of the things that made it possible for them to do so was the assumption that individuals *and* groups share the same kinds of virtues and vices. One moment we find ourselves reading about the acts of an individual, the next moment the narrative turns and we find ourselves reflecting on the acts of a group, and the other way around. These movements can be announced and gradual or unannounced and abrupt. Think of it as the equivalent of having both narrative snakes and ladders at your disposal, with the stakes being the ethical fate of individuals and groups, including your own fate as a writer. Recall some of our universal history makers letting us know about the clumsiness of their attempts to get their level of detail just right.

In this chapter, I want us to think more about this analogy of snakes and ladders as a way of unpacking how history makers switch scales. A history maker can switch scales suddenly, unannounced. They can also build scale in the manner of climbing a ladder, announcing and adding details as they go. We recall from the last chapter Aristotle's further argument in the *Eudemian Ethics* and *Nicomachean Ethics* that when little goods are combined, they make bigger ones. On this view, good can not only be thought of as big and small; it can also be thought of as additive. Little goods add up to big ones. On this view, we reach the idea of histories as made from parts.

Collective biographies and utilitarian ethics **31**

What adds up in history? Well, the answer depends on what you think histories are made of. Some universal history makers, like Polybius (c.200–118 BCE), talked of their works as wholes made from parts. Those parts, to him, were like components of a body, with none able to survive on their own:

> It is impossible to gain this comprehensive perspective from writers of partial histories. This is the same as thinking that all it takes instantly to grasp the form of the whole world, and its order and arrangement in their entirety, is to visit, one by one, each of its outstanding cities—or indeed, to look at sketches of them! Imagine people who think that looking at the scattered parts of a once living and beautiful body is all they need to do to witness the energy and beauty of the actual living creature…. For while it may be possible to get an *impression* of the whole from a part, it is impossible to gain knowledge and precise understanding…. [I]t is only by connecting and comparing *all* the parts with one another, by seeing their similarities and differences—it is only such an overview that puts one in a position to derive benefit and pleasure from history.[3]

There are at least two intriguing ideas in this excerpt. The first is Polybius' claim that there is a beauty and energy to the whole of history that you cannot see in isolated components. This could be an echo of the philosophical idea that everything is connected as one. It could also be an ancient expression of R. G. Collingwood's rejection of what he called a 'scissors and paste' history.[4] In crude terms, this reminds us that you don't get a history from sticking pieces of evidence together. You need a history maker to forge a history like the blacksmith who made the sampo in *The Kalevala*. The second just as interesting idea is that the parts of a history can be like one another, or different to one another. To use Polybius' example, we think of the limbs and organs of an organism as being different to one another. Yet we might also think of the chemical components of an organism as made from a relatively small set of sub-atomic building blocks. An organism can be like a house made of bricks, to put it very simply.

Some ancient history makers viewed their works as made from similar, rather than different, parts. As Jonathan Alonso-Núñez has reminded us, ancient and medieval writers not only made universal histories, but they also made what is known as collective biographies or prosopographies.[5] The earliest collective biographies that we know about are Plutarch's (45–127 CE) *Lives*, Philostratus' (c.172–c.250 CE) *Lives of the Sophists* and Diogenes Laertius' (180–240 CE) *Lives of Eminent Philosophers*.[6] Patricia Cox Miller has argued that what distinguishes collective biographies from universal histories is that they are compilations of like parts.[7] Collective biographies are made from biographies in the way that houses are made from bricks. Yet Miller also stresses that collections or compilations of like things are not uniform works. This is akin to me saying that I noticed the individual differences in the bricks at the Middletown Inn. These differences within collective biographies can be thought of, first, as differences in content. In his collective biographies, for

32 Collective biographies and utilitarian ethics

example, Plutarch wanted to see the 'peculiar colours' of the virtues at play in the lives of different people (*Moralia*, 243b–d;[8] *Aemilius Paulus*, 1.1). The suggestion here is that compilation might capture how different people exhibit the virtues. There is variation but not so much as to make the idea of the virtues themselves meaningless. Second, collective biographies can vary in form, as well as content. Biographies vary in length, use of spatio-temporal scales and narrative type, to name just a few examples. This makes collective biographies more methodologically complex than has previously been considered.

It also, in my view, makes them expressions of *ethos*. *Ethos* in this case is not so much navigation to the virtues as the outcome of *adding* up virtues and vices over space and time. As this chapter will show, the authors of eighteenth- and nineteenth-century collective biographies often signalled that their works could be added up in order to make a more convincing case about the virtues or vices. This makes them dynamic expressions of a kind of moral calculus, which is an idea associated with utilitarian ethics. I'll also complicate that story by showing how the classical Chinese treatment of histories as made from different kinds of parts made it possible to deliver both explicit and oblique judgements about human actions.

Utilitarian ethics

Before looking in more detail at modern collective biographies by women authors, or classical Chinese histories, it is important to say a little about the ethical theory that will be the focal point of this chapter: utilitarian ethics. Utilitarian ethicists suggest that we should act in ways that lead to the most good. This shows us that utilitarian ethicists are interested in the consequences of actions; hence, they are also sometimes called consequentialists. Like virtue ethicists, utilitarian ethicists are interested in the actions of individuals and groups. Moreover, like Aristotle, they see ethics as associated with pleasure. In both his *Eudemian Ethics* and *Nicomachean Ethics*, Aristotle emphasised that virtuous acts are associated with eudaimonia (εὐδαιμονία), which has been translated variously as pleasure, happiness and flourishing. If we connect this idea of eudaimonia with Aristotle's other claims about big goods, and little goods adding up to big ones, then we find some of the key roots for utilitarian ethics.

One of the earliest expressions of utilitarian ethics can be traced to Gottfried Wilhelm Leibniz (1646–1716 CE), who wrote around 1700 that

> [t]o act in accordance with supreme reason is to act in such a manner that the greatest quantity of good available is obtained for the greatest multitude possible and that as much felicity is diffused as the reason of things can bear.[9]

Leibniz associated reason with acting so as to achieve the greatest good for the greatest number of people. Frances Hutcheson further developed this idea in *An Inquiry into the Original of Our Ideas of Beauty and Virtue*, arguing 'that *Action* is *best*, which procures the *greatest Happiness* for the *greatest Numbers*; and that *worst*, which *in like manner* occasions *Misery*'.[10] We can see here that the best action both generates the greatest happiness and the least misery. In cases where both good and misery result, he acknowledged that we might also take into account people's dignity.

Hutcheson argued for a 'mathematical calculation to moral subjects' as an aide for everyday life.[11] With this step, he appeared to depart from Aristotle, who argued that expectations of precision varied between mathematics and ethics. Ethics, we recall from the last chapter, was not expected by Aristotle to be precise. Consequently, he held that navigating to the virtues might involve veering between vices. Jeremy Bentham picked up Hutcheson's ideas in *An Introduction to the Principles of Morals and Legislation* (1789) and made it clear that the principle of greatest happiness applied to individuals, as well as to groups:

> That principle which approves or disapproves of every action whatsoever, according to the tendency which it appears to have to augment or diminish the happiness of the party whose interest is in question: or, what is the same thing in other words, to promote or to oppose that happiness. I say of every action whatsoever; and therefore, not only every action of a private individual, but every measure of government.
>
> *(An Introduction to the Principles of Morals and Legislation*, p. 2)

Happiness could be used to guide the actions of individuals, governments and, as he made clear a little later in the text, humanity (p. 13). It had individual, state and global *utility*, hence the name utilitarianism. Moreover, like Hutcheson, he was interested in the idea of ethical calculus. Consider, for example, the following 'mnemonic doggerel', which he hoped would help his readers to take into account variables or circumstances in their calculations:

> Intense, long, certain, speedy, fruitful, pure—
> Such marks in pleasures and in pains endure.
> Such pleasures seek if private be thy end:
> If it be public, wide let them extend
> Such pains avoid, whichever be thy view:
> If pains must come, let them extend to few (p. 29).

Yet Bentham did not just speak of a moral calculus; he also applied it. His primary focus for application was the determination of punishments for social or legal offenders (pp. 152–336). Bentham's work, however, also discusses a number of historical examples. Ethical calculus could be used to work through people's actions from the past and to suggest 'what ifs' for us to consider in our own times (pp. 78–81; 85–92; 135). It could also be used to pass judgement about the ethical rationality of those in the past. If Louis XIV (1643–1715) had not been religious, we read in just one of his examples, 'France would not have lost 800,000 of its most valuable subjects. The same thing may be said of the authors of the wars called holy ones' (pp. 139–40).

34 Collective biographies and utilitarian ethics

James Mill, in turn, amplified the application of utilitarian ethics to history in *The History of British India* (1817), using utility as the 'grand test of civilisation' to deem that India was in a barbarous state, and thus prior to history making:

> Exactly in proportion as Utility is the object of every pursuit, may we regard a nation as civilised. Exactly in proportion as its ingenuity is wasted on contemptible or mischievous objects, though it may be, in itself, an ingenuity of no ordinary kind, the nation may be safely denominated barbarous. According to this rule, the astronomical and mathematical sciences afford conclusive evidence against the Hindus. They have been cultivated exclusively for the purposes of astrology…which most infallibly denote a nation barbarous.[12]

As this example shows, mathematics in both the content and the form of history making could be used to deem that a people were without history. Places other than Europe and European settler societies suffered much the same fate. James' son, John Stuart Mill, was to temper these and Bentham's views a little by discriminating intellectual and moral pleasures as higher than those of lower sensual or physical pleasures and by acknowledging the contribution of internal sanctions, such as conscience to the determination of which actions to undertake (*Utilitarianism*, pp. 13–16). Martha Nussbaum reads this as an inclination back to Aristotle's virtue ethics: John Stuart Mill knew from the *Nicomachean Ethics* that exercising courage might make you happy, but it might not be pleasurable. In this light, virtues are identified as a higher pleasure in *Utilitarianism*.[13] The idea of ethical calculation and subsequent reckoning of some parts of the globe as having no tally, however, persisted. This can be shown through a range of modern collective biographies.

Women's collective biographies

Poet, novelist and historian Lucy Aikin (1781–1864) was anxious about publishing *Epistles on Women* (1810). After all, she tells us, women and men are not the same, and

> [a]s long as the bodily constitution of the species shall remain the same, man must in general assume those public and active offices of life which confer authority, whilst to women will usually be allotted such domestic and private ones as imply a certain degree of subordination.

(p. v)

She had a right to be nervous, particularly given that *Epistles* was one of the earliest works she published, and she, like many other women history makers, such as Sarah Strickney Ellis (1799–1872) and Mary Cowden Clarke (1809–98), could not count on the right to access libraries and archives. A woman publishing a book might be seen as transgressing from the private to the public spheres and attempting to break into academic and literary circles that she had little or no right to enter. In her

Collective biographies and utilitarian ethics **35**

defence, Aikin—like many women before her—cited service to the 'Great Truth' of a protestant Christian God (viii) and the approach of letting 'the impartial voice of History testify for us, that, when permitted, we have been the worthy associates of the best efforts of the best men' (vi; see also 92).

Yet *Epistles on Women* is not the work of a naïve cipher. Rather, the 'moral of her song' and 'moralizing strain' (pp. viii, 19) is a case for respect and education to be accorded to women. This is achieved via two tactical, apparently disarming, moves. The first is her claim that the lives of women are best understood via their relationship with men. This she positions as a historical claim, for she takes pains to explain that Adam and Eve were equal rather than complementary before the Fall and that the souls of the dead have no sex as they are under 'Virtue's lore' (pp. 23; 57). What this opens up for us is the possibility that inequality is not a universal given. Women can act virtuously in this life to attain 'Virtue's lore' after death. Yet in practice, it means a history in which we expect to read about fathers, brothers and husbands. Moreover, in the abstract, men are discussed on 42 occasions; women are discussed on 54 occasions. The actions of men are also positioned as having far more impact than those of women. Women, necessarily, are part of a history of men. *Epistles on Women* should also, therefore, be understood as epistles on men and, more precisely, women in relation to men.

Second, she sets the expectation upfront that she will cycle through the same methodology of 'argument', 'epistle' and 'notes', turning out commentary on the virtues or vices of women without succumbing to flourishes of creativity. On the face of it, this stems from her decision that it is not practical to recount global human history on one chronological scale. She will vary scales much as universal history makers varied scales in order to bring the 'moral' and 'poetical' into view. As she writes,

> With respect to arrangement, I may remark, that as a strictly chronological one was incompatible with the design of tracing the progress of human society not in one country alone, but in many, I have judged it most advisable to form to myself such an one as seemed best adapted to my own peculiar purposes, moral and poetical.
>
> (p. vii)

The result of these two tactical moves is a dynamic, multi-scale work that is more like three nested, interconnected houses made from hand-wrought parts than a collection of turned-out biographies that can be teased apart and compared. Each 'argument' section recounts the history of a part of the globe in approximately four pages, each 'epistle' section in 60 and each 'notes' section in 16. The arguments resemble the summaries that were used widely as chapter heads in eighteenth and nineteenth-century printed texts. We might think of them as being akin to abstracts, but she presents events in them far more on the scale of societies and humanity as a whole than in the other two sections. She also offers distinctive ethical claims, as with the following advice:

36 Collective biographies and utilitarian ethics

> To Englishmen to look with favour on the mental improvement of females…
> to English women to improve and principle their minds, and by their merit
> induce the men to treat them as friends.
>
> (p. 66)

What sets the epistles off from the other parts of the text is very obviously their
poetic form. The title is a clever double play, conveying the expectation that they
contain poetry and the written thoughts of God's servant. Aikin never deviates from
poetic form, with the scansion of some of the lines sounding quite forced to our ears,
such as her declaration 'such is Savage Man, of beasts the worst, In want, in guilt, in
lawless rapine nurs[ed]' (p. 34). The moral tone of the epistles is stronger than that of
the two other prose sections, as with her judgement of the women of ancient Greece:

> The wives, proud Athens! Fettered and debased, Listlessly duteous, negatively
> chaste, O vapid summary of a slavish lot! They sew and spin, they die and are
> forgot.
>
> (p. 52)

Her focus is on the same societies summarised in the arguments, but she homes in on the
virtues and vices of particular individuals to reinforce her moral judgements. In a manner
akin to the examples presented in Chapter 1 of this book, for example, she uses vices or virtues to switch scales between individuals and groups, and the other way around. Her example of a Native American woman committing matricide, for example, is taken as grounds
for declaring that Heaven bypassed early history and bestowed the virtues upon later times
(p. 43). Responsibility, though, is also sheeted back to Native American men who vacillate
between, as she puts it, 'rage and torpor', hunting and 'jocund' idleness (pp. 34, 37). So too
the 'Asiatic man', for whom 'Self is his God, his wildest will is law' corrupts and renders dull
and lazy women confined to harems (pp. 70, 69). Her history of the virtues is therefore very
clearly coloured—as Plutarch would put it—by her Christian beliefs.

It is the notes section which comes closest to the format of global history built biography by biography. It also contains anthropological vignettes and further judgements on
groups and individuals not contained in either the arguments or epistles sections. Indeed,
in one case, she corrects an argument made in the epistles, noting that it is only rarely
true in her times that Christians still deal in slaves (p. 97; see also p. 40). She also takes aim
at thinkers and writers of history, as seen in her quip that '[c]ertainly Rousseau did not
consult the interests of the weaker sex in his preference of savage life to civilized' (p. 96).

In the aggregate, Aikin sees the triple structure of her work as allowing us to
reckon ethical status. This is not a static state, as she explains in the introduction, for
she is interested in

> the effect of various codes, institutions, and states of manners, on the virtue
> and happiness of man, and the concomitant and proportional elevation or
> depression of women in the scale of existence.
>
> (vii; see also p. 21)

That is, she wants to reckon the fluctuations in women's ethical standing, as calculated primarily through the actions of men. The moral calculus for women is not theirs to determine wholly, or arguably even in the main. So even if more women act in a particular way than men, their moral fate and standing can be determined by them. For Aikin then, there is no single moral calculus. There are at least two and that of men has more weight than that of women by dent of their public lives.

Much of the same message is conveyed in Clarke's *World-Noted Women* (1858) and the Ellis' *The Mothers of Great Men* (1859), though the structure of these later works is much simpler. They are composed of chronologically arranged discrete biographical parts that vary rarely intersect with one another. They are, returning to the analogy that opened the chapter, like the bricks that make a house. Yet neither of these are mass-produced works. Their parts are neither identical in form nor discrete. Each biography varies in length, and as with Aikin's work, women's history is seen as intertwined with that of men. Well over half of the text of Clarke's 17 biographies, for example, is focused on the men who fathered, married, sought a relationship with or who wrote about the selected women. Ellis' subjects are included by virtue of being the mothers of great men. This too is needed to highlight a form of moral calculus, but Ellis' calculus is different to that of Aikin. In her view, the acts of women amplify those of men. As she writes in her descriptions of the achievements of Aspasia (c.470–c.400 BCE) and Laura de Noves (1310–48), for example,

> Such a qualitied helpmate develops a man's faculties, and perfects his genius. She is perhaps even more valuable in this, acting *through* him, than had she been more palpably great in herself. Her intellect operating in enhancement of his, produces probably a larger amount of gained benefit to the world.... It doubles itself, it augments his; and a multiplied emanation of intellectual enlightenment accrues to their fellow-creatures in consequence.
>
> (p. 57)

> She elevated his intellectual faculty; and ennobled his desires—one of the choicest felicities that can befall a woman.
>
> (p. 145; see also p. 113)

The acts of women double, augment, elevate the ethical achievements of men. In crude terms, we might think of them as a multiplying function. This means that the number of women aiding men has an impact on moral calculus. Conversely, the absence of women acting, or acting well, can diminish the moral standing of men. If Isabella I of Castile (1454–1504 CE) had married Richard III (1452–85 CE), Clarke argues, then his sharp intellect 'might have been put to virtuous and valuable use, instead of being exercised in compassing usurpation, treason, and murder' (p. 238).

These ideas of additive or subtractive ethical calculus are also present in large-scale collective biographies composed of hundreds and even thousands of parts. Novelist, frequenter of Jacobin literary circles and friend of Mary Wollstonecraft, Mary Hays (1749–1853), for example, knew that her six-volume *Female Biography,*

38 Collective biographies and utilitarian ethics

or Memoirs of Illustrious and Celebrated Women, of all Ages and Countries (1803) was 'voluminous' (vol. 1, p. viii). Yet in the preface, she stakes out very simple additive language as the major theme of her work:

> Who, to the graces and gentleness of her own sex, adds the knowledge and fortitude of the other, exhibits the most perfect combination of human excellence.
>
> (p. v)

Women add to the acts of men and combine to produce human excellence. So too Lydia Maria Child (1802–80) argued in *Good Wives* (1833) that 'the amount of evil is always in exact proportion to the degree of good which we pervert'. Moreover, she made it clear that she needed to write a history of the world through women's biographies in order to get an 'exact estimate' of their capabilities.[14] But it is to Sarah Josepha Hale (1788–79) that we owe the credit of expressing most clearly the idea of large-scale collective biography as facilitating a global ethical calculus, as these examples from pages ix and 17 of her *Women's Record* (1853) attest:

> In this "Record" are about *two thousand five hundred names*, including those of the female missionaries: out of this number *less than two hundred* are from heathen nations, yet these constitute at this moment nearly three-fourths of the inhabitants of the globe, and for the first four thousand years, with the single exception of the Jewish people, were the world.
>
> (ix)

> Humtan life was shortened; and thus the mother's influence most wonderfully increased. Allow ten years as the period of childhood, when the mother's authority over her sons is predominant; then compare the length of Noah's life with that of Moses, and it will be apparent how greatly female influence was extended when man's life was shortened from 950 to 120 years. In the former case her period of power over her sons was 1 to 95; in the latter, 1 to 12.
>
> (p. 17; see also p. 564)[15]

At play here is the idea we met previously of women adding to or amplifying the good that men can achieve. She also, though, interleaves in calculations of the proportion of Christian women as against those of 'heathen' women, and the value of the length of a woman's life in influencing the actions of men. This further complicates and extends Bentham's 'doggeral' calculation, which factored in the intensity, length, certainty, speed, outcome and public nature of acts. It highlights the view that utilitarian considerations may be amplified or diminished via considerations of gender, religion and place of origin.

Classical Chinese collective biographies

Eighteenth- and nineteenth-century women's collective biographies brought a novel twist to utilitarian ethics. They showed that the 'most good' could be thought of not only in terms of the measurement of acts but also in terms of the additive or subtractive power of those who performed them. Yet whilst their combinatory talk was new, their views were built upon a deep tradition of women's collective biography. The anonymous *Tractatus De Mulieribus Claris in Bello* (*Women Intelligent and Courageous in Warfare*, c. 200 BCE), Plutarch's *Mulierum virtutes*, Baudonovia's *Life of Radegund* (609–14 CE) and Herrad of Hohenbourg's *Hortus deliciarum* (*Garden of Delights*, c. 1176–91 CE), for example, are just a small number of ancient and medieval biographical texts that looked at the acts of women in relation to those of men.[16] There are also many texts from the *querelle des femmes*—the debate about women in sixteenth- and seventeenth-century Europe—which explore the question of whether women were complementary to men or subordinate to them and whether freedoms advanced to women would undermine the virtues of men. Even a quick glance at Ester Sowernam and Joane Sharp's *Ester Hath Hang'd Haman* (1617), Rachel Speght's *Mortalites Memorandum* (1621), Mary Fage's *Fames Roule* (1637) and Bathsua Makin's *Essay on the Antient Education of Gentlewomen* (1673), for example, shows that the virtuous standing of men was understood as relative to the fortunes of women and the other way around.[17]

Nor could it be argued that the authors of eighteenth- or nineteenth-century collective biographies—like Lucy Aikin—were novel in their use of juxtaposed historical 'parts' to make ethical claims. That recognition arguably belongs to Chinese historians, particularly the producers of official dynastic histories. Sima Qian (145–86 BCE), the author of the *Shiji* (*Records of the Grand Historian*), established the pattern of presenting history in five sections—basic annals, tables, treatises, hereditary houses and biographies of notable individuals or groups—that was used in at least 24 subsequent official dynastic histories and documented in Liu Zhiji's historiographical manual *Shitong* (661–721 CE).[18] Sima Qian and subsequent writers used different scales and section lengths, as well as overlaps in content, to make direct and oblique judgements about the acts of individuals and groups. This was particularly the case with the final, collective biography, section, including biographies of women.

The third of the official dynastic histories, for example, Fan Ye's (398–445 CE) *Hou Han shu* (*History of the Later Han*, 445 CE) includes 17 biographies of women out of a total of 90 in the collective biographical section.[19] All of the biographies are categorised by role, characteristic or gender, as with the sections on magicians and recluses. Very little of the *Hou Han shu* is available in English translation, unfortunately, but the text that is available suggests a work in which the complex interplay of parts is used to deliver various ethical judgements about the activities of men and women. A small segment of his sharp observations on how the various people along the silk roads jostled for power, for example, has been translated with much care by John Hill (*The Jade Gate*). He is no less sharp in his biographical observations.

Fan Ye had a high estimation of his talents. He held that his contribution to history making, and to collective biography, was better than anything that had preceded it. We catch a glimpse of these views in a letter he wrote whilst awaiting execution for his part in the plot against Emperor Wen of Liu Song (407–53 CE):

40 Collective biographies and utilitarian ethics

> The Disquisitions in my various biographies embody my painstaking thought and deep purport. I made the language terse because I wanted to restrict the flavour in each of them. But as the for Introductions and Disquisitions in my chapters from the one on scrupulous officials down to those on the six barbarian tribes [last 15 biographies], in those my brush gallops away unbridled. They are the most original writings in this world.... I also wanted to write critiques on various matters within each chapter so as to pass judgement on the right and wrong of the age. My good intentions were never fulfilled.[20]

This makes for an interesting contrast with the views of Orosius from the previous chapter, who presented his efforts as clumsy steps towards the virtuous mean. Fan Ye deemed his level of detail to be just right in making an appraisal of that which was right and wrong, but he also lamented that his full intent would go unrealised on account of his impending execution.

Fan Ye's biographies of 17 women are bookended by an introduction and an appraisal in which he explains the partial nature of his text:

> The discussions in the *Book of Odes* and in the *Book of Documents* of female virtue are from a faraway era. Just as worthy imperial consorts assisted their lords in ruling their states, wise women ennobled the ways of their families; just as accomplished scholars promoted purity, women who exercised proper conduct illuminated the deportment of purity. However, their excellence has not been differentiated. Indeed, the texts transmitted forth from generation to generation are all deficient in this regard. Thus, starting with the Restoration, I have arranged their accomplishments and transmitted them as *Arrayed Chapter on Women*. Women such as the Empresses Ma, Deng, and Liang have received their own accounts, which can be found in the preceding chapters; the likes of Liang Yi and Concubine Li have been appended to the chapters dedicated to their respective households. Women like them will not be included in this chapter. As for the rest, I merely sought out and put in order those whose conduct was exceptional. They did not necessarily engage in only one type of behaviour.[21]

As we can see, Fan Ye's intent was to differentiate the history of women. He wanted to provide details for the lives of particular women, and he wanted to show that not all women acted in the same way.

Yet differentiation is not the same as rendering something discrete. Women's history is not a separate part of the *Hou Han shu*. Every one of the biographies opens with a standard identification sentence which outlines the woman's name and that of her husband, her father, and natal and marital homes. This sets up a message of women's history being part of a whole completed via the inclusion of men, particularly given that none of the men's biographies include marital information and 14 of the 17 women's biographies do. More particularly, it is the role of women as wives or daughters that is identified as the basis for their inclusion and discussion.

Collective biographies and utilitarian ethics **41**

For example, the filial devotion of Cao E (biography 8) and Shu Xianxiong (biography 16) are defined through their suicides via drowning after the drowning of their fathers. This filial devotion extends also to mothers in law, with the wives of Jiang Shi (biography 3, *Lienü zhuan*, in Gonzales pp. 122–4) and Yue Yangxi (p. 6) undertaking multiple acts over their lifetimes to show devotion. Women's biographies document the lives of individuals in the context—and by virtue, expanded scales—of their partners, families and societies.

Wifely devotion, or what is called 'the wifely way' in the biographies of Huan Shaojun and Zhao A (biographies 1 and 4, *Lienü zhuan*, in Gonzales pp. 119, 125; see also the 'way of motherhood' biography 7, p. 135) is seen in eschewing comfort and luxury, wisdom and skill in writing and speech, purity, dutifulness and righteousness (pp. 118, 121, 130, 133, 134, 149, 152–3). Whilst the rules of propriety described in the biography of Cai Yan forbid touch between men and women (biography 17, p. 153), it is also emphasised that wives are responsible for the virtue of their husbands. In the biography of Zhao A, for example, we see that responsibility carried to an extreme end. As she laments,

> 'If I admonish my husband and he does not change, then my father-in-law will believe I did not honour his instructions. The blame will be on me. If I admonish my husband and he does listen, then, as a son, he will have favoured obeying his wife but disobeyed his father. The blame will be on him. In this situation, what can I rely on?' Thereupon she killed herself.
>
> (biography 4, *Lienü zhuan*, in Gonzales pp. 125–6;
> see also biography 9, pp. 137–8)

Yet it would be a mistake to see Fan Ye's text as a straightforward and simple catalogue of virtuous behaviours that women ought to demonstrate. This is not simply because, as with the case of Ma Lun, there is a cross reference to the biography of Wei in another part of the *Hou Han shu*. Rather, there appears at first sight to be no agreed course of behaviour presented regarding widowhood and remarriage. Widowhood is a persistent theme in Fan Ye's biographies of women, and it is dwelt on in some length even in very short entries. Ban Zhao does not remarry, the wife of Liu Changqing mutilates herself to avoid remarriage, the wife of Huangfi is killed by her new suitor and Xun Cai commits suicide in her new household (biographies 5, 12, 13 and 14, *Lienü zhuan*, in Gonzales pp. 126–30, 143–8). Lü Rong, by contrast, kills herself to avoid the advances of an attacker after her husband's death, Li Mujiang remarries and is treated badly in her new household and Cai Yun is kidnapped, ransomed and remarried (biographies 9, 7 and 17, *Lienü zhuan*, in Gonzales pp. 133–8, 151–4). Ana González has argued that Fan Ye's ambiguous stance reflects that of wider Han society. Yet some kind of misfortune befalls all of the women apart from Ban Zhao, who does not remarry. This would suggest oblique criticism of widow remarriage, in line with the trends against remarriage during the course of the Han dynasty, as argued by Jack Dull.[22]

42 Collective biographies and utilitarian ethics

Why remarriage might have been a problem is more fully explained in one of the precursor texts and key sources for the *Hou Han shu*, Liu Xiang's *Lienü zhuan* or *Exemplary Women of Early China*. Liu Xiang's *Lienü zhuan* is a world history of women, as told through a collective biography of 107 women sorted into seven categories of exemplars: the maternal models, the worthy and enlightened, the sympathetic and wise, the chaste and compliant, the principled and righteous, the accomplished rhetoricians and the depraved and favoured. The order reflects the prioritisation of motherhood as a key source for virtuous behaviours, and the exemplars of wickedness are found at the end of the text.

As Anne Kinney has identified, one of the key themes of Liu Xiang's *Lienü zhuan* is how the activities of women contribute to the rise and fall of families and dynasties.[23] Liu Xiang, in turn, developed this theme from Sima Qian's observation in the *Shiji* that the fate of dynasties often sat with a ruler's consorts. The intersection of the individual and the group, and the private and public spheres, and women's movement from one to the other to either strengthen or undercut a family's or dynasty's fortunes is therefore critical to the text. Widowhood could confuse lineage and place the fate of a family or dynasty at risk. Chaste widowhood is therefore promoted as the better course over remarriage. What we witness, as we did for the universal histories in the previous chapter, is Liu Xiang's use of the assumed alignment of individual and group virtues to aid the movement between those spheres. Thirteen of the 15 biographies in the 'worthy and enlightened' section, for instance, show how the admonition of wives against husbands who are lacking in the virtues leads to behavioural reform and an improvement in the fate of a family or dynasty. A good example is seen in Fan Ji, who influences a double change in King Zhuang of Chu (2.5 in *Exemplary Women of Early China*). First, she dissuades him from spending all of his time hunting, and we learn that he 'assiduously applied himself to governmental affairs'. Second, she speaks out against the nepotism of Yu Qiuzi:

> Now Yu Qiuzi has been a minister of Chu for more than ten years, yet the people he has recommended are either his sons or younger brothers or men from his clan. I have not heard of him promoting worthy men or demoting those who are incompetent. This is a case of deceiving one's ruler and obstructing the path of the worthy. To know of worthies and not promote them is disloyal. To be unaware of their worthiness is ignorance.... The king made Sunshu Ao chief counsellor. He governed in Chu for three years, and with his help King Zhuang became hegemon.
>
> (p. 31)

The king's consort moves from the private to the public realm in order to ensure that the fortunes of the dynasty are put ahead of Yu Qiuzi's family. Another example, from the 'sympathetic and wise' section, sees Shu Ji demonstrate her skills at being able to reason by analogy and connect the fates of an individual with that of a family:

When Boshi was born, a serving woman reported it to Shu Ji.... Shu Ji went to look at him, but when she reached the hall she heard his cry and returned, saying 'It is the voice of a wolf. A wolflike child will have a wild heart. The one who destroys the Yangshe lineage will surely be this child'. After this she refused to see him. When he grew up, he and members of the Qi lineage brought about great disorder...and it was because of him that the Yangshe lineage was destroyed.

(p. 57)

Women need the education and position of wife, mother or daughter, Liu Xiang repeatedly suggests, to be able to cut through problems that have much wider implications for social and Confucian notions of harmony. Women act or refrain from acting to ensure that disruptions or perturbations are removed and that social, historical and universal notions of harmony and alignment are restored.

It is also worth noting that the movement between individuals and groups is also supported by the movement in each biography from verse summaries or *song* through to biographical particulars and back to *song* or to summative 'man of discernment' statements which summarise the morality of the tale. Shu Ji's skill in analogy, for example, is noted by 'a man of discernment', and in the following *song*:

Shuxiang's mother
Examined disposition and character.
She extrapolated from the manner of a person's birth,
And was able to know a persons' fate. (pp. 57, 58)

Here, as with Aikin's triple structure of arguments, epistles and notes, *songs* are used as a device to help the reader to move from the consideration of a particular person's acts to a consideration of virtues in the abstract. *Song*, in short, were used as much by the makers of collective biographies as those of universal histories to change spatial and temporal scales.

Back to Middletown

Collective biographies are not simple. They are not the turned-out products of a history maker working to a strict template. They are not historiographical houses made from mass-produced bricks. They, like universal histories, are not written consistently on one scale. They move from singular acts by individuals to calculations of the moral standing of the globe over known history. They are, though, very useful for utilitarian ethicists, including highlighting problems with this approach.

Collective biographies can be useful for utilitarian ethicists because they document the effects or consequences of people's actions at scale. They can highlight via multiple instances whether particular acts maximised net good in the world or at least increased it as against any other alternative. It is possible to even understand the logic that the more examples of acts you include in a collective biography, the

44 Collective biographies and utilitarian ethics

more helpful it might be as a guide to acting in the present. Maximising history might be seen as maximising the likelihood of us navigating to the most good in the present. To unpack this logic even further, collective biographies might be seen also as calculators of the good, particularly if you are assumed to use the same frames of reference or categories—biography and virtues, for example—and to sum the outcomes of individuals' acts.

Yet collective biographies highlight how hard it is to stick by utilitarian logic, at least in its classical form. To begin, none of the biographers we met in this chapter were only interested in consequences. They were interested in actions but also in those who performed those actions. Women's actions, for example, were seen in the context of men's actions. Moreover, they talked of women's intentions as well as actions, as with Xiang Liu's account of the thinking that preceded Zhao A's suicide. They talked of proportional rather than net good, as with Sarah Josepha Hales' reckoning that the length of a woman's life, relative to that of a man, could have an impact on ethical outcomes. That is, the longer women live relative to men, the better the world would be. Their assumptions about consequences were also not universal, for they assumed that women could do the most good by influencing the actions of men and that the fate of women fluctuated with the acts of men. On this logic, women and men act in ethically additive, not discrete, ways. They did not give strictly equal consideration to actions, noting that the lives of Christian men and women, or women in the Chinese court, mattered most.

I could go on, but my point is that collective biographies show us that utilitarian ethics is not simple. They, like universal histories, place a high demand on their audiences. Their danger is that they test the thought, as well as the patience, of their audiences. They offer lengthy, multi-scaled and even conflicting navigational guides. They gesture towards a reckoning of global history but stop short in doing so. Moreover, they mix talk of the virtues in, leaving us to wonder about the role of hybrid ethical views in history making. The expectation remains, as with the histories outlined in the first chapter, that the ethics of history is very much our own making.

This is not just an observation about individuals on the basis of one chapter. With this second chapter, we have begun to see a new perspective on *ethos*. *Ethos* is not just the idea that we as individuals have to work at being ethical over the course of our lives. History makers have also worked at being ethical over the globe and over the course of millennia. Here we see a new story at a bigger scale: the story of a discipline that has not industrialised, that does not turn out precise outcomes. You will not find history celebrated in Winchester's *Exactly*, even though—ironically—it is a history book. This is not the story of history makers as replicating story forms or truths. If this story is made of bricks, then they are the idiosyncratic ones of a building that has turned more than once on its foundations.

Rather, this is a story in which history making is appreciated as ethically generative. Even when two history makers purport to hold to the same ethical view, their dynamic use of spatial and temporal scales complicates things, undercuts attempts to state simple heuristics for what we ought to do and opens up new possibilities for the good, the fair and the just. The rest of this book celebrates this idea of history as *ethos*—as ethically generative—and highlights the headache that it poses for those who want to fix views and the very administration of the ethics of history itself.

Notes

1 Lindsay Schakenbach Regele, 'Industrial Manifest Destiny: American Firearms Manufacturing and Antebellum Expansion', *Business History Review*, 2018, vol. 92, pp. 57–83.
2 Simon Winchester, *Exactly: How Precision Engineers Created the Modern World*, London: Harper Collins 2019.
3 Polybius, *The Histories*, 2 vols, trans E. S. Shuckburgh, intro. F. W. Walbank, Bloomington, IN: Indiana University Press, 1962, 1.5.
4 R. G. Collingwood, *The Idea of History*, rev. edn, ed. W. J. Van Der Dussen, Oxford: Oxford University Press, 1993, pp. 234–5.
5 Jonathan M. Alonso-Núñez, 'The Emergence of Universal Historiography from the 4th to the 2nd Centuries BC', in eds H. Verdin, G. Schepens and E. de Keyser, *Purposes of History in Greek Historiography from the Fourth to the Second Centuries BC*, Leuven: Orientaliste, 1990, pp. 173–92.
6 Plutarch, *Lives*, trans Bernadette Perrin, Cambridge, MA: Harvard University Press, 11 vols, 1914–26, 1914–26; Philostratus, *Lives of the Sophists*, trans Wilmer C. Wright, Cambridge, MA: Harvard University Press, 1921; and Diogenes Laertius, *Lives of Eminent Philosophers*, 2 vols, trans R. D. Hicks, Cambridge, MA: Harvard University Press, 1925.
7 Patricia Cox Miller, 'Strategies of Representation in Collective Biography: Constructing the Subject as Holy', in *Greek Biography and Panegyric in Late Antiquity*, eds Thomas Hägg and Philip Rousseau, Berkeley, CA: University of California Press, pp. 209–55.
8 Plutarch, *Mulierum Virtutes*, in *Moralia*, London: Heinemann, 1927–76, vol. 3.
9 As translated in Joachim Hruschka, 'The Greatest Happiness Principle and other Early German Anticipations of Utilitarian Theory', *Utilitas*, 1991, vol. 3(2), p. 166.
10 Francis Hutcheson, *Inquiry into the Original of our Ideas of Beauty and Virtue* [1725], 2/e, London: J. Darby, A. Bettesworth, F. Fayram, J. Permberton, C. Rivington, J. Hooke, F. Clay, J. Batley and E. Symon, 1726, pp. 177–8. I have updated spelling but retained Hutcheson's use of italics and capital letters in the quotation.
11 Francis Hutcheson, *Inquiry into the Original of our Ideas of Beauty and Virtue*, p. 195.
12 James Mill, *The History of British India*, London: Baldwin, Cradock and Joy, 1817, vol. 1, p. 428.
13 Martha C. Nussbaum, 'Mill Between Aristotle and Bentham', *Daedalus*, 2004, vol. 133(2), pp. 60–8.
14 Lydia Maria Child, *Good Wives*, Boston: Carter, Hendee and Co, 1833.
15 Sarah Josepha Hale, *Women's Record: Or, Sketches of All Distinguished Women, from "the Beginning" Till AD 1850*, New York: Harper and Brothers, 1853.
16 D. Gera, *Warrior Women: The Anonymous Tractatus de Mulieribus*, Leiden: E. J. Brill, 1997; Plutarch, *Mulierum Virtutes*, 242e–f; Boudonivia, *De vita santtae Radegundis liber II*, in *Sainted Women of the Dark Ages*, eds and trans Jo Ann McNamara, John E Halborg and E. Whatley, Durham, NC: Duke University Press, 1992, pp. 60–106; and Herrad of Hohenbourg, *Hortus deliciarum*, eds and trans R. Green, M. Evans, C. Bischoff and M. Curschmann, London: Warbourg Institute, 1979.
17 Ester Sowenam and Joane Sharp (pseuds), *Ester hath hang'd Haman, or an Answer to a Lewd Pamphlet, entitled, The Arraignment of Women* [1617], pamphlet, online at http://www.luminarium.org/renascence-editions/ester.htm, <accessed 13 January 2019>; Rachel Speght, *Mortalites Memorandum, with a Dream Prefixed, Imaginary in Manner, Real in Matter*

[1621], pamphlet, online at http://www.luminarium.org/renascence-editions/ester.htm, <accessed 13 January 2019>; see Mary Fage, *Fame's Rule* [1637], in *The Memory Arts in Renaissance England: A Critical Anthology*, Cambridge: Cambridge University Press, 2016, pp. 309–11; and Bathsua Makin, *An Essay to Revive the Ancient Education of Gentlewomen in Religion, Manners, Arts and Tongues with an Answer to the Objections Against this Way of Education*, London: Thomas Pankhurst, 1673, online at: https://digital.library.upenn.edu/women/makin/education/education.html <accessed 13 January 2019>.

18 Sima Qian, *Records of the Grand Historian*, rev. edn, 3 vols, trans B. Watson, New York: Columbia University Press, 1993. See also Endymion Wilkinson, *Chinese History: A Manual*, 5/e, Harvard-Yenching Monograph Series, Cambridge, MA: Harvard University Asia Center, 2017.

19 On the life of Fan Ye, see Hans Bielenstein, *The Restoration of the Han Dynasty, with Prolegomena on the Historiography of the Hou Han* Shu, 2 vols, Göteborg: Elanders Boktryckeri Aktiebolag, 1953, vol. 1.

20 As translated in Ronald C. Egan, 'The Prose Style of Fan Yeh', *Harvard Journal of Asiatic Studies*, 1979, vol. 39(2), p. 341.

21 Fan Ye *Hou Han shu* 84/74 2781–2806, as translated in 'Arrayed Traditions of Women (*Lienü zhuan*) from the Book of the Later Han (*Hou Han shu*)', partial translation by Ana Gonzalez, 'Strong Minds, Creative Lives: A Study of the Biographies of Eastern Han Women as Found in *Hou Han shu lienü zhuan*', Master's Thesis, McGill University, 2009, p. 115.

22 Jack Dull, 'Marriage and Divorce in Han China: A Glimpse at "Pre-Confucian" Society Divorce in Traditional Chinese Law', in *Chinese Family Law and Social Change in Historical and Comparative Perspective*, ed. David Buxbaum, Seattle: University of Washington Press, 1978, pp. 23–74.

23 Anne Behnke Finney, 'Introduction', in *Exemplary Women of Early China*, trans and ed Anne B. Finney, New York: Columbia University Press, 2014, p. xxvi–xxvii.

Primary texts

Lucy Aikin, *Epistles on Women, Exemplifying their Character and Condition in Various Ages and Nations*, Boston: W. Wells and T. B. Wait, 1810.

Jeremy Bentham, *An Introduction to the Principles of Morals and Legislation* [1823], Mineola, NY: Dover, 2007.

Mary Cowden Clarke, *World-Noted Women; or Types of Womanly Attributes of all Lands and Ages*, New York: D. Appleton, 1858.

Sarah Stickney Ellis, *The Mothers of Great Men*, London: Richard Bentley, 1859.

Mary Hays, *Female Biography; or, Memoirs of Illustrious and Celebrated Women, of All Ages and Countries*, 6 vols, London: Richard Phillips, 1803.

John Stuart Mill, *Utilitarianism*, ed. Roger Crisp, Oxford: Oxford University Press, 1998.

Liu Xiang, *Exemplary Women of Early China, trans and ed. Anne Behnke Kinney*, New York: Columbia University Press, 2014.

Fan Ye, 'Arrayed Traditions of Women (*Lienü zhuan*) from the Book of the Later Han (*Hou Han shu*)', partial translation by Ana González, 'Strong Minds, Creative Lives: A Study of the Biographies of Eastern Han Women as Found in *Hou Han shu lienü zhuan*', Master's Thesis, McGill University, 2009, pp. 115–154, online at: http://digitool.library.mcgill.ca/webclient/StreamGate?folder_id=0&dvs=1546819652373~412 <accessed January 7 2019>.

Fan Ye, *Through the Jade Gate: A Study of the Silk Roads 1st to 2nd Centuries CE*, 2 vols, 2/e, trans John E. Hill, Scotts Valley, CA: CreateSpace, 2015.

4

PHILOSOPHICAL WORLD HISTORIES AND DEONTOLOGICAL ETHICS

Immanuel Kant | Georg Wilhelm Friedrich Hegel | Thomas Hill Green | Robin George Collingwood | Kitarō Nishida | Hajime Tanabe | Keiji Nishitani

BUGIS MASS RAPID TRANSPORT STATION, SINGAPORE. Sound and images burst into the quiet carriage, ferrying a public announcement in concert with the sound of the electric motor. On the screen, a man harasses a woman in a carriage, and, moments later, he is pinned to the ground by at least four transit officers. 'No Molest' scrolls up in four languages. Singapore is famous for its harmonious sense of rules, and I should not be surprised by the film, but I am. Piracy, religious, economic and gender diversity feature heavily in the histories told about Bugis before the organising story of shopping took hold.[1] Stories, like harmonising rules, have origins. They can be broadcast over other older—or different—stories and rules but vestiges remain. And there are different kinds of stories and rules. There are officially announced ones, and there are those which guide and even restrict what we do without as much as a public service announcement. I think back to the video and a sinking feeling sets in.

'Feminazi', 'humourless', 'school ma'am'. Call out harassment and the least you can expect is a collection of labels. This is because, as Kate Manne explains in *Down Girl* and *Entitled*, role transgressions can be policed fiercely.[2] It is not that misogynists view women as other than human; it is that they expect women to behave in particular ways. Step outside of those expectations and disapproval and even violence can ensue. Extend Manne's logic to other roles, and you find yourself in a minefield of consequences for acting and for not acting in particular ways. No moral calculus of consequences can keep track, no matter how big the histories that document it. Much better to air the rules than to lay them bare, boil them down and figure out which ones are good, fair and just?

Immanuel Kant's (1724–1804) *Idee zu einer allgemeinen Geschichte in weltbürgerlicher Absicht—Idea for a Universal History with a Cosmopolitan Aim* (1784)—is 26 pages in its original German.[3] In English, with footnotes, it is 13. In European languages, it is slightly longer, in many Asian languages slightly shorter. Moreover, if you just

DOI: 10.4324/9780429399992-4

48 World histories and deontological ethics

extract the nine summary propositions, you can get it down to a tidy single page. Kitarō Nishida's (1870–1945) *Zen no* Kenkyū—*An Inquiry into the Good* (1911)—is longer at 176 pages, but it does not include any dates, events or even named historical individuals or groups. It offers nothing even vaguely resembling a chronology or timeline. Yet Kant's and Kitarō's works are both world histories of a kind we call philosophical histories.

How Kant and Nishida believed it possible to write such large-scale histories so compactly is the topic of this chapter. They, like the other philosophical historians we will meet, are rule reasoners and catchers. 'Deontologists' is another word we can use to describe them, although, as we will see, that label might be seen as policing activities that are not neat or discrete. In one way, it a chapter of contrasts with the previous one. For Kant and Nishida believed, like Hajime Tanabe (1885–1962), that you could not find the ethics of history via the 'accumulation of individual experiences' or by thinking about consequences alone ('On the Universal', 1916, p. 130). Scaling by stacking biographies and the outcomes of people's actions, to their minds, is no help and might even be a distraction. Rather, philosophy can help us to go one carriage up, if you like, to discern the rules, framework or logic which ought to guide our actions. This is not like the moral calculus of utility or outcomes, but it is, I argue, still an expression of *ethos*. We recall that with *ethos*, we are neither born virtuous nor always virtuous in our actions. Acting ethically takes effort.

The very first history makers saw themselves as aiding this process through the provision of examples of how other people have acted in the past. Scale became a very useful part of their efforts. Some history makers switched scales rapidly, unannounced. I likened this to a game of snakes and ladders, aided by the double belief that we need to look over time to see how people act and over space because individuals and groups can display the same virtues and vices. Other history makers built their accounts from parts. I likened this to building a house from hand-fashioned bricks. Neither analogy is perfect for understanding the *ethos* of histories—they are far too simple to capture the complexities of history making—but I still see them as useful guides for understanding why we have big and little histories. Now I will add a third: that of a matryoshka doll that adds new dolls over time. Matryoshka dolls are sets of wooden dolls that can be opened to reveal smaller and smaller dolls. The dolls can be wholly or partly separated out or nested together within the largest doll. They belong together by virtue of being made to the same graded design, or set of rules, if you like. Typically, they come as a fixed set, but it is possible to imagine that a bigger or a smaller doll can be added. The works described in this chapter are like matryoshka dolls, with nested histories made according to spatial and temporal scales. They fit together by virtue of reflecting the same framework, or set of rules, about the ethics of history. On this view, *ethos* means understanding the nested nature of histories and the ethical rules that allow them to fit together. This is achieved by dint of the assumption that philosophy and history are intertwined, with each shaping the other. It is for this reason that the history makers in this chapter are also philosophers, and the alignment of these two disciplines is the closest we will see in this book.

Deontological ethics

As with the first two chapters, it will help to say a little about the view of ethics which forms the heart of this one. Deontology derives from the Greek words for duty (δέου) and reason (λόγος) and means—in simple terms—reasoning about ethical rules. Deontologists hold that our understanding of what is good, fair and just should be based on reasoned rules or obligations. This is distinct from navigation between vices to virtues in virtue ethics or consideration of consequences such as happiness in utilitarianism. Kant is the thinker most commonly associated with deontological ethics. Across his works, Kant argued for the recognition of the power of human reason and judgement in discerning our duty to the highest good. Kant himself reasoned to what is called the 'categorical imperative', a kind of framework for ethical reasoning to the highest good. It is categorical in that it is unconditional, and it is an imperative because reason leads us to hold that it is our duty to follow it. Kant's first and most commonly cited formulation of the categorical imperative, from *Grundlegung zur Metaphysik der Sitten* (*Groundwork for the Metaphysics of Morals*, hereafter *Groundwork*, 1785), is as follows:

> Act only in accordance with that maxim through which you can at the same time will that it become a universal law.[4]

In applying this imperative, I first think of a reason for acting in a particular way. Second, I think of that reason as a universal law that applies to all rational people. Third, I reflect on whether the second step is possible; and fourth, I ask whether I could act rationally for that universalised action. Kant worked through a series of examples—lying, suicide, keeping promises, developing your talents and contributing to the happiness of others—to test whether actions were good and always made things ethically better. He saw lying, for example, as not something that could be justifiably made a universal law on the grounds that it would harm other people and humanity as a whole.

At this point, you could be forgiven for wondering how deontological ethics might connect with histories. It does, via the idea of *ethos*. Humans are not born virtuous and they are not always virtuous, we recall. They come to an understanding of what is good, fair and just through reasoning over time. They achieve some understanding as individuals, but it is as parts of groups—family, community, state, humanity—that this understanding is strengthened and sustained. Whilst the highest good may be universal, the apprehension of the highest good is a historical process.

Nesting histories and ethics

By the time Kant had expressed the first formulation of the categorical imperative, he had already published *Idea for a Universal History with a Cosmopolitan Aim* (hereafter *Idea*). In *Idea*, Kant proposed that the history of humanity could be understood as the progressive realisation of freedom of will and its culmination in political

50 World histories and deontological ethics

cosmopolitanism as a world federation or republic. That is, he saw history as the story of how humanity had progressively achieved an understanding of ethics via reason and the development of a particular socio-political form. That history would not have a short time frame. This is because he thought short-term fluctuations in the experiences of individuals or groups could mask the unfolding story of ethics. Moreover, he did not agree that the good could be discerned through the aggregation of smaller histories. He did not see ethics as being revealed, for example, biography by biography. Rather, he saw the actions of individuals and groups as both expressing ethics, and that they did so more successfully over time. Simultaneously larger and smaller spatial and temporal scales were needed: nothing less than the history of humanity and of the individual as one in both a moment and over the long course of human history (p. 11).

Kant also identified the driver for humanity's understanding of ethics: its unsociable sociability. He saw the tension and even conflict between humans wanting to individualise and to socialise as sharpening awareness of the nature and limits of particular actions and the good that could be achieve through them (p. 13). How exactly that played out in history was not something he detailed, and he did not see his work as replacing the efforts of historians who worked 'empirically'. As he explained,

> With this idea of a world history, which in a certain way has a guiding thread *a priori*, I would want to displace the treatment of history proper, that is written merely *empirically*—this would be a misinterpretation of my aim; it is only a thought of that which a philosophical mind (which besides this would have to be very well versed in history) could attempt from another standpoint.
>
> (p. 22)

Kant saw *Idea* as another standpoint on the past, albeit one that he saw as leading to a better understanding of the good than its empirical alternatives.

Kant's treatment of *Idea* as a framework—like the categorical imperative itself—opened up the possibility of testing through application and, more importantly, revision. This presented a great opportunity for Georg Wilhelm Friedrich Hegel (1770–1831). Hegel, like Kant, wrote extensively on freedom, mind, ethics and metaphysics, or how we make the most basic sense of the world. History played a key idea in his writings, as well as in his 1822, 1828 and 1830 lectures on the history of philosophical history, published as *Vorlesungen über die Philosophie der Weltgeschichte* (translated as *The Philosophy of History*, 1837). Hegel's basic premise in those lectures is that some approaches to making history are better than others in helping us to reason ethically, and in the opening sections of *The Philosophy of History*, he details a history of the idea of history that encapsulates some of his key philosophical ideas in miniature.

This history of history has three stages—original, critical and philosophical—which may be viewed as both an unfolding and as a hierarchy of the universal idea of history. They are like an ever-growing set of matryoshka dolls. Each of the stages in Hegel's history embodies the idea of history but the later ideas or forms of history realise it more adequately. Each stage suggests the culmination of the idea of history at a particular point; that is, each is thought to represent the best idea of history until it is revealed as inadequate. When that inadequacy is exposed, historians are compelled to adopt a new idea of history.

Original historians like Herodotus (485–25/13 BCE) and Thucydides (460–395 BCE) described what they witnessed (*Philosophy of History*, pp.1–3). This approach to history was not adequate, Hegel informs us, because we know that eyewitness accounts can be wrong or conflicting and that historians can use other kinds of evidence to extend back in time and over space. Consequently, history makers like Polybius (c.200–c.118 BCE) opted for a critical, universal approach, which was the focus of Chapter 1 of this book. Hegel characterised universal history makers as seeking out the connecting 'internal guiding soul of events and actions' (*Philosophy of History*, p. 8). He saw their search as inadequate because they did not know how to figure out what that 'guiding soul' was. This resulted in the fruitless accumulation of details and in misguided efforts at setting and changing spatial and temporal scales. Explicitly reasoning about the 'guiding soul', framework or logic of history denotes the work of the philosophical historian (*Philosophy of History*, p. 9).

Hegel saw himself as a philosophical historian and reasoned that history is the story of our growing understanding of freedom, which he saw as the highest good. Hence his summation that 'the history of the world is none other than the progress of the consciousness of freedom' (ibid., p. 19). The philosophical historian does not just tell the story of freedom, they will ensure that they use reasoning to do so in order to be consistent. A history maker, therefore, is also a philosopher, and the other way around. Hegel historicised philosophy and philosophised history. Having established this framework, or logic, if you like, Hegel stepped beyond Kant's approach and unfurled a history of the world in his *Philosophy of History*.

Hegel's *Philosophy of History* begins with the declaration that the 'oriental world'—including China, India and Persia—is 'outside the World's History' or 'without History' because it has ceased development (p. 116). This infamous claim has spurred much counter-historical research in postcolonial historiography, but for the moment, we note that he sees these civilisations as linked by a belief in ethics as a matter of external regulation. In his view, 'oriental' individuals do not reason to their own moral judgements about right and wrong. Those judgements are acceded to an emperor, a caste system and a judiciary (pp. 116-66; 187–222). It took the victory of the Greeks over the Persians to nudge the development of freedom along (pp. 256–7). The Greeks held to a mixture of internal and external guides to ethics. They bequeathed us the idea of democracy, but they kept slaves and relied on the external authority of oracles for advice on key decisions (pp. 258–68). The Romans, to his mind, tweaked this mixture of internal and external guides to ethics.

The conversion of Constantine (272–337 CE) ushered in 'religious self-con-sciousness' and important questions about the nature and limits of human existence (*Philosophy of History*, pp. 278–333). Yet the further unfurling of freedom, Hegel claims, was minor because slavish adherence to rituals and ceremonies was encouraged

52 World histories and deontological ethics

(pp. 336–41). Hegel thus sees the Christian Middle Ages as a 'long eventful and terrible night' which only ended with 'the all-enlightening Sun' of the Reformation (*Philosophy of History*, pp. 411–12). The Reformation, which was led by the Germanic people—Germany, Scandinavia, Britain, Italy and France—stripped away the power of the Catholic Church and spread the idea that each individual had a direct spiritual relationship with Christ. Individual conscience became the arbiter of truth and people everywhere realised that 'Man in his very nature is destined to be free' (ibid., p. 417). That understanding of freedom was, to Hegel's mind, best expressed in a constitutional monarchy because he held it to offer the best balance of individual and community interests (*Elements of the Philosophy of Right*, §§291–2).

Hegel offered a more detailed account than Kant of the history of humanity. That history of humanity also had nested within it an account of how individuals come to the kind of historical consciousness needed to see that history of freedom. It is thus simultaneously a universal history realised in the world and in the self. Moreover, he developed and adapted Kant's idea of the mainspring of history as unsocial sociability into a dialectic logic that applies to individuals and to groups. In dialectic logic, as we explore an idea (*thesis*), we arrive at its limits and are *necessarily* drawn to a consideration of a diametrically opposed idea (*antithesis*). The ensuing conflict between the thesis and antithesis leads to the contemplation of a new idea, or *synthesis*, which in turn may be taken as a thesis of another dialectical triad. For example, in *The Philosophy of History*, the customary morality of the Greeks—as seen in their consultation with oracles—formed the starting point of a dialectical movement. The inadequacy of this 'thesis' was demonstrated by Socrates, who encouraged the Greeks to embrace independent thought. Customary morality collapsed, and individual freedom looked to triumph in Rome. Individual freedom is the 'antithesis' of customary morality. But this freedom was too abstract: it was not driven by self-reflection and reason. Roman notions of freedom were thus nascent as well. They must be united in a manner that preserves the strong points of each. Hegel believed that the constitutional monarchy in the Germany of his day was a 'synthesis' because he thought that the community and individual were in harmony. At the same time, though, he hinted that America (and possibly even Australia) might see the further unfolding of freedom (pp. 81–91). *Ethos* thus continues with us. The set of matryoshka dolls keeps getting bigger.

Hegel's expansion and transformation of Kant's philosophy put it on a historical footing. Freedom was both in history and of history making. Yet his ideas were, in turn, expanded and transformed in successive generations of philosophies of histories. Karl Marx provided probably the best-known response to Hegel via his argument that economic and material conditions were the key driver of the history of freedom.[5] I would, however, like us to follow two paths less travelled in the remainder of this chapter, from Hegel to Thomas Hill Green (1836–82) and on to Robin George Collingwood (1889–1943) in Oxford, and from Hegel to Thomas Hill Green and on to Kitarō Nishida, Keiji Nishitani (1900–90) and Hajime Tanabe in Japan. These paths illuminate slightly different ideas of *ethos* through a deontological frame.

Green is reasonably well-known for his adaptation and extension of Hegel's ideas on history in his religious and political writings. He was interested in the unfolding story of 'the will of God' or 'eternal consciousness' over time ('On the Different Senses of "Freedom" as Applied to Will and to the Moral Progress of Man', in *Lectures on the Principles of Political Obligation*, pp. 2–27; and *Prolegomena to Ethics*, p. 38).[6] The end point of this development is the social and political form of 'universal Christian citizenship', for 'it is human society as a whole that we must look upon as the organism in which the capacities of the human soul are unfolded' (*Prolegomena to Ethics*, pp. 206, 273). Rather radically, too, he argued that God's manifestation in the world is dependent on the development of our rational will: if we are not conscious of God and act upon that consciousness, then God does not exist for us.[7] This line of thought, though, was tempered somewhat by his argument in the first book of *Prolegomena to Ethics* (1883) that consciousness exists in us regardless of whether we are aware of it or develop it.

The realisation of eternal consciousness is for Green—like Kant and Hegel before him—simultaneously individual, social and human. That is, we develop our ability to reason to the good within nested groups and nested timescales (*Prolegomena to Ethics*, pp. 99, 154). In concrete terms, he sees our ethical development as realised in association with our family, town council or local authorities, the state, and the world community and as part of the development of family, tribes, the state and humanity at points in time and over time (*Prolegomena to Ethics*, pp. 202, 207, 208). We could write history at any of these scales, but they will not be understood until the framework of eternal consciousness is illuminated in them. In practical terms, this makes a history of my family part of the history of humanity, and the history of this point in time part of the long history of the world and the other way around. These histories, therefore, need seem as belonging to the same set by virtue of their illumination of the highest good as eternal consciousness.

A slightly later scholar at Oxford, Robin George Collingwood, drew upon a broad mix of thinkers, including the Italian philosophers Benedetto Croce (1866–1952) and Giovanni Gentile (1875–1944), to try and tease out the nature of these historical relations further. Collingwood is best known for his book *The Idea of History* (1946, revised edition 1993), which is a posthumous aggregation of lectures and parts of *The Principles of History*, which was published first in 1999. In some ways, *The Idea of History* is a critical revisitation of Hegel's *The Philosophy of History*, with Collingwood outlining the dual story of the realisation of rational will and consciousness in the history of history and the realisation of better approaches to history making in the activities of individual history makers. In his framework, the idea of history is first realised in a 'common-sense' or 'scissors and paste' view, in which the history maker is simply a compiler or aggregator of statements by historical agents that are taken to be true (*The Idea of History*, pp. 234–5). The problem with this view, Collingwood tells us, is that the history maker has to take the claims of people in the past as true—even when they are not—and it is not the case that history makers do not select what to include in their works (pp. 278–9). The common-sense view of history thereby gives way to a 'critical' one in which

54 World histories and deontological ethics

the historian engages actively with historical evidence in line with self-authorised principles. Once the history maker comes to reflect upon these principles, they realise that they are subject to strain, change and successive realisation over time, and they adopt a 'constructive' stance to the past (p. 245).

Collingwood thus saw history and philosophy as intertwined and that their relationship provided the 'means of living well in a disordered world'.[8] In his social and political writings, he explored the realisation of rational will and consciousness through the successive unfolding of forms of knowledge—art, religion, science, history and philosophy—and in the realisation of individuals and groups in the family, society and civilisation.[9] He also, however, drew upon the insights of Croce to explain how earlier understandings of rational will and consciousness relate to later ones.

Collingwood did not hold that all people or phenomena evidence qualities like courage equally.[10] Echoing Croce, Collingwood suggested that ideas like being 'good', or being 'civilised', need to be understood through the notion of distinction. Some individuals may demonstrate goodness in a minimal sense, as with an evil person. They are still good but barely so compared with a good person. The same logic holds the other way around. His point is that we cannot understand good without evil or civilisation without barbarism, and we see different degrees of these things in people and groups and over time. In writing this way, he was not suggesting that we navigate a middle course, as with virtue ethics. He thought that individual and collective reasoning would lead us, over time, to accept our duty to act for the good. *Ethos* was not charting a course for the virtuous mean but rather realising the highest good via reason.[11]

Collingwood's other important proviso was that individuals or groups *may* engage in ethical reasoning at a point in time. Over the course of world history, ethical reasoning is realised, but if you zoom in to particular groups or individuals, there may be instances where reasoning appears to stall or even go backwards. Collingwood's twofold point is that you need to look at scale—temporal and spatial—to see the realisation of qualities like civilisation and that the expression of civilisation is not guaranteed or determined in either individuals or groups. Here Collingwood's claims reflect not only the influence of earlier writers like Kant and Hegel—who called this unfolding of freedom over the larger scale 'the cunning of reason'—but also his own times (*The Philosophy of History*, p. 34). In his lifetime, Nazism emerged as a serious threat to freedom, and his was a personal philosophical fight in a near-global war.[12]

Opening up to the smallest history

Critics of Kant, Hegel, Green and Collingwood have seen them as presenting Christianity and European forms of politics as universal rules for the globe. The same complaints have been levelled at Japanese philosophical historians—otherwise known as the Kyoto School—in relation to Buddhism and Japanese nationalism. These are points I will return to in the conclusion of this chapter. For the present, I want to look to the Kyoto School to highlight a critical point: that philosophical histories do not have to write from the individual to the globe, or from the past to the present. We do not have to keep stacking bigger and bigger dolls, to return to my earlier analogy. We can also peel layers of dolls back, writing from the largest scales to the smallest ones. In the world of the Kyoto School, world history can lead back to the individual, to Mahāyāna Buddhist ideas on nothingness, the everyday and even to notions of nihilism. As Nishitani explains it in *The Self-Overcoming of Nihilism*, the 'history of humankind has to be made the history of the self itself' (p. 5).

As a fresh graduate from Tokyo Imperial University in 1894, Nishida read Green with a view to writing a history of ethics. That history was to become *An Inquiry into the Good* 17 years later, and it like Green's work is a simultaneous and open-ended history of the self and of humanity. Yet it also spills out beyond the boundaries of Green's thought, providing a critical rereading of Hegel and Kant and other thinkers such as Johann Gottlieb Fichte (1762–1810), Ernst Mach (1838–1916) and William James (1842–1910). In the preface, for example, we see the ongoing, unfolding interplay of both the self and the world and of experience and philosophy in his own history:

> For many years I wanted to explain all things on the basis of pure experience as the sole reality. At first I read such thinkers as Ernst Mach, but this did not satisfy me. Over time I came to realise that is it not that experience exists because there is an individual, but that an individual exists because there is experience. I thus arrived at the idea that experience is more fundamental than individual differences, and in this way I was able to avoid solipsism. Further, by regarding experience as active, I felt I could harmonize my thought with transcendental philosophy starting with Fichte. Eventually, I wrote what became part II of this book and, as I have said, certain sections are incomplete. [13]
>
> (p. xxx; see also p. 44)

By his reckoning, the world is neither wholly made with our minds—as with some of the more subjective approaches to idealist philosophy—nor wholly made apart from our minds, as with harder approaches realism. What opens up from there in the text is how pure experience grounds the growth in our understanding of the unity of the world—including the unity of our self with the world and the other way around—via our clumsy distinctions and efforts at differentiation. As he argues in a manner akin to Hegel, Green and Collingwood:

> Reality develops into an unlimited unity. From the opposite angle, we can say that an unlimited, single reality develops itself through differentiation from the small to the large, from the shallow to the deep.
>
> (p. 64)

That smaller to larger is the realisation we have as individuals that we belong to and are developed in family, the nation and humankind, including our sense of nature (pp. 139–41). I will return to the implications of Nishida's inclusion of nature in

56 World histories and deontological ethics

history later on in the chapter, as it is worth pausing now to comment on his view of the relations between these things prior to the realisation of the unlimited unity of reality.

How we get from a nascent sense of pure experience as individuals to the unlimited unity of reality is via an expanding sequence of universals that emerge from conflict and contradiction. As he writes,

> In the course of [the development of thinking] various conflicts and contradictions crop up in the system, and out of this emerges reflective thinking. But when viewed from a different angle, that which is contradictory and conflicted is the beginning of a still greater systematic development; it is the incomplete state of a greater unity.
>
> (p. 16)

In simple terms, we develop a sense of ourselves and the world from our attempts at both distinction and unity. We define ourselves as exclusively part of a family, for example, until we become aware of social groupings that both align with and challenge our understandings of the world. We also create distinctions between, say, past and present, subject and object, thought and feeling to help us make sense of the world until we discover that they limit our unity with the world and with others (pp. 3, 7, 17, 23, 33, 47, 49). The relation between our prior and current realisations of unity is one of differentiation.

Earlier in the chapter, we described Collingwood's views on nested forms of ideas such as goodness and civility as turning on distinction. That is, forms contain their opposites and our prior forms. Good, for example, is what it is in relation to evil, and our understandings of good include our earlier attempts at understanding good. This applies to both individuals and humanity, so we can say that both are given shape by the same nested ethical reasoning. Nishida had a similar view, but his use of the word 'differentiation' to describe the relationship between the nested sequence of universals emphasises his interest in a unity brought back to the self through oppositions and conflicts perhaps even more strongly than that expressed in Collingwood. As he explains with the example of the colour red:

> When the motion of material object A is transmitted to object B, there must be a force acting between them. And in the case of qualities, when one quality is established, it is established in opposition to another. For example, if red were the only colour, it would not appear to us as such, because for it to do so there must be colours that are not red. Moreover, for one quality to be compared with and distinguished from one another, both qualities must be fundamentally identical; two things totally different with no point in common cannot be compared and distinguished. If all things are established through such opposition, then there must be a certain unifying reality concealed at their base. In the case of material phenomena, this unifying reality is a physical power in the external world; in the case of mental phenomena, it is the unifying power of consciousness.
>
> (p. 56, see also p. 77)

That unity unfolds through 'larger' and 'deeper' senses of self and community, never leaving them behind but carrying them on, as with the nation becoming part of humanity (p. 141). But it also travels in the other direction, enabling a sense of humanity and the world as made by the individual. This twofold realisation is needed, Nishada concludes, for us to do good demands that we move beyond acting to satisfy either our own desires or those of society. Good arises from the harmony of individuals and humanity:

> We reach the quintessence of good conduct only when subject and object merge, self and things forget one another, and all that exists is the activity of the sole reality of the universe.
>
> (p. 135)

To return to our crude analogy of the matryoshka dolls: there is no doll without each of the other dolls, the set of dolls is not made at once, and the smallest doll defines the largest doll, as well as the other way around.

Whilst I do not agree with Elizabeth Grosz that Nishida's first references to history date from the 1930s, it is fair to say that his thoughts on history unfolded over his lifetime.[14] He started with a philosophical history in the manner of Kant and worked in history and history making as examples like 'The Historical Body' (1937) show:

> Our activity involves us in making things; that is to say, our world of everyday experience is the human-historical world.... It is the world in which we are born, in which we play active roles, and in which we die.
>
> ('The Historical Body', in *Sourcebook for Modern Japanese Philosophy*, p. 38)

The history of modes of making—both what humans make and how the world makes humans—can therefore be read as traces of the unfolding of our consciousness and ability to do good over time ('The Historical Body', p. 40). This, Nishida specifies, includes the smallest of body movements.[15]

Nishida also makes a clearer case in his middle and later writings that knowing history is a means of knowing absolute nothingness: an openness to the particular moments of the world that helps us to develop consciousness and to act for the good. In describing this absolute nothingness as the dwelling in the 'absolute present' that brings us close to God, Nishida acknowledges the influence of Leopold von Ranke's (1795–1886) idea of every epoch being close to God.[16] Zen Buddhism is also clearly an influence, although it is not named explicitly. In *An Enquiry to the Good*, for example, Nishida echoes the ideas of the Edo poet Matsuo Bashō (1644–94) in asking us to display our nature—and our good—just as bamboo or a pine tree display their nature.[17] Sources like this, and Nishida's formal practice under Zen masters in Tokyo as a young man, help us to understand his connection between openness and history.

In a Zen dialogue between Nansen Fugan (748–834 CE) and Joshu Jushin (778–897), for example, we learn that the ordinary mind 'is the Way' and that it is 'vast and boundless as outer space'.[18] Moreover, in an example related more explicitly to history, the Indian poet and writer Rabindranath Tagore (1861–1941) asks us to open our eyes to the everyday historicality in which we live in the moment and see ourselves and the world anew. Tagore cites as examples his wonder as a schoolboy at seeing a cloud and a cow in a field.[19] We might all be able to think of historicality in our own contexts: for instance, Australian fairy-wrens have sung me through the writing of this chapter. These tiny, fleet-footed birds have a way of bringing their songs to your mind in ways that defeat any sense of direction or notion that they are numerable. Their songs seem to travel through you, leaving you wondering about our notion of organisms as distinct. History is the ordinary, lived and embodied experience, as vast as outer space and as seemingly small as the moment of seeing a cloud or of hearing a wren. It is also potential, opening us up to the possibility of new relations between self and the world.

Nishida's call to the open nothingness of history provided fruitful ground for his successors at Kyoto, Tanabe and Nishitani. Tanabe, like Nishida, did not believe that the universal, history, or the good could be understood through a quantitative aggregation of particular phenomena ('On the Universal', 1916, p. 130). Collecting biographies of good people did not warrant the leap that the good was somehow the sum of them. The universal, for him, unfolded through the interrelation of the self and the world over time. So too he saw that unfolding as awakening to nothingness ('On the Universal', p. 134). Tanabe did not, however, see that unfolding as bringing us into immediacy with God because he wanted human free will for the good to be the shaper of history ('Two Essays on Moral Freedom'). As he put it in his reflections on Kant, 'freedom is not "what is given" (*gegeben*) but "what is given to do" (*aufgegeben*)' ('On Kant's Theory of Freedom', p. 155). Consequently, he saw every act as an expression of 'oughtness' ('On the Universal', p. 146).

Tanabe also extended and transformed Nishida's understanding of concentric universals. His 'Logic of the Species as Dialectics' (1946) does more than just betray his background in science and interest in the philosophy of Martin Heidegger. It suggests the amplification of the nation state through the recognition of its dynamic mediation between the individual and humanity in the realisation of nothingness over time. This was not a bald stake for nationalism, though, as Tanabe saw the unfolding of nothingness as halted by the assumption that a nation was in unity with humanity and thus that it could usurp the latter's role. Moreover, he turned the dialectic towards the purpose of salvation through nothingness. As he wrote,

> God does not act directly upon the individual.... This means precisely that salvation of individuals is accomplished only through the mediation of nation and society which already exist as communities of individuals.
>
> (p. 287)

This sense of nothingness and history for salvation is strengthened in his later writings and in particular his best-known work, *Philosophy as Metanoetics* (1945). If noetics is the study of mind in our most basic attempts to make sense of the world in metaphysics, then metanoetics is for Tanabe an exploration of how our confrontation with the limits of reason in facing radical evil can help us to achieve salvation through ordinary nothingness. This is personalised in Tanabe's use of himself to explain openness to salvation in the preface to *Philosophy as Metanoetics*:

> I…shared in all of these sufferings of my fellow Japanese, but as a Philosopher I experienced yet another kind of distress. One the one hand, I was haunted by the thought that as a student of philosophy I ought to be bringing the best of my thought to the service of my nation, to be addressing the government frankly… even if this should incur the displeasure of those currently in power…. On the other hand, there seemed something traitorous about expressing in time of war ideas that, while perfectly proper in times of peace, might end up causing divisions and conflicts among our people that only further expose them to their enemies…. I spent days wrestling with questions and doubts like this from within and without, until I had been quite driven to the point of exhaustion and in my despair concluded that I was not fit to engage in the sublime task of philosophy. At that moment something astonishing happened. In the midst of my distress I let go and surrendered myself humbly to my own inability…. Little matter whether it be called "philosophy" or not: I had already come to realise my own incompetence as a philosopher. What mattered was that I was being confronted at the moment with an intellectual task and ought to do my best to pursue it.
>
> (pp. xlix–l)

In life, we seem to often find ourselves wedged between what seem to be opposites until we relinquish the sense of our own self-power and open ourselves to new ways of experiencing the world and for the world to experience us. We as readers can struggle too between wanting to give Tanabe the benefit of the doubt about his role in the Second World War, and his lack of apparent remorse.[20] We want to read his philosophy, but we also want to speak out against his apparent complicity and that of his teacher in Freiburg, Heidegger. Heidegger, rather infamously, was a member of the Nazi Party and died without openly acknowledging how he might have contributed to the actions of the Third Reich. It could be that our distress, too, might usher in a new sense of the self, the world and the interrelation of the two in history.

The critical role of the self in the realisation of nothingness reaches something of a crescendo in Keiji Nishitani's *The Self-Overcoming of Nihilism* (1949). Taking his cue from Nietzsche, Nishitani argues that 'the history of humankind has to be made the history of the self itself, and history has to be understood from the standpoint of Existence' (p. 5). This is not an abstractly played account of the unfolding of the self but a work in which the author is the embodied focus of the text (pp. 5, 3, 6). Moreover, this is an opening move to nothingness, for the task 'means taking the entirety of history upon oneself as a history of the self, shifting the… ground of that history to the ground of the self, and saying "No" to it in this ground' (p. 7). This

60 World histories and deontological ethics

is *śūnyatā*: the recognition that nothing—including us—is independent. History is therefore the embodied self in the world and world in the self and openness to the dynamic interconnection between both. In short, in history, we pass through the self to the recognition that ours is a world in which there is not a single, discrete thing. We are nothing apart from our own matryoshka world.[21]

If history is not a single thing, then it follows that it is not made from parts; it has no boundaries; it has no spatial and temporal limits. The self, as we have seen, becomes the embodied lens of human history and the other way around. There is also nothing too small as its matter, and the non-human is entailed. We should therefore not be surprised that Nishida's *An Inquiry into the Good* addresses the role of nature in the realisation of absolute nothingness. To his mind, nature unifies and possesses a kind of self. As he explains,

> The various forms, variations, and motions a plant or animal expresses are not mere unions or mechanical movements of insignificant matter; because each has an inseparable relationship to the whole, each should be regarded as a developmental expression of one unifying self.… This unifying activity is found not only in living things, but is present to some extent even in inorganic crystals, and all minerals have a particular crystalline form. The self of nature, that is, its unifying activity, becomes clearer as we move from inorganic crystals to organisms like plants and animals.
>
> (p. 70)

Here we see a movement from smaller to large phenomena, always with a thought to their interconnection.

Nishida's inclusion of nature in history was not novel, even if we acknowledge that the implications of his enfolding of Mahāyāna Buddhism into historiography are yet to be fully appreciated. Hegel, and later Collingwood, also thought about the role of nature in history and in history making. How we might read their views is still a matter of debate, and this has implications for how big history is understood to be. Enfolding nature into philosophical history is not a simple matter as, for example, the lectures and drafts for Collingwood's *The Idea of Nature* show. As David Boucher and Rex Martin identified, there are three variant conclusions to Collingwood's *The Idea of Nature* and notes on lectures that he gave on the topic. Compare his various thoughts on nature from 1934 and 1935:

> Consequently the perfect development of mind would seem to be a real culmination of the process of nature; not leading to any further development, but closing the course of natural evolution. The world of nature would then have fulfilled its function in the life of God, and it [nature] would cease to exist. [At this point God is] pure and absolute being, unqualified and undifferentiated.
> …
> This is too large a question to consider now [that is, the question whether there is any 'difference between the process of human affairs…and the process of nature'].… It will be the underlying theme of my lectures next term, in

which I shall be trying to give an account of history, to describe exactly what it is and how it is known. When that is done, we shall be in a position to consider the question how far the process of nature and the process of history are identical in character, and how far they differ, if they differ at all.[22]

One version treats nature as aligned with humanity in being understood by God, the second opens up the question of their alignment once again. Collingwood's writings fall in favour of historicisation over and over again, which explains why *The Idea of Nature* presents a sequence of understandings of nature over time, much as *The Idea of History* suggests a sequence of understandings of history over time. Nature is in history, and of history and likely part of Collingwood's account of the unfolding of thought towards the interconnection between history and philosophy. Yet Martin, quite rightly, argues that *The Idea of Nature* likely did not have a conclusion.[23] Collingwood either had not worked out a position or was not able to articulate it at his death. As with Hegel's *Philosophy of History*, ethos is signalled as ongoing and needing our engagement.

Back to Bugis

The nested structures of philosophical world histories are complex and dynamic. Yet they also express a simplicity which flows from assuming that historical details can be categorised and expressed as reasoned rules. Kant wrote one of the shortest histories we will find in this book, and yet it is also possible to condense it further, down to even one or two words like reasoned freedom of will. As with the public service announcement I saw in Bugis, however, there is a question about the authority of these efforts. Deferring to or accepting the principles they propose as universals— including the use of reason to determine ethics—is paradoxical. God or the state might be positioned as the sources for their authority, but this assumes a belief in the state or theism on my part, and it still seems to put a limit on Kant's view that ethics proceeds from reason alone. Moreover, there is a risk that philosophical world histories might be read as the final word, without acknowledging the effort we need to put into reasoning to the highest good for ourselves in the present and future. They are, after all, historical artefacts presenting the highest good in the form of Western democracy whilst simultaneously ruling vast swathes of the world to be 'without history'. What at first blush seems incisive and reasonable can be seen as silencing, excluding and even violent by those deemed to be 'without history'. This can apply to the history of those who have lived in Bugis, as well as to the history of women, as I noted in the opening of this chapter. Moreover, there is the worry by those 'without history' that speaking, proposing other rules or contesting the categorical imperative will be framed as transgression. Censure, and even violence, may ensue. Censure is forgetting to say no to a singular and discrete sense of self, separated off from others, as Nishitani argues.

We cannot also be sure of the categorical standing of philosophical world histories written on smaller spatio-temporal scales. Kant, Hegel and Collingwood, for

62 World histories and deontological ethics

example, expressed confidence at being able to discern the unfolding of the good at larger spatio-temporal scales. That confidence stemmed in part from carefully wrought notions of the dialectic and distinction. Their confidence was lesser in the case of actions at a particular time or by particular individuals, nor did they fully acknowledge the dilemma of conflicting duties. We may, for example, face the dilemma of causing harm to others regardless of an action we undertake. In writing about the death of one person in an act of mass genocide, for example, I might be seen as downplaying or even masking a mass catastrophe. Conversely, I may be seen as dehumanising or non-empathetic if I write about the deaths that result from an act of mass genocide and not about the fate of individuals. This is a problem that we will return to repeatedly in this book: there is no clear-cut answer for determining the right or a good scale for considering the experiences of either the dead or the living. I may end up hedging my bets and writing at both scales and not showing due respect to either individuals or groups. Hegel provides little comfort about this, noting that the story of the realisation of freedom is something that we can only discern in the past. Making history is, by contrast, an activity in the present.

The issue is that strict deontologists do not aggregate in the way that Aristotle did in talking of little and big goods. Harms to thousands of people, for example, are not assumed to be a thousand times worse than to those to one person. Threshold deontology has been proposed as a remedy, with degrees of harm recognised for violence against, say, children, or large groups of civilians. There remains an issue, however, with the authority of these thresholds, as well as whether they are absolute or fuzzy. We may not be sure of the boundary between child and adult, between that of large or small groups or between civilians or combatants. When we explore deontological ethics in these ways, it more and more resembles the utilitarian or consequentialist views of the previous chapter.[24] These issues will return when we look to the cosmopolitan ethics at play in global histories and the social contract ethics of microhistories. For the moment, we have to acknowledge that when we think of history as ethically generative that it generates issues as well as opportunities to think of the good in new ways.

Notes

1 Christian Pelras, *The Bugis*, Oxford: Blackwell, 1996; Lynnette J. Chua, *Mobilizing Gay Singapore*, Philadelphia, PA, 2014; and Thum Ping Tjin, Kah Seng Loh and Jack Meng-Tat Chia (eds), *Living with Myths in Singapore*, Singapore: Ethos, 2017.
2 Kate Manne, *Down Girl*, Harmondsworth: Penguin, 2017; id., *Entitled*, Harmondsworth: Penguin, 2020.
3 Immanuel Kant, 'Idee zu einer allgemeinen Geschichte in weltbürgerlicher Absicht', *Berlinische Monatsschrift*, 1784, pp. 385–411, online via http://gutenberg.spiegel.de/buch/idee-zu-einer-allgemeinen-geschichte-in-weltburgerlicher-absicht-3506/1 <accessed 18 January 2019>.
4 Immanuel Kant, Groundwork of the Metaphysics of Morals, in *Immanuel Kant: Practical Philosophy*, trans and ed. M. J. Gregor, Cambridge: Cambridge University Press, 1996, IV, p. 421.
5 See, for example, Karl Marx, 'Economic and Philosophic Manuscripts', *Selected Writings*, ed. David McLellan, Oxford: Oxford University Press, 2/e, 2000, p. 104–18.

World histories and deontological ethics **63**

6 See also T. H. Green, 'Metaphysic of Ethics, Moral Psychology, Sociology or the Sciences of Sittlichkeit [Late 1860s–1870]', in *Unpublished Manuscripts in British Idealism: Political Philosophy, Theology and Social Thought*, ed. Colin Tyler, vol. 1, Exeter: Imprint Academic, 2/e, 2008, pp. 14–71.

7 T. H. Green, 'Faith', in *Works of Thomas Hill Green*, ed. R. L. Nettleship, London: Longmans, Green and Co, 1889, vol. 3, pp. pp. 253–76.

8 R. G. Collingwood, 'The Rules of Life', in *Essays in Political Philosophy*, ed. David Boucher, Oxford: Oxford University Press, 1989, p. 174.

9 R. G. Collingwood, *Speculum Mentis*, Oxford: Oxford University Press, 1924; and *The New Leviathan*, rev. edn ed. David Boucher, Oxford: Oxford University Press, 1992, §§15.1–17.83; and 29.5–29.58.

10 R. G. Collingwood, *An Essay on Philosophical Method*, Oxford: Oxford University Press [1933], rev. edn, eds James Connelly and Giuseppina D'Oro, 2005, p. 81.

11 R. G. Collingwood, *An Essay on Philosophical Method*, p. 88.

12 John Morrow, 'British Idealism, "German Philosophy" and the First World War', *Australian Journal of Politics and History*, 1982, vol. 28(3), pp. 380–90; and D.C. Band, 'The Critical Reception of English Neo-Hegelianism in Britain and America, 1914–1960', *Australian Journal of Politics and History*, 1980, vol. 26(2), pp. 228–41.

13 Grammar in the translation has been retained.

14 Elizabeth McManaman Grosz, 'Nishida and the Historical World: An Examination of Active Intuition, the Body, and Time', *Comparative and Continental Philosophy*, 2014, vol. 6(2), pp. 143–57.

15 Kitarō Nishida, 'Expressive Activity', [1925] and 'The Standpoint of Active Intuition' [1935], in *Ontology of Production: Three Essays*, trans William Haver, Durham, NC: Duke University Press, 2012, pp. 35–63; and 64–113.

16 Leopold von Ranke, 'On Progress in History (from the First Lecture to King Maximilian II of Bavaria, On the Epochs of Modern History' [1854], in *The Theory and Practice of History*, trans Georg G. Iggers and Konrad von Moltke, Indianapolis, IN: Bobbs Merrill, 1973, p. 53.

17 This poem by Bashō is also cited directly by Keiji Nishitani in *Religion and Nothingness*, p. 128.

18 Joshu Jushin, *The Recorded Sayings of Zen Master Joshu*, trans and ed. James Green, Walnut Creek, CA: Altamira, 1998, p. 11.

19 Rabindranath Tagore, 'Historicality in Literature' [1941], in *History at the Limit of World-History*, trans Ranajit Guha, New York: Columbia University Press, 2002, p. 97.

20 On Tanabe's lack of apparent remorse for his wartime activities in *Philosophy as Metanoetics*, see James Heisig, *Philosophers of Nothingness*, p. 151.

21 Bret Davis, 'The Step Back through Nihilism: The Radical Orientation of Nishitani Keiji's Philosophy of Zen', *Synthesis Philosophica*, 2004, vol. 37, pp. 139–59.

22 As quoted in Rex Martin, 'Collingwood's *Essay on Metaphysics* and the Three Conclusions to *The Idea of Nature*', *British Journal for the History of Philosophy*, 1999, vol. 7(2), pp. 343, 340.

23 Rex Martin, 'Collingwood's *Essay on Metaphysics* and the Three Conclusions to *The Idea of Nature*', p. 348.

24 Amartya Sen, 'Rights and Agency', *Philosophy and Public Affairs*, vol. 11(1), 1982, pp. 3–39.

Primary texts

Robin George Collingwood, *The Idea of History*, rev. edn, ed. W. J. van der Dussen, Oxford: Oxford University Press, 1993.

Robin George Collingwood, *The Idea of Nature*, Oxford: Oxford University Press, 1945.

64 World histories and deontological ethics

Thomas Hill Green, *Lectures on the Principles of Political Obligation*, eds Paul Harris and John Morrow, Cambridge: Cambridge University Press, 1986.

Thomas Hill Green, *Prolegomena to Ethics*, ed. David O. Brink, Oxford: Oxford University Press, 2003.

Georg Wilhelm Friedrich Hegel, *Elements of the Philosophy of Right*, trans H. B. Nisbet, ed. Allen W. Wood, Cambridge: Cambridge University Press, 1991.

Georg Wilhelm Friedrich Hegel, *The Philosophy of History*, trans John Sibree, New York: Dover, 2004.

Georg Wilhelm Friedrich Hegel, *Philosophy of Nature*, ed. M. J. Petry, 3 vols, London: Routledge, 1970.

Immanuel Kant, *Kant's Idea for a Universal History with a Cosmopolitan Aim: A Critical Guide*, trans and eds Amélie Rorty and James Schmidt, Cambridge: Cambridge University Press, 2009.

Kitarō Nishida, 'The Historical Body' [1937], in *Sourcebook for Modern Japanese Philosophy: Selected Documents*, trans and eds David Dilworth, Valdo Viglielmo and Agustin Jacinto Zavala, Westport, CT: Greenwood, 1998, pp. 37–53.

Kitarō Nishida, *An Inquiry into the Good*, trans Masao Abe and Christopher Ives, New Haven, CT: Yale University Press, 1990.

Kitarō Nishida, *Place and Dialectic: Two Essays*, trans John W. M. Krummel and Shigenori Nagatomo, Oxford: Oxford University Press, 2012.

Keiji Nishitani, 'My Views on "Overcoming Modernity"', in *Overcoming Modernity: Cultural Identity in Wartime Japan*, trans and ed. Richard Calichman, New York: Columbia University Press, 2008, pp. 51–63.

Keiji Nishitani, *Religion and Nothingness*, trans Jan Van Bragt, Berkeley, CA: University of California Press, 1982.

Keiji Nishitani, *The Self-Overcoming of Nihilism*, trans Graham Parkes and Setsuko Aihara, New York: State University of New York Press, 1990.

Hajime Tanabe, 'On Kant's Theory of Freedom', trans Takeshi Morisato and Cody Staton in *Comparative and Continental Philosophy*, 2013a, vol. 5(2), pp. 150–156.

Hajime Tanabe, 'On the Universal', trans Takeshi Morisato and Timothy Burns in *Comparative and Continental Philosophy*, 2013b, vol. 5(2), pp. 124–149.

Hajime Tanabe, *Philosophy as Metanoetics*, trans Takeuchi Yoshinori, Valdo Viglielmo and James W. Heisig, Berkeley, CA: University of California Press, 1987.

Hajime Tanabe, 'Two Essays on Moral Freedom from the Early Works of Tanabe Hajime', *Comparative and Continental Philosophy*, 2016, vol. 8(2), pp. 144–159.

5

LITTLE WORLD HISTORIES AND SENTIMENT ETHICS

Jawaharlal Nehru | Eileen and Rhoda Power | Ernst Gombrich | John Newbery | Franco-Suisse | Adam Smith | David Hume

FRANKTON, NEAR SUGAR LANE, LAKE WAKATIPU, NEW ZEALAND/ AOTEAROA. Schist stones grip, then shift, under my feet. Their clicks and squeaks press play on auditory memories, like the first time you said 'apple'. I remember thinking that the way you said it was as crisp as what you sought. As your tiny hand stretched up to the tree, I felt that you, too, were growing in this place and that its story was yours to tell. The Māori have a beautiful saying for experiences like this: *ahakoa he iti he pounamu*. Although it is small, it is precious greenstone. Although you are small, you are precious. In Māori, *whānau* is to be part of family, no matter how small you are. You are precious. To be *whānau* is to be connected to people and place, but it also heralds the beginning of something.

The stories that many of us begin with open with the words 'once upon a time'. These words, Ernst Gombrich tells us in *A Little History of the World* (1936), are a bottomless well that we can stop ourselves from falling down by yelling out, 'When?' and 'How?' As our words sing off the stone sides, the story becomes grounded as '*our* story, the story that we call the history of the world' (pp. 1, 4). Gombrich's *A Little History of the World* is a beautiful story told in awful times. It is also one tinged with regret. Gombrich laments his own willingness to believe what he saw and heard in Germany during and after the First World War and the impact of that on his thoughts about history (p. 275). It is natural to seek solace in distance, he tells us, for it lends a new view of things like that of an aeroplane looking down upon a river. That distance is one of both time and of space. But things close to us matter too, as he explains:

> Schoolchildren are often intolerant. Look how easily they make fun of their teacher if they see him wearing something unfashionable that the class finds amusing, and once respect is lost all hell breaks loose. And if a fellow student is different in some minor way—in the colour of their skin or hair, or the way

DOI: 10.4324/9780429399992-5

66 Little world histories and sentiment

> they speak or eat—they too can become victims of hateful teasing and tor-
> menting which they just have to put up with. Of course, not all young people
> are equally cruel or heartless. But no one wants to be a spoil sport, so in one
> way or another most of them join in the fun, until they hardly recognise
> themselves.
> Unfortunately, grown-ups don't behave any better.
>
> (pp. 276–7)

What we feel and think can create and sustain unrecognisable worlds—worlds of
intolerance and cruelty. His remedy is a world history in which children speak and
make the story their own and speak up to make that story ethical.

This chapter is about children, and it is about you. It seeks to unravel the 'once
upon a time' story of how we came to have children's world histories which addressed
their readers directly and made them a part of the past. The heroes of that story are
the eighteenth-century novel, the sentiment ethics of writers like Anthony Ashley
Cooper—the Third Earl of Shaftesbury (1621–83)—Adam Smith (1723–90) and
David Hume (1711–76) and the philosophies of childhood by writers such as John
Locke (1632–1704). Mark Salber Phillips and Jackie C. Horne tell that story beautifully. They illuminate the entanglement of history making with sentiment ethics in
the eighteenth century. That history making fostered the creation of sympathetic
connections between readers and people in the past.[1] It was the collapse of distance
through sympathy, they tell us, that made it possible for children and adults alike
to think about the experiences of people in different times and places. Moreover,
they remind us how novelists provided history makers with the literary devices they
needed to make that shift to sympathy and thus to sentiment.[2] Horne's analysis of
the dialogues and imagined historical children in Jeffreys Taylor's *The Little Historians*
(1824), Agnes Strickland's *Tales of Illustrious British Children* (1833) and Harriet
Martineau's *The Peasant and the Prince* (1841), for example, support her claims well.[3]

Entanglement, though, is not origin. When did writers first address their readers
and invite them into the story? The answer, Lynn Hunt suggests in *Inventing Human
Rights* (2007), also takes us back to the sympathy of eighteenth-century sentiment
ethics and contemporary novels.[4] It is the connection of reader and character, she
argues, that provided the means for people to imagine global human bonds and
declarations of human rights. Human rights imply the human, and with the human
comes human history. So too writers like Tom Brown remind us that playwrights
'broke the fourth wall' and addressed their audiences from at least the sixteenth
century.[5]

Snakes and ladders. Building with bricks. Nested boxes. Breaking through a wall.
This is the fourth analogy we have met in this book, and it, like the previous ones,
can guide our thinking about how history makers have shifted scales to aid our—
and their own—understanding of the ethics of history. In this case, what is brought
to mind is a rupture and the mixing of two worlds. The mixture is one of apparently
quite different things: world histories written on large spatio-temporal scales and
the short lives and small worlds of their child readers.

I am not convinced about this analogy, as I was not convinced about the previous ones. My doubts stem from travelling down the well of a much older and much more prosaic story. My story takes us back to practical, instructional didactic texts, a genre which ranges over books on the sacred, feeding cows, medical remedies, cookbooks, building and maintaining tools and machines and how to get rich quick, to name just a few examples. That tradition, which stretches back to the first instructional texts made in Sumer around 3000 BCE, contributed to notions of what we might call 'joint attention' through use of—among other things—second-person grammatical forms. Put simply, if you want to address someone—and encourage them to act—it helps to personalise your writing through the use of 'you' and 'your'. In this chapter, I will identify joint attention as a feature of children's world histories that are contemporary with Gombrich's *A Little History of the World*, then wind back to the first children's books to illuminate the use of second-person address, and finally look to the connection of world histories with biblical didactics. My account will also be prosaic in that I will acknowledge the cross-promotion of history in networks of texts and toys in the burgeoning book industry fuelled by the enterprise of—among others—John Newbery (1713–67) and note its continuation in examples such as the miniature book *De Grote Gebeurtenisse van de Geshiedenis* (*The Great Events of History*) which was produced by the Franco-Suisse Cheese Company in the mid-1960s. But I will also connect this story back to sentiment ethics and its ancient roots in Plotinus' (205–70 CE) view of the universe as bound together by shared experience. This will lead us to wonder whether there was ever a wall to break and whether ethics only addresses the human world. With this chapter, we see *ethos* as an attempt to reconnect the universe via sympathy, only to see that attempt fall short in the reading of sympathy as a human-to-human fellow feeling.

Sentiment ethics

Sentiment ethicists recognise the sense we have of ourselves and others in understanding ethics. The Third Earl of Shaftesbury offered an account of sentiment ethics in the first edition of *Inquiry Concerning Virtue or Merit* (1699). We can live good lives, he argued, by harnessing feelings, affects and dispositions in the moral sense.[6] In a simple example, I may judge someone negatively if they perform a good act callously. Their act was good, but their disposition was not, displaying what we could call a lack of empathy or sympathy for those they acted in the good for. Whilst they might have reasoned to follow a categorical imperative, or acted for good outcomes, their disposition in acting seems important to us too.

The use of the word 'sentiment' is important to these claims, for this was not just a matter of recognising the importance of empathy or sympathy in people's actions. It also included the sense we can make of our own actions in contributing to the good of our species, to life as a whole and to a 'system of all things, and a universal nature'. Sentimental ethics thus ranged over the universe and even included the possibility that non-human organisms and non-living things might also contribute to the good.[7]

68 Little world histories and sentiment

Here, as with the deontological approaches of the last chapter, we gain a sense of ethics as being about much more than the human. Indeed, it asks us to grapple in *ethos* with the idea that the universe is interconnected and perhaps even indivisible. This, it might surprise you to learn, comes from ancient understandings of sympathy. A key text for this view is Plotinus' (205–70 CE) 'On the Difficulties of the Soul' in his fourth *Ennead*:

> This one universe is bound together in shared experience and is like one living creature, and that which is far is really near.... For the like parts are not situated next to each other, but are separated by others in between, but share their experiences because of their likeness, and it is necessary that something which is done by a part not situated beside it should reach the distant part; and since it is a living thing and all belongs to a unity nothing is so distant in space that is not close enough to the nature of the one living thing to share experience.[8]

This text asks us to think of the universe as being like one living creature, with all of its parts connected by its likeness. Our job is to appreciate that unity through likeness as a part of ethics. This broad understanding of sympathy is that of perception or sense of likeness. This is a physiological and an intellectual endeavour and rational and affective in a unified universe. For Plotinus as for the Third Earl of Shaftesbury, there are no walls to be broken. It is for us to recognise the good that connects the universe.

The fellow feeling of sympathy is part of that interconnected universe. Seventeenth- and eighteenth-century writers talked of the sympathy people can show for objects such as ruins or everyday aids, such as walking sticks.[9] There came to be, though, a particular interest in human–human sympathy, including the details of how it worked. That particular interest remains today and clouds our understanding of what sentiment ethics can be. Smith, for example, offered a definition of sympathy as 'fellow feeling with any passion whatever' and included inanimate objects and the dead in his discussion (*Theory of Moral Sentiments* (1759) I.i.I.5). His interest in how sympathy worked, though, led him to focus on fellow feeling between humans. He saw a role for the imagination in amplifying fellow feeling and made it clear that it could elicit both pleasant and unpleasant experiences, including shock (1.i.2.1–13). Hume also saw the imagination as important, but that it needed proximity of manners, character, country or language to work effectively. As he wrote in *Treatise of Human Nature* (1739),

> We find, that where, beside the general resemblance of our natures, there is any peculiar similarity in our manners, or character, or country, or language, it facilitates the sympathy. The stronger the relation is betwixt ourselves and any object, the more easily does the imagination make the transition, and convey to the related idea the vivacity of conception, from which we always form the idea of our own person.
>
> (*Treatise of Human Nature*, 2.1.11.5)

So too at 2.1.11.13, he noted that the 'praises of others never give us much pleasure, unless they concur with our own opinion' (see also 2.2.4.2). What we can see here is the assumption that we should understand 'like' things in Plotinus' universe as 'same' things, and to define same as alignment of human character, country, language or nature.

Writing you into world history

Hume's account appears to be quite problematic for authors of world histories and for people trying to explain why we might not always sympathise with people like us. He does elaborate that benevolence can be 'counterfeited' by sympathy when we feel pity or concern at the pain of strangers and those unlike us. This happens when we think about another's future states because it taps into the 'general bent or tendency' of benevolence towards promoting another's wellbeing (*Treatise of Human Nature*, 2.2.9.15; see also 2.2.7.1). At the same time, however, he acknowledges that strong signs of suffering can produce a sense of revulsion through horror and some sense that we are happy or good by comparison. That is, extreme experiences might lead us to retreat to our own moral safety (*Treatise of Human Nature*, 2.2.9.18; see also 2.2.9.9). By these lights, making world histories hardly seems possible or even a genuine act.

Strangely enough, world history making boomed at the time that the Earl of Shaftesbury, Smith and Hume wrote their texts. Their times also saw the emergence of world history texts for children. To understand why, we return to the word 'you' and to Gombrich's *Little History of the World*. This word for second-person address, and the use of first-person address, is one of the most striking features of Gombrich's text, which ranges from 'once upon a time' to the contemporary 1930s. 'I' is used 89 times and 'you' 163 times. All but four of the uses of the word 'you' are for second-person address to the reader, and they stand out by being clustered primarily at the start of the book's 40 chapters. They do not, though, all follow the same pattern of usage. Sometimes, for example, Gombrich uses the phrase 'you will remember' to link up parts of the book, as with his distributed accounts of Babylon and the early modern Popes (pp. 27, 180). In these cases, 'you' has a practical literary function. Slightly more frequent, though, are his use of personalised address and analogies to explain abstract concepts to his readers. To explain the upheaval and turmoil that fostered and followed waves of migration, for example, Gombrich asks us to consider our experiences of watching a storm (p. 104). In this way, a global phenomenon is explained by reference to what is close at hand, with the effect of nesting the child reader's history within world history. So too distant time is personalised through the analogy of us stretching up to reach our mother's hand as a tiny child and realising that she too was once a tiny child stretching her hand up. Spatial distance is also personalised through the example of us asking a swallow how far away Egypt is (pp. 1, 10). Likely he thought these good approaches to explaining abstract and large-scale concepts and phenomena for his young readers, but

70 Little world histories and sentiment

regardless of his intentions, the effect is to bring world history into the compass of the child reader's history, and vice versa.

Gombrich does not just personalise systems of measurement and abstract concepts. Beliefs, dispositions and values are personalised in ways that indicate proximity to, or distance from, the reader. We would be shocked, Gombrich suggests, at just how strange the speech, the smell and the values of eighteenth-century men are to us (pp. 213–4). So too Buddhist abstention is explained through the example of how we might be happier by not thinking about the toys and books that we want (p. 56). Similar levels of explanation are not deemed necessary, however, for the precepts of Jesus. This is because Gombrich makes clear his assumption that his readers are familiar with Bible stories (pp. 11, 25, 26, 95, 130, 216). So too the importance of the Enlightenment principles of tolerance, reason and humanity are taken as going without saying (p. 216). These are important steps in the text, for Gombrich's reflections in the final chapter on remedying the violence, fissures and intolerance of his world turn on living Christian and Enlightenment principles. His writing of himself into the final chapter forms the basis of his use of the word 'you' as an invitation for his readers to also write a better future by learning from the past.

I want to say more about Bible stories later on in this chapter, but for the moment, it is worth noting that the use of second-person address as a call to ethical action also characterises the contemporary work *Glimpses of World History* (1934) by Jawaharlal Nehru. Second-person address is used over 1,500 times over the 900 pages of the text—which covers the period 3300 BCE to Nehru's present—with usages weighted heavily at the start of each letter and in the preface to the book. This seems an obvious feature given that the work originated as a series of letters from Nehru to his daughter—Indira Gandhi (1917–84)—during his imprisonment by the British from 1930–33. *Glimpses of World History* is framed by Nehru as a gift from someone who has nothing to give but words and as a means of connecting through the walls of his prison.

Yet the majority of the uses of the word 'you' in *Glimpses of World History* can be read in a manner akin to the kinds of second-person address used in Gombrich's *Little History of the World*. This is due, I believe, to Nehru's admission that his knowledge is partial. His knowledge of the world is partial because his knowledge of Indira, his reader, is partial. Early on, for example, he complains that her request for him to tell her about more history books is hard because she has not told him what she has already read (letter 15, p. 39). He also states his assumption that she knows particular things, as with the anthem 'The Internationale' and William Thackerey's (1811–63) depiction of the corpulent 'nabob' character of Joseph Sedley in *Vanity Fair* (pp. 133, 336). We are, however, not sure that this is the case because we do not have Indira's letters of response. *Glimpses of World History* is literally incomplete because we have only half of their conversation.

It is the absence of Indira's responses which makes it possible for us to read Nehru's 'you' as referring to us, in a manner akin to Gombrich's 'you'. That 'you' is invited to recall details across letters, as with Gombrich's 'you will remember' (for example, pp. 27, 65, 79, 90, 100, 177, 183, 213, 280, 326, 488, 620, 638, 852,

969). Moreover, like Gombrich, Nehru talks in terms of beliefs, dispositions and values that are proximate and distant to that 'you'. Those values stem not from the Bible in his case but from the deep history of India. The embrace of tolerance in India's ancient past, we are told, made it strong. Invasion and colonialism broke that embrace and ossified Indian society into a caste system that made it weak and intolerant. Nehru explains,

> The old Indian outlook in religion and life was always one of tolerance and experiment and change. That gave it strength. Gradually, however, repeated invasions and other troubles made caste rigid, and with it the whole Indian outlook became more rigid and unyielding. This process went on till the Indian people were reduced to their present miserable condition, and caste became the enemy of every kind of progress. Instead of holding together the social structure, it splits it up into hundreds of divisions and makes us weak and turns brother against brother.
>
> (p. 115, see also p. 100)

So too the absence of tolerance explains why Europe has a history of bitter religious, ideological and national disputes and a thirst to subjugate others (pp. 100, 119, 143, 153, 321, 578, 595, 677). It might have professed tolerance in the Enlightenment in a way that Gombrich celebrates, but it never lived it in the way that Nehru holds for ancient India.

Yet like Gombrich's reader, Nehru's 'you' is told about tolerance with the expectation of action. India's and the world's problems, Nehru tells us, will not be solved through sermonising. We have to speak and to talk, as he explains at the opening of the work:

> And so I have always thought that the best way to find out what is right and what is not right, what should be done and what should not be done, is not by giving a sermon, but by talking and discussing, and out of discussion sometimes a little bit of the truth comes out. I have liked my talks with you and we have discussed many things, but the world is wide and beyond our world the other wonderful and mysterious worlds, so none of us need ever be bored or imagine…that we have learned everything worth learning and become very wise.

You talk, go away and reflect on that talk, and you act for the right to make a better world. A different world is made from the personal act of us talking with one another, and the expectation that each of us will act on what we have learned from that talk.

It is tempting to read Nehru's invitation for us to sermonise less and to talk more, like Gombrich's calls for tolerance, as very much reflecting the anxieties at play in 1930s European and Asian politics. Yet talk as a means for illuminating the good is also present in earlier children's world histories like Eileen and Rhoda Power's

72 Little world histories and sentiment

global history of what they call 'Greater Britain' in *Boys and Girls of History* (1926) and *More Boys and Girls of History* (1928, p. vii). Eileen Power is known in the main for her contributions to medieval and economic history and her sister Rhoda Power for her contributions to radio broadcasting and children's literature. Second-person address is a strong feature of their jointly authored history books, as it was for Gombrich's and Nehru's world histories. The 'you' of these two books, though, are not the reader, but fictional and historical conversants. They are a fiction-history hybrid, as the Powers explain in the preface to the first book:

> By taking English children and reconstructing their daily lives, we have tried to secure a more vivid and clear-cut picture that would be obtained by generalised accounts of 'the manor,' 'London life,' 'The Elizabethan stage.' Many of our children...had an historical existence; others have been reconstructed from various contemporary sources; but all, we hope, give a picture which is as accurate as a modern historian can make it, of daily life in bygone times; and in the choice of our little heroes and heroines we have tried to illustrate as wide range of types as possible.
>
> (*Boys and Girls of History*, p. v)

The absence of specific evidence invites fictionalising, as does the need for vivacity and a 'clear-cut' picture of various child 'types'.

By 'types', the Powers mean gender—one-quarter of the chapters are devoted to girls—historical setting and class. The story of the Domesday book (1086 CE), for example, is told through a day in the life of the peasant boy Gurth and contains much speculation on the changes in taxation that might be expected to flow from William the Conqueror's survey of land and land uses (*Boys and Girls of History*, pp. 28–39). In the second volume, 'type' is expanded to include those colonised by the British in various locations around the world, but their experiences—and the world 'through their eyes'—are framed to serve the greater narrative of British 'adventure', as the Powers explain:

> We have tried to see the events described not only through the eyes of the adventuring or conquering English, but those of the little Irish girl, the Red Indian Princess, or the chief's son of Kandy, the Burmese, the Maori and the Australian 'blackfellow', and have attempted to describe their daily lives.... But as every boy and girl likes adventure, and the boys and the girls witnessed or shared in a stirring adventure, the history of England overseas, we hope that this book will be as fortunate in winning their approval as the first.
>
> (*More Boys and Girls of History*, pp. vii–viii)

Indeed, you can shuffle the entries out of chronological order and into a scale of proximity to or distance from English beliefs. The children in *Boys and Girls of History* play—there are over 60 mentions throughout the text of them doing so—and play with toys as the children of the Powers' day do (pp. 3, 7, 245, 251), including the young Queen Victoria (*Boys and Girls of History*, p. 332) and Banganoo the Indigenous Australian (*More Boys and Girls of History*, p. 241). Yet they also pray, even if like Olaf the ninth-century Dane they are not Christian (*Boys and Girls of History*, p. 16). So too they hear Bible stories, as with the example of Stephen of Cloyes, who is thought to have been one of the leaders of the children's crusade in 1212 CE (*Boys and Girls of History*, p. 53). The farther away from Britain geographically, though, the less the child protagonists play and pray, unless—as is the case with the story of South Africa in 1819–20—the chief character is a British immigrant (*More Boys and Girls of History*, pp. 221–36). Those doubly distant to the British—in geography and disposition—are portrayed as strange and as acting in ways contra to reason and Christian precepts. So it is, for example, that seventeenth-century India is described as a land of procrastination and promise breaking (*Boys and Girls of History*, p. 181), the Burmese as easily distracted by luxury, Māori New Zealand as a place where elders can be disobeyed and abused and Indigenous Australians as in thrall to spirit men and unaware of their dispossession at the hands of the British (*More Boys and Girls of History*, pp. 52–65; 184–93, 244–5). The text is not without some judgement of British colonialism, as the knowing comment of the Māori that the British will return and the description of sixteenth-century Ireland as a place of 'living terror' attest (*More Boys and Girls of History*, pp. 70, 192). It hardly escapes our attention, though, that volume one closes out with Queen Victoria's childhood promise to

> become a true Christian, to try to comfort Mamma in all her griefs, trials and anxieties, and to become a dutiful affectionate daughter to her.
>
> (*Boys and Girls of History*, p. 339)

Whilst volume two closes out with the description of the Bantu Tanzanian boy Soko as a 'little ape' by the slave-owning Arab trader Mohammed Ibn Saleh (*More Boys and Girls of History*, p. 270).

So far, we have identified the use of second-person address as an interesting feature of a very small sample of mid-twentieth century histories. How they got to be that way, and how they could make sense in the writing of world history, is still something we have to ascertain. An early clue comes with Mark Salber Phillips' and Jackie C. Horne's writing on eighteenth-century historiography, which I signalled at the opening of this chapter. Both argue for us to consider the entanglement of history with the 'suspect generic category "novel"' and sentiment ethics notions of sympathy.[10] Horne's and Phillips' analyses are rich and have helped to fill out our understanding of the literary innovations at play in eighteenth-century English-language history making. Yet I see the story as much older.

It takes us to the use of second-person address—singular and plural 'you'—in didactic texts. The first instructional texts originate with extant writing, and we have rich traditions of instruction present in writing forms across the planet. Roy Gibson and Alison Sharrock have, for instance, provided a detailed analysis of the use of second-person verb forms in ancient Latin prose and poetic instructional texts by writers such as Lucretius (fl. 94 BCE), Ovid (43 BCE–c.17 CE), Varro (116–27

74 Little world histories and sentiment

BCE) and Cato the Elder (234–149 BCE). Imperative uses of 'you' stand out in Cato's *On Agriculture*, they note, and we strike them early in our reading. Section one, for example, opens in this way:

> When you are thinking of acquiring a farm, keep in mind these points: that you not be over-eager in buying nor spare your pains in examining, and that you consider it not sufficient to go over it once.[11]

Gibson holds that as passive forms were utilised more in educated language than common speech, second-person forms provided a means for dealing with non-elite readers who were expected to carry out the instructions.[12] Use of the word 'you' was an invitation to action, as I suggested in my readings of Nehru's and Gombrich's world histories.

At first sight, this provides us with the beginning of a story that would work in well with analyses of intersections of histories with novels in the eighteenth century. Sympathy, and novels, came to prominence as more women and children learned to read, and book production both accelerated and diversified.[13] 'You' affirmed the rise of the non-elite reader. It is a beguiling story that fits in well with a host of 'ordinary' histories that historiography and the discipline have arguably tried to forget as the notion of a profession took shape in the late nineteenth century. Again, though, Gombrich's caution to his readers about 'once upon a time' stories should give us pause about accepting such explanations. As Harry Hine has argued, there are no clear grounds to draw a firm distinction between practical Roman literature for landholders and their subordinates and poetic works. People could read didactic books even when they were not expected to enact the instructions personally and to get both explicit instructions on how to do things and more passive offerings of advice.[14] As Ralph Keen, Daryn Lehoux, Daniel Markovic and Phillip Mitsis have noted, for example, the ancient Greek poet and philosopher Lucretius uses first- and second-person address every seven lines or so in *De Rerum Natura* 'to put his arm around the reader's shoulder' and to show—or even coerce—them into seeing the vivacity of his subject matter.[15] Second-person address was used across a range of texts, for a range of readers, and in a range of ways within texts.

The Roman-era Greek writer Longinus (fl. 30 CE) provides us with more specific information on the nature and purpose of second-person address in history making *On the Sublime*:

> A change of person is equally realistic. It often makes the reader fill himself in the midst of the dangers described.... Herodotus writes: 'From Elephantine you will sail up the coast, and you will then reach a flat plain. You will cross this, then embark again for a two-day voyage which will bring you to a large city called Meroe.' Do you see, my friend, how he gets a hold on your mind and leads it through these places and makes you *see* what you only hear? Such passages, by addressing the reader directly, place him in the middle of the action.[16]

Here we see second-person address described as 'placing' the hearer or reader—or them placing themselves—in the action, and later on in the text he reiterates that it both excites and helps the attention of the hearer or reader.[17] This is seen as not coming at the cost of the realistic, but as enhancing it. Polybius, on the other hand, explicitly eschewed techniques of this kind in *The Histories*, and his writing shows a preference for the indefinite pronoun 'one', as in the instruction to historians in 1.14 that 'one must not shrink either from blaming one's friends or praising one's enemies'. In the same clause, however, he switches to second-person address to offer one of his most important instructions: 'if you take truth from History what is left but an idle unprofitable tale'.[18] This example shows us that second-person address was not restricted to the 'placing' usage suggested by Longinus. We do also find Plutarch and Lucian praising historians such as Thucydides for using second-person address to make the reader feel like a spectator and to enhance the vivacity of a text, but we have to remember that Lucian's views on history were often satirical.[19]

With thanks to Kristine Gilmartin's detailed analysis of the distribution of pronoun types in Greek and Roman historiography, we know that second person was used rarely in Greek histories and more frequently in Roman histories. She also demonstrates, however, that use of the second person in the manner encouraged by Longinus, Plutarch and Lucian did not account for the majority of uses in Roman texts. 'You' was more often used to ornament descriptions and to include the reader as a fellow historian in the judgement of the character of individuals. This analysis leads to her conclusion that Greek writers probably viewed second person as inappropriate in scientific texts and that the Romans drew upon it in varied forms to drive home the sense of history as connected with the reader's fate or destiny.[20] Gilmartin's analysis helps to explain, first, why second person is not a feature in Aristotle's writing, but this needs to be balanced with Edward Jeremiah's helpful account of how he—along with other ancient Greek writers—developed a range of reflexive pronouns to promote personal reflection on rationality and personal and political autonomy, as well as participants in the creation of public rationality.[21] Second, Gilmartin's conclusion accords with what we saw at the opening of this chapter: that 'you' includes but is much more than an invitation to sympathise. Our children's world historians wanted their readers to connect with them in a variety of ways in order to drive home the sense of history as being in their hands, as well as them being participants in the narrative.

Creating children's world histories

Where Gilmartin's two conclusions appear to come together is in seventeenth-century philosophies of childhood and education by writers like John Locke. As Locke writes in *Some Thoughts Concerning Education* (1693), for example,

> But of all the ways whereby children are to be instructed, and their manners formed, the plainest, easiest and most efficacious, is, to set before their eyes the *examples* of those things you would have them do or avoid. Which, when they

are pointed out to them in the practice of persons within their knowledge, with some reflection on their beauty or unbecomingness, are of more force to draw or deter their imitation than any discourses which can be made to them.[22]

Like Aristotle, Locke argued for the preeminent role of reason in ethics.[23] In *Some Thoughts Concerning Education*, though, he teased that idea of rationality further out by arguing that it can be developed in children through adaptation of content—use of 'few and plain words'—and that such adaptations can serve as the foundations of knowing 'right and wrong.'[24] An example that Locke gives to support his view is a suggested shift away from question and answer catechisms and the presentation of Bible stories:

> There are some parts of the Scripture which may be proper to put into the hands of a child to engage him to read; such as are the story of Joseph and his brethren, of David and Goliath, of David and Jonathan, etc. And others that he should be made to read for his instruction, as that *What you would have others do to you, do you the same unto them*; and such other easy and plain moral rules, which being fitly chosen, might often be made use of both for reading and instruction…be inculcated as the standing and sacred rules of his life and action.[25]

The interesting thing is that the producers of books for children were already ahead of him in promoting the adaptation of materials to develop reason and moral development, and they used a range of second-person addresses to do so. Didactic thumb—small and miniature—Bibles and Bible primers were the loci of that development.[26]

The earliest extant thumb Bible is John Weever's (1576–1632) *An Agnus Dei* (1601), which presents the life of Jesus in verse form six lines at a time across 128 pages measuring 3.3 by 2.7 cm. John Taylor's *Verbum Sempiternum and Salvator Mundi* (1611) extended the textual range further by offering a verse summary of the old and new testaments and prayers for daily use in pages measuring 3.2 by 2.8 cm. Taylor's work includes notes to the reader at the opening of the book and the beginning of the new testament section, and in these, we can see the use of first and second person:

> With care and pains out of the sacred book,
> This little abstract I for thee have took.
> And with great Rev'rence have I cull'd from thence,
> All things that are of greatest consequence.
> And all I beg when thou tak'st it in hand,
> Before thou judge be sure to understand.
> …
> Man's sinfulness, and God's exceeding grace
> thou here may'st see and read, in little space.[27]

These verses are particularly lovely invitations for the reader to see a big story 'in little space' and to be the judge of that little space only as an afterthought. That reader
is assumed to be young or poorly literate, for the adult literate might be expected
to read the Bible without edits or the need for verse form.[28] By the time we reach
the burgeoning London book trade of the mid-eighteenth century, the reader is
addressed explicitly as young and sometimes even distinguished from the parental
or guardian reader of a text's preface. Nathaniel Crouch's (pseud. Robert Burton,
c.1632–c.1725) *Youth's Divine Pastime* (c.1720), for example, offers 40 illustrated
Bible stories in verse, with an opening in which second-person address is prevalent.
The first lines make it clear that the young reader will benefit from knowing about
the biblical past:

> Sweet children, Wisdom you invites
> To hearken to her Voice;
> She offers to you rare Delights,
> Most worthy of your choice.
> Eternal Blessings in her Ways,
> You shall be sure to find;
> Oh, therefore in your youthful days,
> Your great Creator mind.[29]

The book offers a summary of Christian sacred history, but it also contains cross
advertisements for large-scale secular histories. First mentioned is Samuel Crossman's
(c.1624–84) *The Young Man's Calling* (1713), a collective biography which highlights the 'virtues and piety' of various children in the past, and second is Crouch's
own *The Vanity of the Life of Man*, which presents a seven-stage universal history in
the manner of Orosius which aimed to 'expose the follies of every age'.[30]

The same cross-promotion and thereby connection of adapted biblical and secular
history is seen in the works of the well-known children's writer and publisher John
Newbery (fl.1713–d.1767). Newbery's *A Compendious History of the World from the
Creation to the Dissolution of the Roman Republic* (1775) is written predominantly in passive impersonal form, but third person pronouns are utilised in the preface to address the
reader in a way that indicates joint judgement with the author. Consider this example:

> As the history of each of the following nations is supposed to have been writ-
> ten by an inhabitant thereof, an uniformity of style, of method, and of senti-
> ment is not to be expected; nor will the same fact be always stated in the same
> manner, or with equal force; for we may suppose that most historians have
> some degree of partiality for their native country.
>
> (*A Compendious History of the World*, p. v)

Newbery expects his readers to see what he does: that histories are written from a position and therefore that the variation and unevenness of his sources will in part shape
his work. Where he believes he can shape the material most is in casting a light on the

78 Little world histories and sentiment

virtues and vices at play in the actions of individuals, whether they be the Roman emperor Commodus' (161–92 CE) 'monstrous vices and extravagances' (vol. 2, p. 10) or Cyrus II of Persia's (600–530 BCE) 'noble and engaging behaviour…wit and vivacity' (vol. 1, p. 62).

Newbery's earlier work *Holy Bible Abridged* (1757) is dedicated directly to the parents, guardians and governesses of his readers in the hope that a shared knowledge of God will 'cement us together in society' and generate happiness (pp. iv, vi). Here we see, like the *Compendious History*, the expectation that his readers will join him in contributing to society via the study of the past, and that they will achieve happiness by doing so. The good is the pleasurable, as Aristotle reminds us. It is, however, in Newbery's first children's book—*A Little Pretty Pocket Book* (1744)—that we most clearly see his use of personal address across different text types and objects to reinforce a shared sense of ethical action as shaping the past and the future. *A Pretty Little Pocket* Book is dedicated to parents, guardians and governesses in a manner nearly identical to *Holy Bible Abridged*. What follows, however, is a second-person address to parents, guardians and governesses on the food, clothes, exercise and education needed to raise hardy and virtuous children (pp. 5–12). One part of that address harks back to Locke and Aristotle. 'Your' sons should be taught to reason early, he writes, by the study of 'Mankind':

> Show him the springs and hinges on which they move; teach him to draw consequences from the actions of others; and if he should hesitate or mistake, you are to set him right; But then take care to do it in such a manner, as to forward his enquiries, and pave this his grand pursuit with pleasure.
>
> (pp. 7–8)

Two fictive letters—one addressed to Tommy, the other to Polly—then follow from Jack the Giant-Killer in which second-person address is used to reinforce the option advertised on the cover of buying an accompanying ball or pincushion, 'the use of which will infallibly make Tommy a good boy, and Polly a good girl' (p. 1) How that good is to be achieved is spelt out to the child reader in second-person address. Here is an excerpt from the letter to Polly on the pincushion:

> In order that you may be as good as possible, I have also sent you a Pincushion, the one Side of which is Red, and the other Black, and with it ten Pins; and I must insist upon making this Bargain, that your Nurse may hang up the Pincushion by the String to it, and for every good Action you do, a Pin shall be stuck on the Red Side, and for every bad Action a Pin shall be stuck on the Black Side. And when by doing good and pretty Things you have got all the ten Pins on the Red Side, then I'll send you a Penny, and so I will as often as all the Pins shall be fairly got on that Side. But if ever the Pins be all found on the Black Side of the Pincushion, then I'll send a Rod, and you shall be whipt as often as they are found there. But this, my Dear, I hope you'll prevent by continuing a good Girl, that everybody may still love you, as well as Your Friend, Jack the Giant-Killer.
>
> (pp. 18–20)

Little world histories and sentiment **79**

The letter to Tommy on the ball points out that it, too, is two-toned and that it comes with pins for counting the good and the bad (pp. 14–21). The book connects to an object; the book and the object connect the child to the 'springs and the hinges' of the right and the pleasures of achieving the right.

The commercial dimensions of Newbery's didacticism may surprise us, for we perhaps expect text and object cross-promotion to be features of the modern capitalist world (1800–). Newbery hoped that you would buy all of his texts—whether they be sacred history, secular world history, children's games, rhymes and stories—and the cross-promoted objects. There are no object tie-ins with the world histories I described at the opening of the chapter, but there is at least one example I have found from the twentieth century that reverses the object-miniature world history relationship for children.

De grote gebeurtenissen van de Geschiedenis (*The Great Events of History*) is an 8.5 by 5 cm illustrated prose text that summarises world history in 32 pages. The exact date of publication is unknown, but we know it to be one part of more than a 50-book series produced by the Belgian Franco-Suisse cheese firm between 1965 and 1973. For eight cheese tokens, you could send away for a miniature book on major sporting figures, chemistry, household electricity and wiring, etiquette and public speaking and the history of flight, cars, explorers or the major events of the Second World War.[31] In other promotions, Franco-Suisse offered lapel pins and cut figures. *The Great Events of History* is written in predominantly passive impersonal style, but the preface uses third person to indicate the notion of shared judgement about historical evidence and a shared project. We read:

> Many historical facts have a great reputation. They alone are famous, while there are others who are often less well-known, but which have brought a major turnaround in the history of human distinction. It is this last one, which we will deal with in these summarized stories, which together can be regarded as a fresco of Western civilization.
>
> We have left aside some older facts that are sometimes based on legendary or hypothetical data. (p. 2)[32]

That project, we learn on the last page, seems a very prescient one:

> Thanks to his military genius and his conquests, Napoleon took his Code to the far corners of Europe, which meant an application of…Human and Civil Rights. For a long time, he had dreamed up his dream: a distant Europe, founded on peace and wellbeing. England, opposed to such a plan, did everything in its power to cause it to shipwreck, but notwithstanding Waterloo, the grain of the French Revolution has sprouted, at least as far as European unity is concerned.
>
> (p. 29)

Notwithstanding English 'shipwrecking', Europe displays a tendency towards a unity built upon human and civil rights.

80 Little world histories and sentiment

How many copies of *The Great Events of History* were produced is unknown, and the Franco-Suisse company no longer operates. What we do know is that *Great Events of History* is part of a long history of tokens that includes both sacred and secular uses, from sixteenth-century tokens used to restrict attendance at protestant communion, through to commercial exchange and trade tokens. The Franco-Suisse tokens were clearly designed to promote the purchase of cheese and dairy products, but they also offered the promise of a future build upon human rights. Moreover, we know from surviving copies and edition numbers of the books by Newbery and Croucher that sacred and secular world histories sold well, travelled across to settler societies and were adapted or reproduced via local presses for usage in both homes and burgeoning systems of organised schooling.

Sarah Trimmer's *An Easy Introduction to the Knowledge of Nature* and *Reading the Holy Scriptures* (1770), to take just two examples, ran to over 15 editions, sold around 750,000 copies and were on curriculum lists in the UK and the USA for close to a century. Trimmer's text is constructed on the basis of a series of hypothetical field walks and conversations that lead an unnamed mother to introduce Charlotte and Henry to the beauties and utility of animals, plants and rocks as reflecting the beauty and utility of the scriptures. She, again like Croucher and Newbery, uses second-person address in the dialogue between the mother and her children and to bring them and the world into closer compass, as this extract shows:

> When you were very little children, I dare say, you thought the world was no bigger than the town you live in, and that you had seen all the men and women in it; but now you know better, for I think I have told you that there are thousands and tend thousands of people; you have seen a great many at church, but they are only a small number of what the earth contains. When you go to London you will be quite astonished at the multitudes.... The world is an exceedingly large globe, and this [globe] before us is a kind of miniature picture of it…it is not possible to draw every part of the great world on a globe, any more than it was for the painter to mark every hair of the eyebrows on this small picture on my bracelet.[33]

That miniaturisation was achieved by the selection of content, but literal miniaturisation also made it possible for small hands to hold and even to hide knowledge. Moreover, that miniaturisation invites the child reader to connect their world to the abstract one described and brings that world back to the child as a moral agent who shapes the future through good action.

Back to Frankton

Trimmer's *An Easy Introduction to the Knowledge of Nature* introduces world and biblical history through field walks with children. If we think of sentiment ethics in the broader senses suggested by the Earl of Shaftesbury and Smith, we ought not be surprised. If the universe is one, then we ought to sense the good in nature,

Little world histories and sentiment **81**

as well as those who wander its trails. But that sensing, R. G. Collingwood argued, comes down to whether we see the good as numerable or not. Collingwood noted that distinction in explaining how re-enactment is possible. He, like Aristotle in the *Categories*,[34] observed that some things are discrete and countable, and some things are not. Thoughts and feelings are not discrete things and countable. When we say that we have 'fellow feeling' or share the 'same' thought as someone else, therefore, we do not expect them to count as literally the same, as one.[35] Sympathy is not precise, quantifiable.

We recall Collingwood as one of the thinkers featured in the previous chapter, as the creator of a nuanced philosophical history. His views, like those of the Kyoto School, led me to question the adequacy of the 'nested boxes' analogy I used to open that chapter. Philosophical world histories are unified: it is not possible to separate them into discrete parts. This positions our understandings of ethics as one with family, community, the state and humanity and as across time. I also presented Collingwood as someone who had not determined how he could think of nature in his philosophical sense of history. Well, extending Collingwood's logic, we need to ask whether we see nature as numerable or not, and numerable in distinction from a non-numerable sense of human thoughts and feelings. To return to Frankton, I can count schist pebbles. I can also, though, say that they are like one another. In the former sense, I treat them as discrete, in the latter I do not: quantitative and qualitative if you like. I can call greenstone small and precious, and I can call my child those things too. I may not be using an analogy when I do so. Both are good, both worth nurturing and looking after. But I can also treat them as intimately connected, and the health of one as related to the health of the other. As we will see in Chapter 11, Māori history makers see the human and the non-human as connected and the idea of a discrete human history as problematic.

This holistic sense of connection, and ethics that can shape it and be shaped by it, has not fared well in our histories of children's world histories. We have tended to see them, as well as contemporaneous world histories for adults, as texts that turned on human-to-human sympathy. 'You' has a much older and broader history, as this chapter has shown. Moreover, whilst our treatment of histories as kindred to novels and plays has supported the key story of the emergence of human rights, the question of how to consider the non-human world in ethics has not gone away. As the rest of this book will show, the non-human has continued to remake our senses of history as ethos and to challenge our ideas of the ethics of history. The stones keep shifting, and in Chapters 10 and 11, we will see them as holistically connected with human history.

Notes

1 Jackie C. Horne, *History and the Construction of the Child in Early British Children's Literature*, Abingdon: Routledge, 2011, xx; and Mark Salber Phillips, *Society and Sentiment: Genres of Historical Writing in Britain, 1740–1820*, Princeton, NJ: Princeton University Press, 2000, pp. 26, 28.

82 Little world histories and sentiment

2 Jackie C. Horne, *History and the Construction of the Child in Early British Children's Literature*, ch. 3.

3 Jeffreys Taylor, *The Little Historians: A New Chronicle of the Affairs of England in Church and State, by Lewis and Paul: with Explanatory Remarks, and Additional Information upon Various Subjects Connected with the Progress of Civilization; also Some Account of Antiquities*, London: Baldwin, Cradock, and Joy, 1824; Agnes Strickland, *Historical Tales of Illustrious British Children*, London: N. Hailes, 1833; and Harriet Martineau, *The Peasant and the Prince (the Playfellow)*, London: Charles Knight and Co, 1841.

4 Lynn Hunt, *Inventing Human Rights: A History*, New York: W. W. Norton, 2007.

5 Tom Brown, *Breaking the Fourth Wall: Direct Address in the Cinema*, Edinburgh: Edinburgh University Press, 2012, pp. 4–5.

6 Anthony Ashley Cooper (Third Earl of Shaftesbury), *An Inquiry Into Virtue and Merit* [1699], in *Characteristicks of Men, Manners, Opinions, Times*, vol. 2, ed. Douglas den Uyl, Indianapolis, IN: Liberty Fund, 2001, 3.1.1–2.

7 Anthony Ashley Cooper (Third Earl of Shaftesbury), *An Inquiry Into Virtue and Merit*, 2.1.19–20

8 Plotinus, *Ennead IV*, trans A. H. Armstrong, Loeb Classical Library, Cambridge: Harvard University Press, 1984, 4.4.32.14–22.

9 Marnie Hughes-Warrington, '*How Good an Historian Shall I Be?': R. G. Collingwood, the Historical Imagination and Education*, Thorverton: Imprint Academic, 2003, ch. 2.

10 Jackie C. Horne, *History and the Construction of the Child in Early British Children's Literature*, p. 127.

11 Cato and Varro, *On Agriculture*, Loeb Classical Library, Cambridge, MA: Harvard University Press, 1934, 1.1.

12 Roy Gibson, 'Didactic Poetry as "Popular" Form: A Study of Imperatival Expressions in Latin Didactic Verse and Prose'; Alison Sharrock, '*Haud mollia iussa*', in *Form and Content in Didactic Poetry*, Nottingham Classical Literature Studies, ed. Catherine Atherton, Bari: Levante, 1998, pp. 67–98, 99–115.

13 See for example Ian Jackson, 'Approaches to the History of Readers and Reading in Eighteenth-Century Britain', *The Historical Journal*, vol. 47(4), 2004, pp. 1041–54.

14 Harry M. Hine, '"Discite…Agricolae": Modes of Instruction in Latin Prose Agricultural Writing from Cato to Pliny the Elder', *Classical Quarterly*, vol. 61(2), 2011, pp. 624–52.

15 Ralph Keen, 'Lucretius and his Reader', *Apeiron*, vol. 19(1), 1985, pp. 1–10; Daryn Lehoux, 'Seeing and Unseeing, Seen and Unseen', in *Lucretius: Poetry, Philosophy, Science*, eds D. Lehoux and A. D. Morrison, Oxford: Oxford University Press, 2013, pp. 131–52, quote at p. 137; Daniel Markovic, *The Rhetoric of Explanation in* De Rerum Natura, Leiden: Brill, 2008; and Phillip Mitsis, 'Committing Philosophy on the Reader: Didactic Coercion and Reader Autonomy in De Rerum Natura', *Materiali e discussioni per l'analisi dei testi classici*, no. 31, 1993, pp. 111–28.

16 Longinus, *On Great Writing (On the Sublime)*, trans. G. M. A. Grube, Indianapolis, IN: Hackett, 1991, 26.1.

17 Longinus, *On Great Writing (On the Sublime)*, 26.3.

18 Polybius, *The Histories*, 2 vols, trans. E. S. Shuckburgh, intro. F. W. Walbank, Bloomington, IN: Indiana University Press, 1962, 1.14.

19 Plutarch, 'On the Fame of the Athenians', in *Moralia*, trans. F. C. Babbitt, Cambridge, MA: Harvard University Press, 1936, 347a; and Lucian, 'How to Write History', in *Lucian*, trans K. Kilburn, vol. 6, Cambridge, MA: Harvard University Press, 1959, 51.

20 Kristine Gilmartin, 'A Rhetorical Figure in Latin Historical Style: The Imaginary Second Person Singular', *Transactions of the American Philological Association*, vol. 105, 1975, pp. 99–121.

21 Edward T. Jeremiah, *The Emergence of Reflexivity in Greek Language and Thought: From Homer to Plato*, Leiden: Brill, 2012.

22 John Locke, *Some Thoughts Concerning Education and Of the Conduct of the Understanding*, eds Ruth W. Grant and Nathan Tarcov, Indianopolis, IN: Hackett, 1996, §82.

23 John Locke, *Essays on the Law of Nature and Associated Writings*, ed. Wolfgang von Leyden, Oxford: Oxford University Press, 1954, §13.

24 John Locke, *Some Thoughts Concerning Education and Of the Conduct of the Understanding*, §82.

25 John Locke, *Some Thoughts Concerning Education and Of the Conduct of the Understanding*, §159.

26 Scott Mandelbrote, 'The Bible and Didactic Literature in Early Modern England', in *Didactic Literature in England 1500–1800*, eds Natasha Glaisyer and Sara Pennell, Abingdon: Routledge, 2016, pp. 19–39.

27 John Taylor's text can be read in the ninth edition of *The Bible*, printed by Fay and Davison, pp. 8–10, 166–7, National Library of Israel, online: http://rosetta.nli.org.il/delivery/DeliveryManagerServlet?dps_pid=IE56617803&change_lng=&_ga=2.245743303.237833670.1553569854-1780202479.1553569854 <accessed 26 March 2019>.

28 Kristina Myvold and Dorina Miller Parmenter (eds), *Miniature Books: The Format and Function of Tiny Religious Texts*, Sheffield: Equinox, 2019.

29 Nathaniel Crouch (pseud. Robert Burton), *Youth's divine pastime. In two parts. Part I. Containing forty remarkable scripture histories, turn'd into English verse. With forty pictures proper to each story; very delightful for young persons, and to prevent vain and vicious divertisements. Also several scripture hymns upon various occasions*, 15/e, London: A. Battersworth and C. Hitch, 1732, p. 1.

30 Samuel Crossman, *The young man's calling: or the whole duty of youth. In a serious and compassionate address to all young persons to remember their Creator in the days of their Youth. Together with remarks upon the lives of several excellent young persons of both sexes, as well ancient as modern, noble and others, who have been famous for piety and vertue in their generations. With twelve curious pictures, illustrating the several histories. Also Divine Poems*, 7/e, London: Nathaniel Crouch, 1713; and Nathaniel Crouch (pseud. Robert Burton), *The vanity of the life of man. Representing the seven several stages thereof, from his birth to his death. With pictures and poems, exposing the follies of every age. To which are added, several other poems upon divers subjects and occasions*, 5/e, London: A. Bettesworth and J. Batley, 1729.

31 Information on the *Mijn Bibliotheek* series can be found at the miniature book collection at the University of North Texas library: https://digital.library.unt.edu/search/?q4=%22Franco-Suisse%22&t4=dc_publisher&src=ark&searchType=advanced <accessed 27 March 2019>.

32 Excerpts are my translations.

33 Sarah Trimmer, *An Easy Introduction to the Knowledge of Nature, and Reading the Holy Scriptures. Adapted to the capacities of children*, 9/e, London: T. Longman, G. G. and J. Robinson, 1796.

34 Aristotle, *Categories*, in *The Complete Works of Aristotle* trans. J. L. Ackrill and ed. J. Barnes, Princeton, NJ: Princeton University Press, vol. 1, pp. 3–24.

35 Marnie Hughes-Warrington, 'How Good an Historian Shall I Be?'

Primary texts

De Grote Gebeurtenisse van de Geshiedenis [Dutch], Mijn Biblioteek vol. 12, Brussels: Franco-Suisse, c.1965–73.

Ernst Gombrich, *A Little History of the World*, trans. Caroline Mustill, New Haven: Yale University Press, [1936] 2005.

84 Little world histories and sentiment

David Hume, *Enquiries Concerning Human Understanding and Concerning the Principles of Morals*, Oxford: Oxford University Press, [1748] 1995.

Jawaharlal Nehru, *Glimpses of World History*, 2 vols, Allahabad: Oxford University Press, 1934–5.

John Newbery, *A Little Pretty Pocket Book, Intended for the Instruction and Amusement of Little Master Tommy, and Pretty Miss Polly: With Two Letters from Jack the Giant-Killer; as Also a Ball and Pincushion; The Use of which Will Infallibly Make Tommy a Good Boy, and Polly a Good Girl*, 10/e, London: F. Newbery, [1744] 1760.

John Newbery, *The Holy Bible Abridged; or, the History of the Old and New Testament Illustrated with Notes, and Adorned with Cuts*, London: T. Carnan and F. Newbery, 4/e, [1764] 1775.

John Newbery, *A Compendious History of the World from the Creation to the Dissolution of the Roman Republic, with a Continuation to the Peace of Amiens 1802*, London: Darton and Harvey, 1804.

Eileen and Rhoda Power, *Boys and Girls of History*, Cambridge: Cambridge University Press, 1926–8.

Adam Smith, *The Theory of Moral Sentiments*, ed. Knud Haakonssen, Cambridge: Cambridge University Press, [1759] 2002.

6

GLOBAL HISTORIES AND COSMOPOLITAN ETHICS

H. G. Wells | Charles Morazé and Georges-Henri Dumont | Leften Stavrianos | Sebastian Conrad | Kwame Anthony Appiah | Martha Nussbaum | Onora O'Neill

OLD SAN JUAN, PUERTO RICO. Bomba and Latin trap tapped through the beads, relaying a hum from jewellery store to jewellery store down to where the cruise boats docked. Groups of people wended their way up the Calle Tanca, following the hum to the expected jewellery purchase that would perhaps define their connection to Puerto Rico. Hurricane Maria had complicated that connection. The island had struggled to restore power and water supplies because not everyone saw it as part of the USA. Puerto Rico became a US territory in the late nineteenth century. The right to citizenship and limited power to vote followed, but Puerto Rico is still not represented in the Congress that governs it. Maria had exposed disputed forms of personal, national and international entanglement that defied any sense that the road to recovery would be quick, clean and without hurt. Barely a year after I visited, the port would close again. Coronavirus, too, threatened to rupture and to reinscribe senses of regional and global identity that had been stitched together by cruise excursions.

Just over 70 years before Hurricane Maria, people around the globe thought that being part of something bigger would help individuals and nations, but personal, regional and national senses of distinctiveness complicated that desire too. In the aftermath of the Second World War, and as tensions began to escalate in a new 'cold' war and a succession of regional conflicts, governments, cultural agencies and historians saw the big picture as the key to world peace and prosperity. That big picture history making entailed, in Leften Stavros Stavrianos' (1913–2004) words, nothing less than adopting 'the perspective of an observer perched on the moon rather than ensconced in London or Paris or Washington'. This, he hoped, would bring an end to the 'intellectually indefensible' and 'pedagogically disastrous' effort of simply piling more national histories into histories of Western civilisation ('A Global Perspective in the Organization of World History', p. 8).

DOI: 10.4324/9780429399992-6

86 Global histories and cosmopolitan ethics

From space, you can see natural boundaries between Earth's continents. Moreover, from low orbit, and under good optical conditions, you can see a Spanish greenhouse complex, a US copper mine and the Great Wall of China. Even from the biggest global view, ours is a world of ports, borders, boundaries and structures. We underestimate this fact repeatedly, the ethicist Onora O'Neill (1941–) writes in *Justice Across Boundaries* (2016), and in our forgetting, we can get tangled up in trying to figure out what a global sense of ethics might mean, let alone whether it is achievable or even desirable.

This chapter is on the fences, boundaries and structures that lurk in and complicate the ethical globalism or cosmopolitanism of a range of global and human histories from the twentieth- and twenty-first centuries by writers such as H. G. Wells (1866–1946), Stavrianos, Sebastian Conrad (1966–) and the UNESCO history of mankind—later 'humanity'—team led by Charles Morazé (1913–2003) and Georges-Henri Dumont (1920–2013). A variety of writers have argued that global histories are distinctive from the large-scale universal, world, collective biographical and philosophical approaches already explored in this book and from the big and deep approaches we will look at from Chapter 8. Of the various attempts at definitional distinction between these labels, Bruce Mazlish's identification and explanation of the following passage from Michael Geyer and Charles Bright's 'World History in a Global Age' is perhaps the most useful starting point:

> What we have before us as contemporary history grates against the familiar explanatory strategies and analytic categories with which scholars have traditionally worked.... This is a crisis, above all, of Western imaginings, but it poses profound challenges for any historian: the world we live in has come into its own as an integrated globe, yet it lacks narration and has no history.... The central challenge of a renewed world history at the end of the twentieth century is to narrate the world's past in an age of globality.[1]

Mazlish turns the leap from world to globe in this passage over, noting that the first refers to comprehensive descriptions of human existence—real or imagined—from within those worlds of existence. The second, by contrast, connotes a 'heavenly body' and thus the notion of looking at the human—and more—from the outside. He then goes on to explain,

> It occupies a different valence, deriving from the Latin, *globus*, the first definition of which is 'something spherical or rounded,' like a 'heavenly body.' Only secondarily does the dictionary offer the synonym, earth. Global thus points in the direction of space; its sense permits the notion of standing outside our planet and seeing 'Spaceship Earth.'[2]

This usage accords well with Leften Stavrianos' idea of history written from the view of the moon, and it will provide us with the first steps of our analysis in this chapter. As this chapter will also highlight, however, there are two other features of Geyer and Bright's and Mazlish's descriptions that are worth drawing out. First, there is the notion of historians responding to a 'crisis of Western imaginings' by connecting the reshaping of world history into global or human history with the creation of a more peaceful and just world. Second, there is the fact that a view of the globe from the moon or from a satellite is a view from low orbit and thus a view that captures—and still might be captive to—existing structures in the shape of forms of historical training, concepts, sources of evidence and determinations of periodisation and scope. These aspects, as I will show, turn out to be crucial in explaining the struggles of global historians to promote and sustain cosmopolitan ethics, which focuses on justice in promoting understandings of the good. Recalling the notion of *ethos*, though, I will note that not all history makers have accepted ethics in its cosmopolitan form. They continue to push for the end of boundaries between humans and other living things, and even living and non-living things. These will be the focus of our journey from Chapter 9, culminating in an acknowledgement of place in our search for good histories.

Cosmopolitan ethics

A good starting point for understanding cosmopolitan ethics is Onora O'Neill's *Justice Across Boundaries*, which opens with Robert Frost's poem 'Mending Wall'. The imagined dialogue of neighbours in the poem sees Frost rehearse the reasons for not mending a wall that is no longer needed, and the rebuttal by his neighbour that good fences make good neighbours. This dialogue about the necessity of fences, O'Neill observes, is also a dialogue we need to have about ethics. People have built all kinds of walls—literal and conceptual, firm and fuzzy—for a long time, and we need to explore whether the inclusions and exclusions they establish and sustain make for a more or less good and just world (*Justice Across Boundaries*, pp. 2–3; 99–119; see also *Bounds of Justice*, 2000, pp. 168–85).

Supporters of cosmopolitan ethics commonly argue for the removal or opening up of structures and boundaries in the service of the creation of a just, fair and peaceful world, but few endorse or manage their removal altogether. Why? O'Neill answers the question in two ways. Her first answer is historical: political philosophy—at least in its Western form—has long been shaped by the almost unquestioned idea that justice is internal to and therefore bounded by human communities. This means that few people have thought through the conceptual and practical implications of exiting this idea in realising cosmopolitanism. This takes us to O'Neill's second answer, which is practical: there is no notion of justice without the agents and agencies who have the obligation to enact it. This leads her to argue

> that the practical tasks of enacting and securing justice should not question specific borders, but should focus on the capabilities for action of the agents and agencies that are to respect or realise justice. In particular, a practical approach to rights needs to take account both of the specific powers and of the diversity of non-state actors, many of them not intrinsically territorial, whose activities often cross state and other boundaries.
>
> (*Justice Across Boundaries*, p. 8)

88 Global histories and cosmopolitan ethics

This is not to suggest that O'Neill blithely accepts existing structures, as her critical appraisal of health provision as too focused on the individual doctor-patient relationship and too little focused on public health suggests (*Justice Across Boundaries*, pp. 211–24). Rather, she wants to start with what we have—practically, conceptually, institutionally and globally—to work through global ethical issues.

Rationality plays a key role in O'Neill's advice on addressing global and local problems. Kant—rather than the sentimentalists of the last chapter—is influential in her choice of stance, with her acknowledging both the power of his idea of people as acting out of an unsocial sociability, and consequently as interdependent, and reasoning as practical. That is, the purpose of reasoning is to 'provide *standards* or *norms* that thought, action and communication can (but often fail) to meet' (*Constructing Authorities*, 2015, p. 2; see also *Bounds of Justice*, pp. 11–28; 50–64). This highlights that cosmopolitan ethics is a form of deontological ethics, although one that its proponents would argue is more fitting for a global age. Moreover, she interprets Kant's claim that reasoning must be universal as *followable* reason: that is, 'the norms of reasoning…must be norms that can be used by a *plurality* of agents' (*Constructing Authorities*, p. 2). Universal does not mean one take on ethics; it means intelligibility. You and I may disagree about particular things, but we can agree on how we come to our understanding of these things. This reminds us of Kant's 'framework' approach to ethics and to history, where writing the details is our responsibility. O'Neill's is thus an account of the framework or logic of cosmopolitanism, of ethics and of ethical reason. She explains this idea in relation to Kant:

> Kant sees those circumstances as arising when a plurality of potential reasoners finds that their communication and interaction are not antecedently coordinated (for example, by instinct, divine plan, pre-established harmony or other sorts of authority). Uncoordinated agents who may disagree with one another can at least *offer* one another reasons for believing their claims or following their proposals for action. But they can only do this if they put forward considerations that (they take it) others *could follow in thought*, so understand, or *could adopt for action.*
>
> (*Construc.ting Authorities*, p. 3)

This account of the circumstances of ethics leads O'Neill to argue that a plurality of agents cannot follow or enact principles that cripple or destroy the agency of some of its members (*Constructing Authorities*, pp. 48–50). The burden, therefore, of making a global or human history, as for working through ethical dilemmas, is reasoning to intelligibility and action. Hers is not a view of ethics which turns on empathetic connection with those close or near to us or second-person address. Indeed, she returns to Kant in noting that the sources and nature of our moral reasoning may be inscrutable (*Constructing Authorities*, p. 141).[3] Nevertheless, practical reason works to make sense of the world, and the duty of practical reasoning is unending. This means recognising the historical and dialogical nature of reasoning and the possibility of truth and ethical actions as altering over time.[4] We cannot expect, therefore, to write the history of humanity or global history once.

Global histories and cosmopolitan ethics **89**

If reasoning to intelligibility and action are the strengths of O'Neill's vision of cosmopolitan ethics, then it is also, Martha Nussbaum (1947–) suggests, its exclusionary Achilles' heel. The characterisation of ethical agents as rational, she holds, restricts ethics and the flow on effects for social, political, economic and cultural life unnecessarily. This makes it all but impossible for us to consider people with disabilities, or nonhuman animals, and 'normal' people as they go through stages of development and decline, as contributing to our understanding and actions in the name of justice, the good and the fair (*Frontiers of Justice*, 2006). Looking back to Aristotle, and then more recently to the economist-philosopher Amartya Sen, Nussbaum opens up a list of 'capabilities' that includes rationality but which is not exhausted by it. These are defined in the broad as 'claims to a chance for functioning, claims that give rise to correlated social and political duties' (*Women and Human Development*, 2001, p. 84).[5] They can be basic capabilities, such as an ability to move around and mature conditions of readiness, such as the ability to play or to reproduce, but the exercise of either is not just dependent upon the nature of the individual but also upon the environment in which they live. A severely disabled child, for example, may not be able to play or to express joy if they do not get access to suitable care and education (*Women and Human Development*, p. 85; *Frontiers of Justice*, pp. 96–223). Nussbaum takes the further step of naming 11 human capabilities which ought to be recognised and enshrined by every state to ensure the dignity of all persons: (1) life, (2) bodily health, (3) bodily integrity, (4) senses, (5) imagination and thought, (6) emotions, (7) practical reason, (8) affiliation, (9) living with and concern for other species, (10) play and (11) control over one's environment (*Frontiers of Justice*, pp. 76–8). Along similar lines she argues that animals are capable of dignified existence and that such an existence would mean at minimum adequate opportunities for nutrition and physical activity; freedom from pain, squalor and cruelty; freedom to act in ways that are characteristic to the species; freedom from fear and opportunities for rewarding interactions with other creatures of the same species and different species; and the chance to enjoy light and air in tranquillity (*Frontiers of Justice*, p. 326). There is some overlap in the two lists, particularly on the matter of nutrition, but the human list includes more mental and affective states, and the animal list outlines more negative freedoms ('freedom from'). This difference in terms of mental and affective states and negative freedoms will turn out to be a significant one in the discussion on responsible and accountable agents in Chapters 8 and 9 on varieties of big histories and information and entanglement ethics.

Nussbaum's lists of capabilities are cosmopolitan in that she presumes that they apply to all humans and all living entities. At the same time, she characterises the capabilities as minimum thresholds (*Frontiers of Justice*, p. 76) and as an open-ended list that is open for revision (*Women and Human Development*, p. 77; *Frontiers of Justice*, pp. 71, 76). This means that she does not spell out how groups are to deal in practice with inequalities above the threshold (*Frontiers of Justice*, p. 75). Nussbaum's account suggests equal weighting across the capabilities, but she does not rule out the possibility of multiple capability theories of justice, and therefore, ways of realising it. This, we presume, includes the practical reasoning view of O'Neill, but we could

90 Global histories and cosmopolitan ethics

also imagine the principle of empathy outlined in the sentimental theories of the last chapter. This plurality could bring with it a clash of principles and distribution practices, and that raises a question about the principles that will be used to work through them. Nussbaum prioritises the principle of dignity, whereas Ronald Dworkin looks to the ideas of equal respect and concern.[6] It is also possible to envisage autonomy as a guiding principle, but as both Onora O'Neill and Kwame Anthony Appiah (1954–) observe, understandings of autonomy are sometimes highly individualistic and not at all cognisant of the social circumstances of practical reasoning or considerations of dignity.[7]

Appiah also raises the concern that theories of justice underestimate the deep— and even stubborn—connections people have with notions of belief, country, colour, class, culture and gender. The various interests of those who contributed to the multi-author human or global histories in this chapter show us this point. This may not just be a case of Hegel's observation of contingencies—the non-universal—getting in the way of world peace. Indeed, in *The Philosophy of Spirit*, Hegel makes it clear that the ethical 'ought' to arise from the contingent 'is': we cannot get above the context of our histories and lives in reasoning to following and action.[8]

Appiah notes in *As If* (2017) that the contingent only becomes a problem when we magnify it to a totalising 'as' rather than an 'as if'. His point is that we navigate life with a bundle of complex, overlapping, even contradictory, idealisations about the world and heuristics for managing them. Where we hit problems is in treating any one of these with an exclusionary status. I do not agree with Appiah's view entirely, as this chapter will show. Multiple views can be courted non-exclusively, but some can be treated as better than others. Moreover, we might aspire to a cosmopolitan view, but our heuristics might be national or even personal. In simple terms, we might want to make a global history, but the practises we undertake might undercut that effort. We might want a view from the moon, but not be able to escape the orbit of conventional approaches to history making and ethics.

From world to global history

The penultimate illustration in H. G. Wells' *The Outline of History* (1920, hereafter *Outline*) is a map of the 'old world in the future'. Some features of that map are indeed old world, as with the use of colours to denote oceans and kinds of vegetation and the familiar labels 'Australia', 'Europe', 'Asia' and 'Africa'. These serve as background for a single, more unfamiliar label, 'The United States of the World'. Ironically, North and South America are excluded from the map. To our eyes, this simultaneous act of inclusion and exclusion is jarring, even unthinkable. How can there be united states without the United States? Wells' text confirms that the label and the exclusion were deliberate because to his mind there was no world in 1920. This judgement was not simply a reflection of his point in the final line of the book, that the US was not represented at the first meeting of the League of Nations (vol. 2, p. 761). His more substantive point was that the League was not worldly. Rather, he tells us, it is at present a mere partial league of governments and states. It emphasizes nationality; it defers to sovereignty. What the world needs is no such league of nations as this nor even a mere league of peoples, but *a world league of men*. The world perishes unless sovereignty is merged and nationality is subordinated. And for that the minds of men must first be prepared by experience and knowledge and thought.

(Vol. 2, p. 752)

Wells believed that the future could be different—worldly—and that the League might be a step in the right direction. Indeed, he acknowledged that 'several partial leagues may precede any world league' (vol. 2, p. 753) and that this course of development was a human necessity:

Our history has traced a steady growth of the social and political units into which men have combined. In the brief period of ten thousand years these units have grown from the small family tribe of the early Neolithic culture to the vast united realms—vast, yet still too small and partial—of the present time.… Our true State, this state that is already beginning, this state to which every man owes his utmost political effort, must now be this Federal World State to which human necessities point.

(Vol. 2, p. 750)

Wells' assumption of little structures nested within bigger ones, and of the unfolding of bigger structures over time, illuminates his lineage with the philosophical world histories of Chapter 4. Indeed, he acknowledges his debt to Kant in the introduction to the book (vol. 1, p. 2). Both Kant and Hegel wrote about the possibility of a future world League of Nations and its ability to staunch conflict. Kant thought that a league might be formed with the purpose of seeking an end to all war forever but that this true condition of peace was unlikely on account of the vast regions of the world that would need to be protected. Any league in practice would therefore be an approximation rather than ideal.[9] Hegel was more circumspect and even accepting of the role of conflict in driving the realisation of freedom because he saw the treaties of nations as expressing particular contingencies, not as moving above them.[10] Wells' treatment of the League of Nations as an iteration suggests his closer alignment with Kant, but their views do not coincide entirely. There is every sense in which Wells sees a world league as possible, despite the vast swathes of territory that would be entailed. Moreover, that possibility became a necessity for him and humanity after the experience of a world war that was 'blind' to the protection of civilians (vol 1, p. 2).

Wells envisaged the 'world league of men' as regulating financial, labour, educational, health and flight activities and as reigning in the 'increasing destructiveness and intolerableness of war waged with the new powers of science' (vol. 2, p. 753). Conversely, he saw it as enabling a universal religion, universal education, universal scientific research, free literature of discussion and criticism, democracy and the

92 Global histories and cosmopolitan ethics

economic harnessing of the natural world for the common good (vol. 2, p. 754). Yet he also appreciated the difficulty of appreciating this because of the contingent need of nations. Success turned on structural change, beginning with the way that people understand the world.

Enter history. In Wells' view, national and global peace and prosperity were not possible without 'common historical ideas.' As he explains,

> Without such ideas to hold them together in harmonious cooperation, with nothing but narrow, selfish, and conflicting nationalist traditions, races, and peoples are bound to drift towards conflict and destruction.… A sense of history as the common adventure of all mankind as necessary for peace within as it is for peace between nations.
>
> (Vol 1, p. 2)

Hence an 'outline' of history in the sense of it being a framework akin to Kant's *Idea for a Universal History with a Cosmopolitan Aim*. *Outline* was published in 24 fortnightly illustrated instalments in 1919 and then as a two-volume book in 1920 which sold over two million copies worldwide. His insistence on telling the story of efforts to devise and implement a life of common humanity clearly rang a chord (vol. 1, p. 77). Yet there is much 'old world in the future' of Wells' vision of the past. An adventurous range of chapters on the origins of the universe, earth and life in which events are dated millions of years ago gives way rapidly to the story of humans told through the then conventional dating system of BC and AD (Before Christ and *Anno Domini*). So too a mix of early human history with thematic overviews in accordance with familiar themes of language, race, religion and civilisation leads to conventional treatments of almost all of the topics you would expect to see in a Western civilisation text: for example, the Ancient Greeks, the Crusades, the Renaissance, the American and French Revolutions, Napoleon and the First World War. This is not to suggest that Wells had an uncritical stance towards the materials he handled, with good examples seen in his dismissal of the idea of pure races in Chapter XII of volume one and his criticism of Christianity for failing to keep the peace over its long history (vol. 1, p. 378). Yet it is hard to see the leap from these customary markers—and the boundaries they can imply—to a fair and peaceful democratic world of one religion, system of research and free expression and education.

The mismatch between Wells' intent of making a common history and achieving it in *Outline* might be explained in at least two ways. First, and rather pragmatically, *Outline* owed a great debt to existing universal histories such as Friedrich Ratzel's three-volume *Anthropogrographie*, translated into English as *The History of Mankind* (1897), and Ellen Churchill Semple's *Influences of Geographic Environment, on the Basis of Ratzel's System of Anthropo-Geography* (1911).[11] Wells acknowledged as much in the introduction to his work, noting his preference for single-author works that provided a more unified account of the nature of the past. In this way, we might think of *Outline* as a transcription of existing approaches to history. Yet it is not a precise transcription, as neither his chapter headings nor main lines of argument owe all of their shape to

Ratzel or Semple. His is a selective inheritance of historiographical tradition, along with his selective inheritance of Kant's and Hegel's main lines of thought on world government, conflict and peace. This leads us to the second potential explanation, which concerns the way that Wells, along with Kant and Hegel, thought that freedom would be realised. We recall from Chapter 3 that Kant and Hegel, along with other philosophical world historians, saw freedom as realised over time and through the dialectic juxtaposition or even clash of views of the world. This view emphasised both continuity in the unfolding of freedom through history and discontinuity in the clash of opposites in the dialectic. The play of continuity and clash is also present in Wells' *Outline*, and they serve to tell the unfolding story of a sense of humanity, beginning with the oldest human tools (vol. 1, p. 42) and extending into the future thanks to the energy that will be unleased in a world league of humanity (vol. 2, p. 754). Wells' 'old world in the new' is therefore both a pragmatic and a philosophical feature of *Outline*.

Outline is not an isolated example of 'old world in the new' in global or human history. Leften Stavrianos also openly acknowledged the difficulties of moving or even removing structures and boundaries in trying to articulate a satellite view of the past in a cold war world. Stavrianos provides us with a useful point of comparison with Wells because he taught and wrote global history and the smaller-scale history of the Balkans singly, and in teams, from the late 1950s to the late 1990s. This allows us to further explore the reasons for my preliminary observation that the structure of global history is a case of 'old world in the new', and to see what form of boundary and structural changes might be at play across time, in multiple single- and multi-author texts and multiple editions. In simple terms, for instance, do his works exemplify Wells' and the philosophical world historians' view that ideas are realised through time in a dialectical clash?

Stavrianos' engagement with history was driven by his desire to make people aware of the growth of global inequality and his later acknowledgement that talk of peace and international institutions had not quelled the suspicions and hatreds driving the seemingly incessant conflicts of the twentieth century (*Lifelines from Our Past*, pp. 5, 8). Like Wells, he saw the way history was written and taught as a key part of addressing inequality and achieving peace. To his view, this was not a case of bolting on historical phenomena from outside of the West, as that would generate bigger books and courses without addressing the underlying message that the globe was the West and everything else. Stavrianos argued for history to be addressed to the present and for it to include advanced studies in specific regions. Most importantly, however, he like Wells wanted there to be a shift to a sense of history that was common to humanity. As he wrote, global history

> should include an overview of the entire history of humanity from a consistent global viewpoint. This is essential in order to make clear the dynamics of world history and its regional interrelationships. Compartmentalized study of a given region loses much of its value if it is not preceded by an understanding of the relationship of that region with others and with world history as a whole.
>
> ('A Global Perspective in the Organization of World History', p. 9)

94 Global histories and cosmopolitan ethics

Stavrianos worked to enact this approach as a university teacher, curriculum designer sole and team author, first in *A Global History of Man* (1962) and then in other major works such as *The World Since 1500: A Global History* (1966) and *The World to 1500* (1970; both reprinted as the single-volume *Global History*), *The Epic of Modern Man: A Collection of Readings*, *The Promise of the Coming Dark Age* (1976), *Global Rift: The Third World Comes of Age* (1981) and *Lifelines of Our Past: A New World History*, as well as in his regional works on the history of the Balkans and Ottoman Empire, including *The Balkans Since 1453* (1958).[12]

Stavrianos saw the teaching of world history as critical to the success of achieving a global view. This for him meant just not what was taught but also how it was taught. In a world history course, he wrote,

> It would not suffice to have the specialist on Asia, followed by the specialists on Europe, Africa, Latin America, etc., and thus cover the globe and assume that the course is global. This would be a superficial and worthless hodge-podge of fragments of existing courses. Rather it is essential that one person invest the time and thought required to really integrate the course and to master the interrelationships and inner dynamism that inevitably would be overlooked in a vaudeville-style course.[13]

There could be no globalising of world history texts or curriculum without globalising the people who taught it, and this observation, Gilbert Allerdyce notes, helps to explain the resistance that Stavrianos encountered in implementing his plans. Moreover, it allows us to expand our pragmatic explanation for the persistence of boundaries and structures in global history to include the kinds of training that history makers receive, as well as the sources upon which they rely.

A struggle with 'vaudeville-style' history making is also signalled four pages into the group authored *A Global History of Man*, with the authorship of segments and regional areas of specialisation identified. Stavrianos, we learn from the listings, is both the senior integrating author and the producer of 'parts 1 [Man's Physical World], 2 [Man Before Civilization], 4 [Civilized Man Lives in Global Unity], Unit 6 Soviet Union, and Unit 8 Middle East' (*A Global History of Man*, p. iv). Yet despite not being the integrative author of part three, Stavrianos presents the work as offering the 'composite fabric of a true global history' (p. v). The tension remains throughout the work, with the flashback technique of tying past events to the present and on overview of the forces uniting and splintering the world and the role of the United Nations in fostering peace and unity bumping up against the traditional division of much of history into ancient and classical, medieval and modern sections (part two) and an overview of national and regional histories (part three). Over the eight editions of *The World Since 1500* and *The World to 1500* (also sold as *Global History: From Prehistory to the Twentieth Century*), the number of chapters increased in proportion to the global reach of the text, but the periodisation (to 500 CE; 500–1500; 1500–1763; 1763–1914; 1914 to today), topics and division of sections into world regions is far more suggestive of a history of Europe and the rest of the world than *A Global History of Man. The Epic of Modern Man* suggests the theme of multiple revolutions—scientific, industrial and political—but the periodisation and demarcation of an imperial Europe from the rest of the world is similar to that of *The World from 1500* and *The World to 1500*. The mirror twins of these texts are *The Balkans Since 1453* (1958) and *Global Rift* (1981) which both harness European periodisation to tell its history from the outside in, from the perspective of an Ottoman or third world periphery that is kept in a state of historiographical and economic underdevelopment. More adventurous is *The Promise of the Coming Dark Age*, which outlines the case for the present as a dark age akin to those of the past and its remediation through worker control, participatory democracy and individual and group self-determination. Finally, *Lifelines from Our Past* simplifies historical periodisation into kinship, tributary and free-market forms of social organisation and looks at each through the lens of ecology, gender relations, social relations and war.

Looking at this overview, it is tempting to treat *Global Rift* (1981) as the dialectical antithesis which generated the shifts in periodisation and topics in *The Promise of the Coming Dark Age* (1976) and *Lifelines from Our Past* (editions from 1989–2015). If we were to do so, however, then we would ignore the precedent text *The Balkans Since 1453* (1958) and the long and overlapping print history of that text (1958–2005, with the fourth impression being released after Stavrianos' death) and the more traditionally structured *A Global History of Man* (1962–74) and *The World Since 1500/The World to 1500/Global History* (1966–99). This textual history shows us that while Stavrianos may have rearranged the boundaries and structure of his global histories, the popularity of some of his works as textbooks probably meant that earlier, more traditional boundaries and structures were sustained and transcribed, often with only small changes. The overlapping, even messy, nature of the history of these boundaries and structures suggests something at play other than dialectical development. Pragmatically, for example, book reviews, the comfort and training of people teaching a text, what school boards recognise as history and lack of resources to replace texts can all lengthen or shorten the life of a text. Theoretically, change in the making of global history might therefore be more akin to the rope analogy Ludwig Wittgenstein used to describe the idea of conceptual family resemblance than the idea of a trip to the moon:

> We find that what connects all the cases of comparing is a vast number of overlapping similarities, and as soon as we see this, we feel no longer compelled to say that there must be some one feature common to them all. What ties the ship to the wharf is a rope, and the rope consists of fibres, but it does not get its strength from any fibre which runs through it from one end to the other, but from the fact that there is a vast number of fibres overlapping.[14]

The UNESCO *History of Humanity* project helps us to explore the suitableness of Wittgenstein's idea further, both because of the scale and distribution of the writing team and its production over two major editions across half a century (1966, 2009). The formal decision by UNESCO to create a history of humanity—first

96 Global histories and cosmopolitan ethics

expressed as mankind—dates from 1947. As Frederico Mayor, the director general of UNESCO during the formulation of the second edition saw it, the *History of Humanity* provided the necessary 'truly universal work of international cooperation' to address the grave dangers arising from ignorance of the world's 'matrix of our collective destinies' (*History of Humanity*, second edition, vol. 1, p. v). As Paul Duedahl has noted in careful detail, however, the politics of the project were delicate and complicated from the first moment.[15] Those politics are written into the two editions of the text. They are seen most obviously, for example, in the division of the European chapters across the two editions via the inclusion or exclusion of the Soviet Union and 'former Soviet Union'. Yet the volumes also straddle old and new boundaries and structures and navigate differences of methodological approach. Charles Morazé acknowledges as much in outlining his decision in favour of a chronologically arranged history with thematic and then regional divisions as the 'lesser of two evils' (*History of Humanity*, vol. 1, p. x). Disputed regional names and period divisions are acknowledged as part of the issue, but he also raises doubts about the possibility of producing a cosmopolitan universal history for methodological and ethical reasons. He writes,

> The analytic nature of historical research today blocks the way to synthesis, to the kind of approach required in the writing of a history that can be considered truly universal.… We should not count on the diffusion of a universalism, which is the subject of reflection by a very small, privileged minority, as long as all cultures are not equally represented and historians from all parts of the world are not endowed with the same means and cannot claim the same status, social and otherwise.… Since this history could not reach the highest common factor, it had to tend towards the lowest common multiple.
>
> (*History of Humanity*, vol. 1, p. x)

Morazé's characterisation of 'analytic' historical research—the production of small-scale, chronologically arranged regional or national histories—as an obstacle both to historiographical progress and to world peace echoes the complaint of both Wells and Stavrianos (*History of Humanity*, vol. 1, p. x). It is clear that none of them saw the parts of existing historical research as capable of being aggregated up to a global whole in the manner of the collective biographers we read about in Chapter 2. He also, however, raises a second objection that is latent in Stavrianos' choice of writing topics: the idea of universal history as expressing and securing a concentration of power in the hands of the few. In simple terms, his complaint is that universal history is not cosmopolitan history; it is the amplification and imposition of the will of a 'small and privileged minority'. His remedy was to settle on the least upon which all could agree. That approach clearly ran to editorial guidance, as the variable length and structure of the chapters attest. Some of the contributing authors arranged their materials chronologically, others via thematic headings and still others via a nation-by-nation survey. Europe garners the most attention, South Asia the least. Morazé alerts us that these were matters that elicited strong emotions and that the team adopted a collaborative and light touch in asking for updates, corrections and revisions to materials. Clearly, that did not always work, and editorial redress is sometimes offered through footnotes. Most commonly, these are used to highlight differences of opinion across chapters, as with note three of Chapter 10, volume one, which contests the author's claims about the Neanderthals. In a smaller number of cases, though, they signal Morazé's concern about universal history as a concentration of power, as with this note at the end of Chapter 18—on the early history of *Homo sapiens*—in volume one:

> The views here [that Homo sapiens sapiens appeared 40,000 years ago] seem to be obsolete, except for Europe.
>
> (*History of Humanity*, vol. 1, p. 181).

None of the editorial decisions or interventions negate the possibility or ideal of universal history; it is rather that present professional practice and global inequalities prevent its realisation. This might be seen as a chicken and egg problem, but the UNESCO team, in a manner akin to Wells, clearly saw iterative improvement as a means to cosmopolitan ends.

The UNESCO *History of Humanity* remains singular in the size and global spread of its authorship, and it might be treated—on its own terms—as an iteration that has not triggered the realisation of a universal ideal. Indeed, it might be treated as adding new fibres to an already thickening 'rope' of cosmopolitanism. This is despite the burgeoning growth of global histories across the latter half of the twentieth century and the beginning of the twenty-first century. These take the form, predominantly, of single-author books and journal articles. The reasons for the continued growth of global history in this form, Sebastian Conrad reflects, may be connected back to people needing to understand the global processes driving present-day conflict and terrorist attacks, migration and forms of inequality. This, in a way, is a continuation of Wells' request—like that of other large-scale writers—that history be a part of our endeavours to understand the present and to act for the global good. Moreover, Conrad, like Wells, Stavrianos and the UNESCO team, sees the discipline of history as blighted—like the rest of the humanities—by two 'birth defects' (*What Is Global History?*, p. 3). These are, respectively, the connection of modern disciplines with the nation state and the Eurocentric positioning of Europe as shaping world history (*What Is Global History?*, p. 4). In *Global Geschichte*, he rules out the possibility of there being a universal, cosmopolitan global history. There is, rather, a constellation of perspectives that includes works with a global horizon, histories that tell of global entanglements and histories written against the background of global integration (*Global Geschichte*, pp. 10–11). The English translation of *Global* Geschichte—*What Is Global History?*—offers an even firmer constriction of aspiration via the ruling in favour of the history of integration over big history—the subject of Chapter 8—and histories of global connections (*What Is Global History?*, p. 6). Conrad's decision turns on his appraisal, first, of big and deep historical approaches as vulnerable to determinism and subsumption by the natural sciences (*What Is Global History?*, p. 145). This is a reading of big and deep approaches that I will unpick from Chapter 8. Work on entanglements, on the other hand, is blighted on Conrad's view by the practice of history via national and area studies. Global integration is preferred by Conrad because of the methodological and perspectival sophistication he sees in its work to revise the organisation and institutional order of knowledge (*What Is Global History?*, p. 4). Integrative global histories are therefore presented as boundary and structure breakers.

In *Globalisation and the Nation in Imperial Germany*, for example, Conrad works to revise the idea of nation and globe as mutually exclusive or as one preceding the other. Looking at debates on labour mobility, he presents a case for nationalism and globalisation as dependent upon one another (*Globalisation and the Nation in Imperial Germany*, p. 3). His goal is therefore not so much to remove existing concepts that structure and bound histories as to revisit the relationship between them. This suggests, for example, that the presentation of thematic, then regional and national overviews in the UNESCO *History of Humanity* and Stavrianos' *A Global History of Man*, misses the opportunity for us to understand them primarily through their relationship with one another. So too he takes aim at the idea of the Enlightenment as a Western phenomenon that was transposed upon world history. This view of history, he argues, overplays the isolation of European intellectuals and underappreciates the extent to which the Enlightenment was a response to cross-border interaction and global integration.[16] These works show a strong programme of revising existing notions that the world is Europe and 'the rest' and that nation and globe are either mutually exclusive or in a causal relationship. In these ways, his work extends and complements that of Jürgen Osterhammel in works such as *Globalization: A Short History* (2005), *The Transformation of the World: A Global History of the Nineteenth Century* (2008) and *Unfabling the East: The Enlightenment's Encounter with Asia* (2018).[17]

Yet it is in Conrad's and Osterhammel's one major work together—as editors of the fourth volume of *A History of the World, An Emerging Modern World 1750–1870*—that we see the least evidence of that revisionist intent in play. As with Stavrianos and the UNESCO team, they had to work with other writers who might not have shared their views entirely. Moreover, reader reports and user demand might have expected something more familiar than the works they wrote as sole authors. *An Emerging Modern World 1750–1870*, for example, is arranged under familiar thematic headings that also coincide with traditional histories of history making—that is, the imperial, economic, political, cultural and social. Within those headings, contents are arranged either via further themes (parts 1, 3, 4) or via world regions (part 2). In these ways, Conrad and Osterhammel's work reinforces the usefulness of historiographical change as rope making: the idea that new threads of ideas might be added but that these are intertwined with and play off with older, overlapping notions. The question this raises for us is whether this rope view—which I have suggested as being at play in Wells', Stavrianos' and the UNESCO team's work in various ways—is a practical necessity, or whether it needs to be surpassed in history making.

Returning to Old San Juan

Global histories are expressions of a desire to exit the forms of training, expression, periodisation, scaling and so on that marked the histories made in a conflict-ridden, unequal and local-looking world. The path to that exit is not quick, clean or even without hurt. You can have principles in mind for negotiating that exit—practical reason, empathy, autonomy, dignity or even Conrad's notion of integration—but not everyone might be on the same page as you. You can't exit because not everyone is *following* you in that exit, as O'Neill would put it. Moreover, not everyone might agree that you make histories and therefore that you belong to the discipline of history and can speak for it. Some of these views might be quite strident, bringing to mind Appiah's observation that ethics is difficult when people totalise. But you might also not pull that exit off, for all your desire to do so. This is because while your view of history might be global and cosmopolitan, your training and approaches to communication might see you return to individuals and particular socio-political forms and thus spatial and temporal scales. It is not the case, as with Appiah's claim, that a totalising view has taken hold; it is more the case that one idealisation gets the upper hand over another in what could be a lifelong tussle. The consequences of this tussle can be profound, as with the lack of aid afforded Puerto Rico. Not all tussles, however, have predetermined outcomes. *Ethos* prevails. As Chapters 9 and 10 will show, the historicisation of the sciences and the consequent production of scientific histories provides another avenue for communication, albeit one that not all history makers accept. Moreover, Chapter 9 highlights the role of teaching in shaping new visions of history and the ethics of history. It may even provide the more radical stamping ground for *ethos* than the research activities we commonly associate with the production of new knowledge.

While O'Neill, Nussbaum and Appiah all acknowledge the possibility that their cosmopolitan principles might be subject to refinement and change, they do not say why or how. When I looked at the histories in this chapter, I suggested a picture of them being tied to the earth in low orbit by a Wittgensteinian rope. New structures, boundaries and horizons were suggested, but they both replaced and overlapped with existing structures, boundaries and horizons. Indeed, some persisted stubbornly, undermining the efforts at a different view by the various writers canvassed. When you look at global and human histories, you see time capsules of ideas from different times and places. The same may be true of agents working to enact practical reason, dignity and the cosmopolitan. Another way of thinking about this is Hegel's notion of the dialectic—picked up by Wells—the realisation of freedom via a series of conceptual and practical conflicts in which former views are not left behind but transformed into more and more cosmopolitan ones. Hegel has a cosmopolitan principle—freedom—but it is not presumed to be universally followed or acted in all times and places. We might not agree with his *how*, but at least he has one.

Hegel amplified the contingent. This, I believe, is significant. We may hold reason, dignity, autonomy, empathy and idealisation to be universal principles to be at the forefront of a cosmopolitan ethics. Perhaps, though, they are all ancillary to the

100 Global histories and cosmopolitan ethics

cosmopolitan principle of change, and it needs to be at the forefront of how we identify the good, the right and the just. In the context of this book, that means changes in both spatio- and temporal scales, as well as in levels of abstraction, techniques for researching history, choice of topics, headings and forms of expression, and notions of subjects and objects, and so on.

Notes

1 Michael Geyer and Charles Bright, 'World History in a Global Age', *American Historical Review*, 1995, vol. 100(4), pp. 1037, 1041 [1034–60], as quoted in Bruce Mazlish, 'Global History to World History', *The Journal of Interdisciplinary History*, 1998, vol. 28(3), pp. 389–90 [385–95].

2 Bruce Mazlish, 'Global History to World History', p. 390. See also Bruce Mazlish, 'Terms', in *Palgrave Advances in World Histories*, ed. Marnie Hughes-Warrington, Basingstoke: Palgrave Macmillan, 2005, pp. 18–43.

3 On Kant and the inscrutability of the origins of freedom and radical evil, see Immanuel Kant, *Prolegomena to Any Future Metaphysics that will be Able to Come Forward as a Science*, trans and ed. Gary Hatfield, Cambridge: Cambridge University Press, 1997, p. 144. See also Evgenia Cherkasova, 'On the Boundary of Intelligibility: Kant's Conception of Radical Evil and the Limits of Ethical Discourse', *The Review of Metaphysics*, 2005, vol. 58(3), pp. 571–84.

4 Onora O'Neill, 'Action, Anthropology and Autonomy', *Constructions of Reason*, Cambridge: Cambridge University Press, 1989, pp. 72–80.

5 See, for example, Amartya Sen, *The Idea of Justice*, London: Allen Lane, 2009.

6 Ronald Dworkin, *Sovereign Virtue: The Theory and Practice of Equality*, Cambridge, MA: Harvard University Press, 2000.

7 See, for example, Onora O'Neill, *Autonomy and Trust in Bioethics*, Cambridge: Cambridge University Press, 2002.

8 G. W. F. Hegel, *Elements of the Philosophy of Right*, §8.

9 Immanuel Kant, 'Toward Perpetual Peace', in *Practical Philosophy*, Cambridge edition of the works of Immanuel Kant, Cambridge: Cambridge University Press, 1999, §8, p. 357; and 'The Metaphysic of Morals: Doctrine of Right', in *Practical Philosophy*, §61, p. 487.

10 G. W. F. Hegel, *Elements of the Philosophy of Right*, ed Allen W. Wood, Cambridge: Cambridge University Press, 1991, §333.

11 Friedrich Ratzel, *The History of Mankind*, trans. A. J. Butler, 2/e, New York: Macmillan, 2 vols, 1897; and Ellen Churchill Semple, *Influences of Geographic Environment, on the Basis of Ratzel's System of Anthropo-Geography*, New York: Henry Holt, 1911.

12 See primary texts and Leften S. Stavrianos, *The Ottoman Empire: Was It the Sick Man of Europe?*, New York: Rinehart, 1957; *The Balkans since 1453*, New York: Reinhart, 1958; *The Balkans 1815–1914*, New York: Rinehart and Winston, 1963; *Balkan Federation: A History of the Movement Towards Balkan Unity in Modern Times*, Hamdon, CT: Archon, 1964; *The World Since 1500: A Global History*, Englewood Cliffs, NJ: Prentice-Hall, 1966; *The Epic of Modern Man: A Collection of Readings*, Englewood Cliffs, NJ: Prentice-Hall, 1966; and *The Promise of the Coming Dark Age*, San Francisco, CA: W. H. Freeman, 1976.

13 L. S. Stavrianos to Northwestern University Faculty, memorandum 14 April 1961, Wild Papers, Northwestern University Archives, as quoted in Gilbert Allerdyce, 'Toward World History: American Historians and the Coming of the World History Course', in Ross E. Dunn, Laura J. Mitchell and Kerry Ward (eds), *The New World History: A Field Guide for Teachers and Researchers*, Berkeley: University of California Press, 2016, p. 53.

14 Ludwig Wittgenstein, *The Blue and the Brown Books*, Oxford: Blackwell, 1958, p. 87.
15 Paul Duedahl, 'Selling Mankind: UNESCO and the Invention of Global History, 1945–1976', *Journal of World History*, 2011, vol. 22(1), pp. 101–33.
16 Sebastian Conrad, 'Enlightenment in World History: A Historiographical Critique', *American Historical Review*, 2012, vol. 117(4), pp. 999–1027.
17 Jürgen Osterhammel, *Globalization: A Short History*, Princeton, NJ: Princeton University Press, 2005; *The Transformation of the World: A Global History of the Nineteenth Century*, Princeton, NJ: Princeton University Press, 2014; and *Unfabling the East: The Enlightenment's Encounter with Asia*, Princeton, NJ: Princeton University Press, 2018.

Primary texts

Kwame Anthony Appiah, *As If: Ideals and Idealization*, Cambridge, MA: Harvard University Press, 2017.
Kwame Anthony Appiah, *Cosmopolitanism: Ethics in a World of Strangers*, New York: W. W. Norton, 2007.
Kwame Anthony Appiah, *The Lies That Bind: Rethinking Identity*, London: Profile, 2018.
Sebastian Conrad, *Global Geschichte: Eine Einführung*, Munich: C. H. Beck, 2013.
Sebastian Conrad, *What Is Global History?*, Princeton, NJ: Princeton University Press, 2016.
Sebastian Conrad, *Globalisation and the Nation in Germany*, Cambridge: Cambridge University Press, 2010.
Sebastian Conrad and Jürgen Osterhammel (eds), *A History of the World: An Emerging Modern World 1750–1870*, volume 4 of *A History of the World*, eds Jürgen Osterhammel and Akira Iriye, Cambridge, MA: Harvard University Press, 2018.
Charles Morazé and Georges-Henri Dumont (eds), *History of Humanity*, London: Routledge and UNESCO, 7 vols, 1994–2008.
Martha Nussbaum, *Frontiers of Justice: Disability, Nationality, Species Membership*, Cambridge, MA: Harvard University Press, 2006.
Martha Nussbaum, *Women and Human Development: A Capabilities Approach*, Cambridge: Cambridge University Press, 2001.
Onora O'Neill, *Bounds of Justice*, Cambridge: Cambridge University Press, 2000.
Onora O'Neill, *Constructing Authorities: Reason, Politics and Interpretations in Kant's Philosophy*, Cambridge, Cambridge University Press, 2015.
Onora O'Neill, *Justice Across Boundaries: Whose Obligations?* Cambridge: Cambridge University Press, 2016.
Leften Stavros Stavrianos, Loretta Kreider Andrews, George Blanksten, Roger F. Hackett, Ella C. Leppert, Paul L. Murphy and Lacey Baldwin Smith, *A Global History of Man*, Boston: Allyn and Bacon, 1962.
Leften Stavros Stavrianos, 'A Global Perspective in the Organization of World History', [1964] in *Teaching World History: A Resource Book*, ed Heidi Roupp, New York: M. E. Sharpe, 1997, pp. 8–9.
Leften Stavros Stavrianos, *Lifelines from Our Past: A New World History*, New York: Pantheon, 1989.
H. G. Wells, *The Outline of History*, London: George Newnes, 2 vols, 1920.

7

MICROHISTORIES AND SOCIAL CONTRACT ETHICS

Carlo Ginzburg | Natalie Zemon Davis | István M. Szijártó | Sigurður Gylfi Magnússon | Claire Judde de Larivière | John Rawls | David Gauthier | Charles W. Mills | Carol Pateman

OXFORD, ENGLAND. Twice a day, a polite form of misrule plays outside my hotel window. Students walk out of their final exams in regulation subfusc: dark suit, bowtie, gown and red carnation. They stand behind a barrier on the street and wait for their friends to cover them with the hallmarks of a party. Confetti, glitter, saffron-coloured flour, silly string, shaving cream and prosecco are thrown this way and that, coating the cobblestones of Merton Street. When I was a student, 'trashing' meant flour thrown on the run to avoid the wrath and the fines of the proctors, the bowler hat–wearing faces of university order. These days, the university and the students seem to have come to some sort of uneasy agreement, despite the practice still being against the code of conduct and subject to fines. Depriving the homeless of food and environmental damage are cited as reasons not to do it. Yet students continue to stand behind a university-mandated barrier in university-mandated dress. They throw objects from a prescribed list of things, checked with a bag search, with an 'environment' option offered. The street is swept clean every evening, yet trashing persists through time.

Trashing is the kind of strange and seemingly singular material that the Icelandic historian Sigurður Gylfi Magnússon (1957–) would see as the necessary start for a microhistory. Microhistory, Magnússon argues repeatedly through his writings, is the strange singular. It begins with a past event or phenomenon that we find puzzling or do not understand. Our being puzzled or not understanding that phenomenon is a sign that the way that we make sense of the past and our world might not be right but more importantly ethical. His point is that we should not expect to explain phenomena—past or present—with a pre-set, general or abstract set of 'big' assumptions or methodologies. That is, we should be open to the experiences of those who participate in trashing rather than jump to categorise their experience under headings such as 'misrule'—as I did in the opening of this chapter—or explain them under approaches such as cultural or social history. If we are open to

DOI: 10.4324/9780429399992-7

peoples' experiences, we may change our understanding of 'misrule' or challenge the validity of the concept altogether. Indeed, trashing may be so strange as to change our understanding of the world. In this way, seemingly small phenomena can be ethically important, whether the 'small' in these cases refers to geographical or historical scale, or the number of people involved or any combination of these three elements. Conversely, applying general or 'big' concepts or methodologies to explain phenomena can be 'downright dangerous', Magnússon advances in 'The Singularization of History', since

> [t]he subjects themselves, by whatever name they are known, are liable to disappear. Even microhistorians have their work cut out to remain faithful to their subject matter in the face of academic demands, and so put heavy emphasis on presenting links between their research and larger wholes. All this tends to produce a final form that is a distortion of general history.
>
> (p. 720)

At play here is the idea that you cannot necessarily explain the little with the big without some ethical loss or even harm. It is not simply that the small goes out of focus as you change scales; it is that it disappears.

Magnússon's claim appears to sit a long way from the larger-scale and scale-shifting histories we have explored so far in this book. His writing pulls us up and suggests that what holds at one scale may be lost in another, that they may be different ethically in kind, as well as degree. A very rough analogy would be the observation that quantum—rather than classical—physics is needed to explain the world at a microscale. On this view, microhistories cannot simply be slotted into larger-scale histories, as with the collective biographies we looked at in Chapter 3, and we cannot expect to use the virtues to pivot between one scale and another, as suggested in the universal histories explored in Chapter 2. Unlike the quantum analogy, however, Magnússon's argument is not just that the micro and the macro are different; it is also that they *should* be different. On these terms, an argument for the micro is an argument from ethics.

This chapter tests Magnússon's claim for the distinct ethics of microhistories. I will argue that microhistories, like all of the histories I have surveyed in this book so far, are spatio-temporally dynamic. They include multiple scales and shifts, from the little to the big, and the other way around. The Hungarian historian István M. Szijártó (1965–) uses the word 'multiscopic' to describe this feature of microhistories (*What is Microhistory?*, p. 4). This provides us with another analogy—alongside snakes and ladders, bricks, nested boxes and a rope—with which to explore the scales and the ethics of history. A multiscope simulates a 3D representation of a thing through the bundling of images taken from slightly different angles. It is a neat analogy which inclines us towards thinking about history making as capturing the past through a shifting photographic lens. For all the neatness of this explanation, though, I will show in this chapter that the lens of microhistory moves neither smoothly one way or the other or across a broad range. Rather, it tends to larger scales for its explanations of the past, and they do not range smaller than the human.

104 Microhistories and social contract ethics

I need to be more specific here and note that microhistories do not canvas isolated humans or phenomena smaller than the human. That is, they assume an ethics in which humans are agents or the initiators of ethical beliefs, dispositions or acts *and* the recipients of ethical beliefs, dispositions or acts. That is, microhistorians are interested in the ways in which people act in connection with one another. People act ethically towards others and the other way around. Moreover, they may act in agreement for the sake of what they hold to be ethical. It is, therefore, reasonable to ask whether microhistories simply reflect in miniature the abstract or general assumptions and methodologies of human-oriented ethics and in particular what is called social contract ethics.

Social contract ethics

Social contract ethics is associated with, among others, the writings of Thomas Hobbes (1588–1679), John Locke (1632–1704), Immanuel Kant (1724–1804) and Jean-Jacques Rousseau (1712–88). We have looked a little at these writers in Chapters 4 and 5. In this chapter, I want to focus on the recent revival of this approach to ethics encouraged by writers such as John Rawls (1921–2002) and David Gauthier (1932–). They hold, in a basic sense, that our notions of what is ethical are shaped by the idea of a contract or form of agreement. In 1971, Rawls published a book called *The Theory of Justice* in which he argued for the scaling down of our discussion of ethics to understand some of its most important features. Rawls' scaling entailed the description of an 'incomplete', 'simple' and hypothetical framework that he thought would tell us much about justice and the glue or bond of civic friendship (*Theory of Justice*, pp. x, 4, 17). Rawls' framework imagined a group of 'free and rational' and 'autonomous' people coming together to collectively select principles of justice from behind a 'veil of ignorance' (pp. 9, 11, 19). That is, he asks us to imagine a group of rational human agents who do not know their dispositions or place in society—and who are therefore assumed to be in a position of initial equality—and to further imagine what fundamental terms of association they determine. Rawls saw this as a fundamentally fair framework by dint of the veil of ignorance involved. That is, no one knows their position in society and therefore they cannot protect it; rather, they will act from the assumption that distributing goods to the least advantaged will be a fair agreement or bargain for all (p. 11). In sum, notions of the just stem from the agreement of rational humans.

Rawls acknowledged three features that made his model incomplete and thus hypothetical. First, he acknowledged that there is no society in which it can be assumed that all persons associate freely and equally. As he explained,

> No society can, of course, be a scheme of cooperation which men enter voluntarily in a literal sense; each person finds himself placed at birth in some particular position in some particular society, and the nature of this position materially affects his life prospects. Yet a society satisfying the principles of justice as fairness comes as close as a society can to being a voluntary scheme,

for it meets the principles which free and equal persons would assent to under circumstances that are fair.

(p. 13)

Second, Rawls understood that the idea of a social contract could be useful for agreeing on principles additional to justice. Indeed, be believed that it could be a means for agreeing on all of the virtues. Rawls' point here encourages us to see the just as part of the good but not equal to it in meaning. Third, he saw his social contract as based on the assumption that participants were possessed of the 'requisite intellectual capacity' needed to determine the principles of justice. They, he believed, could make 'paternalistic' decisions on behalf of those not at the age of reason or who are not able to decide rationally, such as children or the intellectually disabled (pp. 46, 93, 143, 209). Feelings such as envy, humiliation and shame were also left out as 'complications' (pp. 142–50, 530–4).

Criticisms of Rawls' theory pick up on his exclusions, but they also suggest further refinements and arguments that might challenge it in deeper ways. In the last chapter, for example, we learned of Martha Nussbaum's view that social contracts should assume the participation of those excluded by Rawls—namely, children, the intellectually disabled and even animals. To this we might add Linda Barclay's argument that exclusion from the social contract perpetuates the unjust treatment of people with disabilities and Sophia Wong and Leslie Francis and Anita Silvers' argument that individuals with severe intellectual impairments can collaborate with others to develop principles of what is good and what is just.[1] So too Andrew Cohen has argued that moral standing might be given to animals and therefore taken into account by those seeking to agree the principles of justice. In this case, we have an agent- or human-oriented ethics that bestows moral worth on animals rather than the entity- or recipient-oriented views of ethics we will explore in the next two chapters which hold animals to be ethically accountable, even if they are not rationally responsible.

Extensive criticisms by Carole Patemen and Charles W. Wills illuminate the non-neutrality of Rawls' terms for the articulation of the principles of justice. Patemen argues that Rawls' idea of the social contract renders invisible what she calls the sexual contract and the patriarchal right that flows from it. He paints his portrayal of rational agents as simultaneously disembodied and sexless but also as the heads of families. This cements the domination of men over women. Charles W. Mills argues that whites have a contract to enforce the supremacy of whites. He writes of the blindness that supposedly flows from Rawls' postulation of his contract as a hypothetical contract:

> Rawls, an American working in the late twentieth century, writes a book on justice widely credited with reviving postwar political philosophy in which not a single reference to American slavery and its legacy can be found.... The silence of mainstream moral and political philosophy on issues of race is a sign of the continuing power of the Contract over its signatories, an illusory colour

blindness that actually entrenches white privilege. A genuine transcendence of its terms would require, as a preliminary, the acknowledgement of its past and present existence and the social, political, economic, psychological, and moral implications it has had both for its contractors and for its victims.

(*The Racial Contract*, p. 77)

The defence that Rawls' model is purely hypothetical underestimates how rationality may function to subject women and blacks.

Rawls notes that the parties are indistinguishable from one another, and therefore, one party can represent all of the rest. This means that we need only one person behind the veil of ignorance, or as he writes, 'We can view the choice [contract] in the original position from the standpoint of one person selected at random' (*Theory of Justice*, p. 139). This is not something that he unpacks in detail (p. 58). This point will turn out to be quite important in our exploration of microhistories in this chapter.

Singling out microhistory

The appearance of microhistory is dated repeatedly to 1976. This date recognises the publication of one of the best-known microhistories, Carlo Ginzberg's *Il formaggio e i vermi. Il Cosmo di un mugnaio del '500*—later translated as *The Cheese and the Worms: The Cosmos of a Sixteenth-Century Miller* (1980). *The Cheese and the Worms*— which uses trial transcripts to reconstruct how the miller Dominico Scandella or Menocchio (1532–99) made sense of the world—had a shaping influence on many of the microhistories that followed. Moreover, the selection of 1976 as a starting point makes it feasible to develop a relatively comprehensive historical overview of microhistories. It is, though, a problematic date by virtue of all of the works that it excludes, including Ginzburg's earlier microhistory, *I Bernadanti: Stregoneria e culti agrari tra Cinquecento e Seicento* (1966, translated as *The Night Battles: Witchcraft and Agrarian Cults in the Sixteenth and Seventeenth Centuries*, 1983). The collective biographies which I traced back to at least the Roman world in Chapter 3, for example, also have good claim to be described as aggregations of microhistories. They are micro both in their word length and in their focus on individual lives or individual actions.

A closer look at the claim for 1976 by writers such as Szijártó suggests that there is a difference between collective biographies and microhistories. He puts this difference down to the appearance and refinement of the assumptions and methodologies at work in the fields of social and cultural history. This difference is hinted at in his definition of microhistories in *What is Microhistory?* Microhistorians, he writes,

[t]ry to show the historical actors' experiences and how they saw themselves and their lives and which meanings they attributed to things that had happened to them, while they also try to point to deep historical structures, long-lived ways of thinking and global processes using a retrospective analysis—factors that were absent from the actors' own horizons of interpretation.

(p. 7)

In this definition, a nod is given to cultural history in the suggestion that microhistorians respect the individual life experiences of historical agents, and a nod is given to social history in the idea of microhistorians pointing to deep structures, thoughts and processes beyond those envisaged by people in the past. In expanding his definition, Szijártó leans to the side of social history and thereby characterises microhistories as the 'exceptional normal'. This, put simply, means the expectation that a micro-investigation will lead to macro-level conclusions about social structures, thoughts or processes or, more commonly, that macro-level methodologies and ways of thinking about society will be used to deep dive into the detail of microhistories (pp. 7, 8). Szijártó thus refines his definition of microhistory, as we noted earlier, to describe it as the bidirectional or multiscopic exploration of the 'exceptional normal'.

Szijártó's definition of microhistory is at odds with that of Magnússon, as a number of the reviewers of their joint book, *What is Microhistory?* (2013) have noted.[2] Magnússon leans more heavily on the connection between cultural history and microhistory and therefore denies that microhistories are multiscopic vehicles for understanding social structures, thoughts or processes. Rather, he argues for their status as the 'strange singular'. This leads him to urge microhistorians to eschew the idea of microhistories as necessarily nested within larger-scale histories or on the small end of a range of history sizes. Microhistorians, he argues,

> [h]ave been too concerned with the 'great historical questions,' or what I term the 'grand narrative.' Instead of focusing on studying as minutely as possible the fragments they have in their hands, they fall into the temptation of conventional history, of contextualising their findings.... I urge microhistorians to ignore the grand narrative as far as possible, and to concentrate on… the 'singularization of history.'… In my writings I have stated my firm conviction that it is not possible 'to step into the same stream twice,' to use the metaphor that Socrates is supposed to have attributed to Heraclitus to capture his doctrine that everything is in motion and subject to constant change.… Historians will…just have to accept that the past will never be within their grasp. Recognising this is, to my mind, history's most powerful defence.
>
> (p. 158)

Magnússon's concern is that any predetermined big story or methodology can hinder the historian's ability to allow individuals the singularity, idiosyncrasies, contradictions and inconsistencies of their experiences. Historians may be so concerned with seeing the larger-scale course of the stream—to use his metaphor—that they fail to see its motion. In short, larger-scale approaches like social history are ethically problematic when applied to small phenomena because general or abstract explanations and methodologies may freeze or fail to reflect shifts or differences at play in people's experiences.

The idea that larger-scale histories can blind us to the voices, needs and experiences of particular individuals motivates much of the historiography that we would today label as 'postmodern' or 'postnarrativist'. Postmodern and postnarrativist historians and

108 Microhistories and social contract ethics

history theorists such as Joan Wallach Scott, Keith Jenkins, Jouni-Matti Kuukkanen and Claire Norton and Mark Donnelly hold that the use of larger-scale or general narrative structures, concepts, assumptions and methodologies can also blind us to our own voices, needs and experiences as the makers or audiences of histories and to the fact that our lives are neither abstract nor infinite.[3] No history maker is above or outside of time or space. The concepts, methodologies and narrative structures they use reflect ethical assumptions about the world in which some phenomena are treated as good, fair and just and others not. This is an important point about just how pervasive ethics is in history. Every decision, every word, for example, reflects a determination about the way the world *ought* to be. Theorists like Ethan Kleinberg and Jacques Derrida also highlight the impossibility of escape from this pervasive ethics of history and the burden of decisions that it entails.[4] Every moment of our lives matters and by extension every moment of our history making and every moment in which we connect with histories. This impossibility is not acknowledged by Magnússon, but it nevertheless haunts his work in ways that we and he might not expect.

An uneven multiscope

Szijártó's description of microhistories as multiscopic captures the dynamic scale shifting at work in microhistories. This is a feature that they share in common with the histories explored throughout this book. His analogy does not, however, capture the unevenness of that dynamism. Scale shifts do not happen evenly throughout microhistory narratives. Nor do microhistorians shift evenly across time and space. In my view, microhistories tend towards broader or larger methodologies, concepts and evidence to explain the experiences of individuals and or groups. A good example that highlights the ways that microhistories tend towards the big is Magnússon's own 'The Doctor's Tale', which can be found in *What is Microhistory?* 'The Doctor's Tale' explores an extended family's experience of mortality in Iceland and more specifically infant mortality, as well as inter- and intra-family relationships. It does not start with the singular strange, as with the description of trashing which opened this chapter. Rather, it opens with general comments on the spatio-temporal setting—Strandasýsla, north-west Iceland in the late nineteenth century—on the kinds of sources that will be used (autobiographies and letters) and on the historical drivers of infant mortality (p. 80). These comments frame 'The Doctor's Tale' as belonging to nineteenth-century cultural and social history. Magnússon then plunges into a short description of the everyday experiences of the Jónsson and Halldórsdóttir family of Kirkjuból, but he shifts scales frequently to provide broader observations on the nature of Icelandic autobiography (p. 80), domestic or proto industrialisation (pp. 81–2), the economic structure of Iceland in the late nineteenth century (p. 82) and Icelandic rates of literacy (p. 83), to name just a few examples.

So too the second section opens with a general introduction to infant mortality rates in Iceland in the nineteenth century, including government statistics (p. 86) and reports from district medical officers (pp. 84–5). This helps Magnússon to frame his argument that '[t]he ubiquity of death in nineteenth-century society presumably had a profound impact influence on the character of those who survived' (p. 89). This is not to suggest that the letters or autobiographical materials from the family are unnecessary for his account; it is simply that he uses materials on a variety of scales to ensure that we develop a good understanding of how families felt about losing their children, about death and about family ruptures. His conclusion is that despite the frequency of infant mortality in nineteenth-century Iceland and the matter-of-fact ways in which family records of those deaths were kept, we cannot assume that people from the past did not love their children.

It is not the case, though, that Magnússon builds up from specific to broader phenomena to reach those conclusions. Big goods are not built from little ones, to return to Aristotle's way of putting it. Rather, he starts with and returns to broader phenomena, and he shifts frequently, but not at all evenly, between social-historical observations and extracts of evidence from the particular experiences of the Jónsson and Halldórsdóttir family. You could imagine him, though, opening with the speci-ficities of an experience, as I did at the opening of this chapter. So why didn't he? I believe that Magnússon's microhistory is moored in broader phenomena—as I believe other microhistories are moored in general phenomena—because they are interested in the interactions between people.

Another way of putting this idea is that microhistories like Magnússon's have a scale floor. They do not look to isolated individuals or the parts of an individual's body at a particular time or even organisms that are smaller than humans. Compared with the histories that we will examine in Chapter 9, microhistories are big. Pulling these threads together, it is reasonable to describe microhistories as human histories that explore the experiences of individuals in relation to one another. Those rela-tions may include the creation, affirmation or breaking of relational bonds. It is, therefore, worth exploring whether microhistories are social contract histories. This is not just because they explore the ways in which humans bond with one another and act in ways that Rawls would call just. Microhistories more often explore the breaking of social bonds. They focus on what we might call breaches of the social contract or breaches of justice. Ginzburg's *The Cheese and the Worms*, for example, builds up a picture of Menocchio's view of the world from his heresy trial tran-script. So too *The Night Battles* explores how pagan beliefs collided with those of the Christian authorities. Magnússon's 'The Doctor's Tale' uncovers an affair that split two families apart. These much-studied works provide us with food for thought about the bonds of justice that connect and split individuals, and I will say a little more about them in a moment. For the present, I would like to foreground a more recent microhistory: Claire Judde de Larivière's *La révolte des boules de neige* or *The Revolt of Snowballs* (2018). My reasoning is that Judde de Larivière's account of the moment in 1511 when residents of Murano pelted snowballs at the outgoing Venetian podestà highlights the complexities of justice in ways that can inform our reading of older microhistories and social contract ethics.

The Revolt of Snowballs opens with general observations in the manner of Magnússon's 'The Doctor's Tale'. She informs us that the story comes from an archival record of trial transcripts, and she locates Murano via words and a map of

110 Microhistories and social contract ethics

the Venetian Lagoon (pp. xi, xiii). Before reading a page of her history, we, therefore, know that someone went to trial, that Murano has a main canal and that we are about to read about a 'revolt'. From there, she reverts to a short description of the snowball-throwing incident (pp. 1–7), before shifting spatio-temporal scales to explain the nature of the Murano economy (pp. 8–28) and how it was governed by Venice and governed itself (pp. 29–48). Moreover, she takes pains to explain how the annual ceremony of the incoming and outgoing podestà played out in an exceptionally cold winter in which there was repeated conflict between Venice and the League of Cambrai. Murano residents were not only taxed to meet the costs of these skirmishes; they were also repeatedly mobilised (pp. 49–79). Relations between Venice and Murano, we come to understand through Judde de Larivière's examination of larger-scale phenomena, were particularly tense during a biting winter. Against that tense background, the throwing of snowballs could be interpreted as a revolt. Judde de Larivière then shifts scales to home in on the finer details of the trial before shifting scales again to highlight how the throwing of snowballs was a statement of misrule by the *populo*—ordinary people—against a state that could not sustain a fair, good or just social contract (pp. 80–28). I will unpick the idea of this contract in a moment, but for now, it is important to note that Judde de Larivière's scale shifting is not evenly distributed. Within each of the chapters, she shifts scales in a manner much like Magnússon to explain the meaning of everyday practices in Murano and how those practices tell us about wider relations with Venice and groups beyond the Venetian Lagoon. Her history tends towards larger or more general phenomena and never travels below scales in which humans interact with one another.

Frequent scale shifts are also seen in the older microhistories of Ginzburg and Davis. Ginzburg's *The Cheese and the Worms*, for example, offers, for example, analyses of the various ways in which Venice supported peasants of the Fruili region to contain local elites (pp. 13–15), the kinds of books and ideas Menocchio might have accessed (pp. 28–32) and the contemporary importance of oral tradition and reading (pp. 77–80). Within each of the short chapters, too, Ginzburg takes the time to explain the nature of religious trials in sixteenth-century Italy, the nature of the local economy and the structure of local governance, as well as key ideas from contemporary theological texts. All of this provides the backdrop to show how Menocchio navigated complex social interactions. Ginzburg's play of scales, therefore, serves to highlight the agency of Menocchio in a way that a general history of the Fruili might not. Indeed, it might be argued that Menocchio is so peculiar as to not be illuminative of any macro trends, but the book shows how he broke the social contract, and in so doing, it illuminates that contract. This same theme travels through Ginzburg's earlier work *The Night Battles*, in which he makes a case that the witch trials of the Benandanti ('night walkers') reveal the fusion of pagan fertility rites and Christian beliefs in local ritual. That case, as with *The Cheese and the Worms*, is built up via dynamic scale shifting.

Davis' work to locate the writings and life of the Berber diplomat al-Hasan ibn Muhammad al-Wazzan al-Fasi or Joannes Leo Africanus (c.1494–c.1554) is also a dynamic play on micro- and macro-scales. *Trickster Tales* (2006) provides a contextualised account of how al-Wazzan's views of religion, diplomacy, literature, philosophy and sexuality capture in microcosm the connections and conflicts between Africa and Europe in the sixteenth century and how his *Descrittione dell'Africa* (*Description of Africa*) fuelled European curiosity about the boundaries of the known and the unknown world. Yet there is less confidence in Davis' assertions about al-Wazzan's 'exceptional normality' or 'strange singularity' than we encounter in Ginzburg's or Magnússon's texts. This is deliberate on Davis' part. She wants us to know about the silences and contradictions in his life and about the importance of the historian's conditional, described in the following terms:

> Throughout I have tried to make use of the conditional—'would have,' 'may have,' 'was likely to have'—and the speculative 'perhaps,' 'maybe.' These are my invitations to the reader to follow a plausible life story from materials of the time.
>
> (*Trickster Tales*, p. 13)

This is her way of signalling that not even the micro delivers certainty and sense. Individual lives are marked by gaps in the evidence record, as well as contradictions and even untruths.

Zemon Davis makes sense of the micro first via the announcement of gaps in the historical record, second via the insertion of fictional dialogues to express her view on what might have been—as with the opening of *Women on the Margins* (1995)—and third via a scaling up to larger phenomena and trends. All three are at play in the work for which she is probably best known, *The Return of Martin Guerre*. *The Return of Martin Guerre* stands out from other microhistories as a product of frustration at another microhistory being simultaneously too micro and following a single macro- or metanarrative too stringently: the historical film *Le retour de Martin Guerre* (1982). The sixteenth-century account of a man impersonating the husband of Bertrande de Rols, her acceptance of him and the eventual return of Martin Guerre was, as Davis argues, perfect for filmic representation. Yet Davis was ultimately dissatisfied with Daniel Vigne's production on account of it not being able to handle uncertainties, details and the big picture. As she writes,

> The film was departing from the historical record, and I found this troubling. The Basque background of the Guerres was sacrificed; rural Protestantism was ignored; and especially the double game of the wife and the judge's inner contradictions were softened. These changes may have helped to give the film the powerful simplicity that had allowed the Martin Guerre story to become a legend in the first place, but they also made it hard to explain what actually happened. Where was there room in this beautiful and compelling cinematographic recreation of a village for the uncertainties, the "perhapses," the "may-have-beens," to which the historian has recourse when the evidence is inadequate or perplexing? Our film was an exciting suspense story... [b]ut where was there room to reflect upon the significance of identity in the sixteenth century?
>
> (p. viii)

112 Microhistories and social contract ethics

Davis' reflection on film having no room to reflect on the topic of identity in the sixteenth century is particularly interesting for our purposes. This is because there may be two issues at stake in her comments. The first, suggested by her description of the film as 'an exciting suspense story' is that *Le retour de Martin Guerre* had a metanarrative and that it did not have room for a second. That metanarrative might have reflected the first narrative presentations of the Martin Guerre story in works such as *Arrest Memorable* by the trial judge Jean de Coras (1565). We might also, however, read Davis' comments as a reflection on the kinds of narratives favoured in twentieth-century film production. On this view, a change in scale from the micro to the macro might be from many historical details to a small number of or even a singular narrative frame. This might be a variation on the complaint that in writing macrohistory, details thin out, as with Magnússon's argument against metanarratives at the opening of this chapter.

The second reading, hinted at in Davis' complaint of 'no room' for a sixteenth-century story on identity in *Le retour de Martin Guerre*, is the idea that film might operate within a smaller range of scales than a written history. This restricted range of scales might suggest avoidance, as with D. Desser and G. Studies' complaint that US Vietnam War films focus on the personal in order to avoid a painful political past.[5] Yet it might also say something about the limitations of visual history in relation to written history. There is something really interesting in Davis' complaint that film might not be able to talk about the identities of groups and individuals. It is hard to deny the challenge of inserting big picture observations in films without the use of opening titles, as with 'Afghanistan, 13th Century' (*Padmaavat*, 2018) and 'She wants everyone to know she is a good mother' (*I, Tonya*, 2017) or the use of maps, or dates or instructional dialogue by a character. These devices are used, however, and variation in attention to authenticity across sound, visual effects, costume, hair, makeup, bodily movement and dialogue, to name just a few examples, can mean that a wide temporal frame is present in every filmic scene. Historical films might tell a big temporal story, and one that says a lot about identity from the late nineteenth to the early twenty-first centuries. They might be less adept, though, at telling a story about identity from the larger range of the sixteenth to the twenty-first centuries.

Sizing up justice

Davis' 'one big story' and 'too little detail' complaints about *Le retour de Martin Guerre* illuminate an important ethical point. Not telling a big story can mean avoidance, as has been claimed of US Vietnam War films. Not providing enough detail, however, can also suggest avoidance, as well as a pragmatic decision about what viewers can cope with. Written histories, no matter how small, do not avoid these problems, as we noted in our discussion of Orosius in Chapter 2. You can veer this way and that in trying to highlight the good, the fair and the just. The complaint that could be made of all the microhistories canvassed in this chapter so far, for example, is that they are too big. They all focus on lifetimes, or on significant events for individual humans. As Michel Foucault argues, we can question this 'floor' for microhistory. He writes, 'As the archaeology of our thought easily shows, man is an invention of a recent date. And one perhaps nearing its end'.[6] Foucault encourages us to scale down further, focusing for example on Martin Guerre's foot, which was lost in the Spanish attack on Saint Quentin in 1557, and the cobbler's testimony that Arnaud du Tilh—the imposter—had smaller feet than Guerre. Or we could scale down even further, focusing on the sorghum stalks in *The Night Battles*, or on the snowballs in *The Snowball Revolt*. As we will see in Chapter 10, multiple large-scale histories have been written about physically small non-human entities. What these examples highlight for our purposes in this chapter is that microhistories are *human* histories and that the ethics at play in Magnússon's championing of microhistory is agent or human oriented. Ethics is human. It might be contested whether microhistory has a scale ceiling, but its floor in the human seems to go largely without saying.

Contra this view, though, is the simultaneous complaint that microhistories are too small. This complaint is at play in Robert Findlay's 1988 review of *The Return of Martin Guerre*, which highlights the narrative differences between Jean de Cora's roughly contemporary account and Davis' reading of events:

> Coras's focus was on the marvellous deception perpetrated by Arnaud, and in the many subsequent retellings of the tale, the emphasis was similarly on the arch-trickster, the sly thief of sexual favours and property. Davis presents a radically different interpretation in which the focus is on Bertrande de Rols or, rather, on her relationship with the impostor.... These two versions of the story of Martin Guerre could hardly be more different. The traditional account is a narrative of greed and deception, of perverted talents and a duped woman, of great ability in the service of fraud and theft. Davis's book tells a tale of devotion and collaboration, of love and identity, of how an invented marriage was destroyed by a hard-hearted man with a wooden leg.[7]

Findlay's point is that the key figure in the history of events concerning Martin Guerre is open to interpretation and that the selection of a key figure may say more about the writer of the history than about its subject. Davis' rebuttal quite rightly emphasises her access to a wider range of evidence than that used by Coras, and her work to give voice to the aspirations and actions of individuals that might have been passed over in earlier versions of the story.[8]

The meaning of Findlay's and Davis' responses to one another is not explained by the common complaint that microhistorians have, as Magnússon captures it well, 'a tendency to expand their generalizations far beyond the material with which they are working' (*What is Microhistory?*, p. 128). Neither Davis nor Findlay overstretched. Theirs was a difference of interpretation, and it highlights for us—in crude terms— that there is no tight fit between evidence and explanation in history, even when you make microhistory. Even when you look at the tiniest of human actions, choice and interpretation are not diminished. As we will see in the next chapter, the same is true of history made on the largest scales. The sources do not suggest a history; the historian must make decisions about what sources to use, how to connect them and how to tell their history. This supports Hayden's White's view of us needing to pay attention to the content of the form or the nature of history telling, as well as the sources that are used. Yet the telling of history is 'baggier' than even White suggests, and that 'bagginess' is constricted by the historian not simply out of narrativist virtuosity. This is because narratives are not ethically neutral.

White's *Metahistory* rather famously presented a gridlike typology of emplotment, argumentation and ideology—which can be read vertically, horizontally and diagonally—to explain forms of history telling in the nineteenth century. One of these tropes—'synecdoche'—seems to fit microhistory well, as Magnússon observes (*What is Microhistory?*, p. 152). Hayden White defines synecdoche in a way that is very useful for our purposes in this book. He writes,

> By the trope of Synecdoche…it is possible to construe the two parts in the manner of an *integration* within a whole that is *qualitatively* different from the sum of the parts and of which the parts are but *microcosmic* replications.[9]

As the previous chapters have shown us, how 'parts', 'sum' and 'integration' are understood is a matter of ethics, of interpreting Aristotle's advice to think with carpenter's logic about big and little goods. As an example of synecdoche, for example, White offers us 'he is all heart'. Yet I can also say 'he is all ears', 'he is all hands', 'he is all nerves', 'he is all legs' and the meaning—and ethical stance—of each of these varies. This is most clearly seen by contrasting the meaning of 'he is all heart', which we would take to be a positive statement about someone, with 'he is all hands', which we would take to be a negative statement about someone. They are all examples of synecdoche, and they all share the same stem. If I change the saying slightly, to 'he is all atoms', the meaning might also suggest atomism and thus integration as aggregation, as with collected microhistories featured in Chapter 2. It can also present a person as something other than human, as, for example, emotionally cold. If the saying sounds strange, I can change it to the more familiar 'we are all stardust' to make the same point, and in this case, it can be read either in a positive sense—that we are somehow bigger than our bodies in being connected to the universe—or in the negative sense that we are assembled from the remnants of long-gone entities. We are, in short, either connected to an ever-expanding universe or finite, small leftovers.

What this shows us is that there are at least two Martin Guerre histories that can be, or *ought to be*, told. One can focus on the outrage against Martin Guerre, the other on the complicity of a wife with an imposter. Yet we need not stop there. One can further focus on the motivations of the imposter, another on the puzzlement of the judge, another on the outrage of Bertrande's family and so on. Martin Guerre will be the topic of histories—including visual ones—for years to come. White suggested as much in highlighting the ideological setting of history telling, but ethics was not at the forefront of his argument. The variety of ethical views canvassed in this book so far suggest that his work on narrative is unfinished business. What this tells us, importantly, is that restricting the size of a history does not restrict options for telling and that the telling will not just be a matter of narrative virtuosity.

Differences in the telling of microhistories also reflect differences in ethical view. This means that microhistory is not *an* ethical stance, as Magnússon suggests. Scaling down does not protect you from telling a story that comes at the expense of others and from rendering the experiences of some individuals invisible. Microhistory does not deliver us from ethical decisions, and it does not protect all voices and render them visible. A ten-minute snowball fight need not be understood in one way.

Judde de Larivière's story, for example, points towards the frustration of a male population repeatedly called to defend Venice's interest. Yet she also notes that children threw snowballs too. Did they see things in the same way as adults? They will have felt the effects of taxation and conscription or even been conscripted themselves. We do not know their views as we do those called to trial. We know even less about the views of women on Murano or whether one side of the island saw things in the same way as the other. We also know that different cultural and religious groups resided in the Islands of the Venetian Lagoon at various times and that they might not have been treated in the justice system in the same way as the accused we learn about through the trial transcript in Judde de Larivière's story. We do not know because these individuals and groups did not have their voices captured. History is often unfair in that way.

A captured voice in a justice system does not necessarily speak with justice, however. Individuals burst into voice in trial transcripts, articulating their views on how the world is and ought to be. Yet they are also an ethically problematic source in that we do not know the conditions under which ordinary people spoke. Their words may reflect deprivation of sleep or hunger or even torture. Moreover, they can reflect grief, outrage, scepticism, joy and so many more dispositions that can be hard to pin down in the written word. The written word is not fixed to a single reading, and so it is that the story of Martin Guerre, the doctor, the witches of the Fruili and the snowball throwers of Murano might be told and re-told in different ways. The microverse of microhistory seems bigger than we might have previously thought and an open-ended effort in the manner of *ethos*.

Back to Oxford

We return to a sunny day in Oxford, where prosecco, party poppers, shaving foam and yellow dye mark the end of exams. This little event might be seen through the lens of misrule, where people turn the tables on those who govern them in order to remind them of their freedom. I was once one of those students, however, and had only the foggiest idea of who the 'university' might have been on that occasion. Trashing was just a way of letting off steam after stressful exams. It was also a way of signalling the end of a degree before the long wait commenced for a seat in a graduation ceremony at which your friends might not be present. Yet it also marked a moment of resistance against those were sceptical about whether women could be philosophers. Those trashing and being trashed were neither abstractions nor singular: many stories could be told, as I could tell my own story many ways. All of them would involve shifting bonds with a variety of people.

116 Microhistories and social contract ethics

So too the decision makers of Rawls' world are not abstractions who can be relied upon to deliver bonds of justice that will serve all singly and fairly. He notes as much in describing his theory of justice as a simplified hypothetical. His positioning of their decisions as paternal suggests that women, blacks, children and the disabled might not expect to be those decision makers. Yet we know from history that women can take up with imposters; children can throw snowballs. Going through a decision-making process with the veil of ignorance does not guarantee a singular ethical outcome, no matter how rational it is. Moreover, every moment in that decision-making might generate good or harm. The burden of ethics and the need for *ethos* remains with us and not Rawls' veiled figures. These are all well-known criticisms of social contract ethics. What Rawls highlights is that the work of ethics is not that of isolated individuals, even if he did make the throwaway comment that a single person could make a social contract. This suggests a scale floor for ethics, with the actions of two or more people. This seems to make a lot of intuitive sense. Doing what is good, fair and just will be doing with others.

The question is, though, whether those 'others' are human and whether the scale floor for the ethics of history should therefore rest with the human. The snowball fight, after all, involved snow. We will unpick this assumption in Chapters 9–11. Ahead of that though, I want to take a closer look at whether there are temporal boundaries to the ethics of history, beginning with the idea that the smallest timescales are the ones we need to navigate some of the most grievous acts of harm humans have undertaken against each other.

Notes

1 Linda Barclay, *Disability with Dignity: Justice, Human Rights and Equal Status*, Abingdon: Routledge, 2018; Sophia Isako Wong, 'Duties of Justice to Citizens with Cognitive Disabilities', *Metaphilosophy*, vol. 40(3–4), 2009, pp. 382–401; and Anita Silvers and Leslie Pickering Francis, 'Justice through Trust: Disability and the "Outlier Problem" in Social Contract Theory', *Ethics*, vol. 116(1), 2005, pp. 40–76.

2 See, for example, Tamás Kisantal, Review of *What Is Microhistory?*, *The Hungarian Historical Review*, vol. 4(2), 2015, pp. 512–7.

3 Joan Wallach Scott, *Gender and the Politics of History*, New York: Columbia University Press, 2/e, 1999; Keith Jenkins, *Rethinking History*, London: Routledge, 1991; Jouni-Matti Kuukkanen, *Postnarrativist Philosophy of History*, Basingstoke: Palgrave Macmillan, 2015; and Claire Norton and Mark Donnelly, *Liberating Histories*, Abingdon: Routledge, 2019.

4 See for example Jacques Derrida, 'A Certain Impossible Possibility of Saying the Event', *Critical Inquiry*, 2007, vol. 33(2), pp. 441–61. For a helpful exploration of Derrida's views in relation to the ethics of history, see Ethan Kleinberg, *Haunting History: For a Deconstructive Approach to the Past*, Stanford, CA: Stanford University Press, 2017.

5 D. Desser and G. Studies, 'Never Having to Say you are Sorry: Rambo's Rewriting of the Vietnam War', *Film Quarterly*, 1988, vol. 42(1), pp. 9–16.

6 Michel Foucault, *The Order of Things: An Archaeology of the Human Sciences*, trans A. Sheridan, London: Pantheon, 1970, p. 387.

7 Robert Findlay, 'The Refashioning of Martin Guerre', *The American Historical Review*, vol. 93(3), 1988, p. 555.

8 Natalie Zemon Davis, 'On the Lame', *American Historical Review*, vol. 93(3), 1988, pp. 572–603.
9 Hayden White, *Metahistory: The Historical Imagination in the Nineteenth Century*, Baltimore, MD: Johns Hopkins University Press, 1973, p. 127.

Primary texts

Natalie Zemon Davis, *The Return of Martin Guerre*, Cambridge, MA: Harvard University Press, 1983.

Natalie Zemon Davis, *Trickster Travels: In Search of Leo Africanus A Sixteenth-Century Muslim Between Worlds*, New York: Faber, 2006.

Natalie Zemon Davis, *Women on the Margins: Three Seventeenth-Century Lives*, Cambridge, MA: Harvard University Press, 1995.

David Gauthier, *Morals by Agreement*, Oxford: Oxford University Press, 1986.

David Gauthier, *Moral Dealing: Contract, Ethics, and Reason*, Ithaca, NJ: Cornell University Press, 1990.

Carlo Ginzburg, *The Cheese and the Worms: The Cosmos of a Sixteenth-Century Miller*, trans. John and Anne Tedeschi, Harmondsworth: Penguin, 1982.

Carlo Ginzburg, 'Microhistory: Two or Three Things that I Know about It,' *Critical Inquiry*, 1993, vol. 20(1), pp. 10–35.

Carlo Ginzburg, *The Night Battles: Witchcraft and Agrarian Cults in the Sixteenth and Seventeenth Centuries*, 2/e, Baltimore, MD: John Hopkins University Press, 2013.

Claire Judde de Larivière, *The Revolt of Snowballs: Murano Confronts Venice, 1511*, trans Thomas V Cohen, Abingdon: Routledge, 2018.

Sigurður Gylfi Magnússon and István M. Szijártó, *What Is Microhistory?: Theory and Practice*, Abingdon: Routledge, 2013.

Sigurður Gylfi Magnússon, 'The Singularization of History: Social History and Microhistory within the Postmodern State of Knowledge', *Journal of Social History*, vol. 36(3), 2003, pp. 701–735.

Charles W. Mills, *The Racial Contract*, Ithaca, NJ: Cornell University Press, 1997.

Carole Pateman, *The Sexual Contract*, Cambridge: Polity, 1988.

Carole Pateman and Charles W. Mills, *Contract and Domination*, Cambridge: Polity, 2007.

John Rawls *A Theory of Justice*, Cambridge, MA: Harvard University Press, 1971.

8

SLICE HISTORIES AND INFINITE ETHICS

Boubacar Boris Diop | Tierno Monénembo | Véronique Tadjo | Abdourahman A. Waberi | Garrett Graff | Mitchell Zuckhoff | Richard Drew | Henry Singer | David Hein | Irene Sankoff | Emmanuel Levinas

NEW YORK CITY, UNITED STATES OF AMERICA. You walk around the tiniest of wood path bends, and you see it. Heavy shod brass feet and hands extended to cradle the curled pages of a weighty book and the frame of a storyteller who leans towards a duckling who might or might not be within reach. Two plaques fixed to the ground. Hans Christian Andersen, which I expected. A much smaller one below that remembering all the children who lost parents on September 11, 2001. Unexpected. I really wanted to see Central Park but could not face going to Ground Zero. Sometimes, as a history maker, you feel the weight of the heavy boots that John Safran Foer writes about in his novel *Extremely Loud and Incredibly Close* (2005).[1] Present what you find with honesty. Respect differences. Treat others with care, including the dead. Parents and children. So many of them, globally: a story we ought not have. Unrelenting ethical imperatives that collapse upon you and which leave you feeling that you should not, have no right, cannot speak. Ours is an age in which it appears that there is no ethical high line to be reclaimed.

Wood paths like the one I took in Central Park, as Martin Heidegger reminds us, can lead us to dead ends or to clearings.[2] His philosophy was an invitation for us to dwell, to make and re-make our understanding of the good, the fair and the just without resorting to known or customary paths such as rules, virtues or calculations of the 'most good'.[3] When we do so, he thought, we recognise every moment of our lives as the making of history, as open to choices about what we will and will not do in the name of others or ourselves. On this view, the ethics of history cannot be written for me, they cannot be assumed, and they can never be forgotten.[4]

Oftentimes, we don't have the choice to dwell, even if we want to. I have often thought that not only about Heidegger's writings but also about the ethical theories canvassed so far in this book. Aristotle saw ethics as practical, as the practise of *ethos*. He also talked of big goods and little ones. He did not, however, provide advice

DOI: 10.4324/9780429399992-8

on whether the phenomena we encounter might seem too big or too small for us to make ethical sense of them. Nor did he comment on moments where we feel we have no time to deliberate on what we ought to do. I expect he thought that the practice of *ethos* would hold us in good stead. If we practise ethics—*ethos*—we might come to exercise good judgements in the way that an athlete develops muscle memory. As this book has shown, history makers have long seen themselves as playing a part in the appreciation and development of *ethos*. This is because it is assumed that history allows its makers and audiences to explore the actions of others without experiencing their hurts and acts of harm. In this sense it is like those advertisements you see for vehicles made under controlled conditions of the 'do not try this at home variety'. The controlled conditions of histories include the scales of telling. History makers can shift spatial and temporal scales to emphasise the good—or otherwise—that they see in the activities of individuals or groups over short or long time frames.

History making does not necessarily, however, provide refuge or a place of dwelling. Harms and hurts do not pause for our reflections or reckonings as history makers. They may even seem to pile up, collapse in on us, and overwhelm us. In this chapter, we are going to take a look at this question of whether phenomena can overwhelm the attempts of history makers to make ethical sense of them and whether this breakdown or collapse in sense making is where we find the ethics of history. In distinction from the previous chapter, our focus will be on histories of large-scale phenomena that are explained via short temporal scales. More specifically, my focus will be slice histories of mass murder and genocide.

Slice histories provide an account of past phenomena at a 'slice' or a moment in time. They are akin to a computerised tomography or CT scan which splits the human body out into layered images. This adds yet another analogy to our exploration of the scales of history, and like all of the others, I think that it is a useful yet imperfect way of thinking about the ethics of history. It is useful in that it highlights how we may focus in on a component of a complex phenomenon to explain it. In slice histories, time is that component: events are narrated over the course of days, hours or even minutes. Slice histories, though, often also look to the experiences of small groups of people or individuals. In this chapter, for example, we will look at how some history makers look to the experiences of individuals when talking about acts of mass harm. This does not imply that slice history makers believe in common, layered or even 'stackable' human virtues or vices which can be used to scale their histories up to bigger stories, as with the collective biographies of Chapter 3. The individuals they look to are not always expected to be representative. Rather, they see the stories of individuals as important because they stress or even break customary ethical explanations. They challenge our understanding of the ethics of history. Often children are the focus, as with the memorial in New York's Central Park. This is not because they are always innocent, although most are. Sometimes they are so young that they cannot even be said to know how or why they were harmed or murdered. In this way, they might be seen as highlighting the power of what Emmanuel Levinas (1906–95) called infinite ethics.

In infinite ethics, as we shall see, coming face-to-face with another person can humble us and remind us to be open to ethics in every moment. This is the radical openness of Heidegger's ethics but very much forged through an acknowledgement of frenetic acts of mass harm and murder. Ironically, though, we will also discover that infinite ethics has its limits. It is not clear, for example, whether the face of another always leads us to ethical responsibility or whether non-human faces or entities without faces can humble us and lead us to new ethical explanations. I will argue that Levinas' various arguments are for a human-oriented ethics, thus leaving out the possibility of harms writ upon the non-human world. This limitation will be challenged as we examine the reorientation from human-oriented to object-oriented, entangled or relational views of ethics in Chapters 9–11. In those chapters, I will canvas big, non-human and Indigenous histories. I will argue for them as a reorientation rather than a recent shift in thinking, for the entanglement of humans and place in ethics dates back to views of the world that pre-date Aristotle. In this way, I will argue that a commitment to *ethos* must include the acknowledgement of multiple approaches to history making and the possibility of new ones to come, as well as multiple and new ways of approaching the ethics of history.

Before I say a little more about infinite ethics, I want to note that 'slice history' is not a broadly used term. We can also use the variants 'vertical' or 'moment in time' histories. I note that in the context of this chapter, too, the term 'slice' also has painful connotations. It is hard not to wince when using the word 'slice' to account for histories of the Rwandan genocide of 1994, given that machetes were used so often in the killing of 800,000 to a million Tutsis in around 100 days. Nor is it comfortable to think about the four passenger planes that sliced into the Twin Towers, the Pentagon and a field in Shanksville, Pennsylvania, on September 11, 2001, killing just under 3,000 people in 102 minutes. These are acutely painful histories, and ones that Levinas helps us to see as never far away. The Senegalese writer Boubacar Boris Diop (1946–) captures this sentiment well for us in his novel on the Rwandan genocide, *Murambi, The Book of Bones* (2006):

> I suffered from these things without really feeling involved. I didn't realise that if the victims shouted loud enough, it was so I would hear them, myself and thousands of other people on earth, and so we would try to do everything we could do so that their suffering might end. It always happened so far away, in countries on the other side of the world. But in these early days of April 1994, the country on the other side of the world is mine.

(p. 11)

In infinite ethics, as we shall see, there is no place to dwell apart from the harms of our world. One of the ways that slice histories do this—as I will show through examples from African and US history makers using written and audiovisual media—is by harnessing the power of *oratio recta* and *oratio obliqua* or, put crudely, histories told in fact and in gist, respectively.[5] They do so to involve us in their histories and to show that the ways that we make histories are open to ethical scrutiny.

Infinite ethics

The idea of infinite ethics is most strongly associated with Emmanuel Levinas. Levinas wanted ethics to be appreciated not as a theory or series of abstractions but as a fine-tuned description of our encounters with other people. More specifically, he wanted us to be attuned to the spontaneous acts we undertake for others ahead of formulating notions of the good, the fair, the just, virtue and vice. Ethics, for him, meant returning to our face-to-face encounters with others and realising how they call our experiences and assumptions about customary approaches to ethics into question.[6] In this sense, he held ethics to be practical and personal. He did not see ethics as a matter of virtues, rules or calculations of the 'most good', as with the approaches explored so far in this book. We might also think of his ethics as being open to wonder, allowing moments in which we cannot make sense of the world, and thereby allowing for new approaches to understanding and to action.[7]

Yet Levinas also believed that ethics was more than personal. This is because he saw our openness to face-to-face encounters with others as interrupting our customary ways of seeing and judging the world. Other people are beyond, or transcend, our experiences: they challenge our understandings of ourselves and unravel the assumptions we make about what it means to act ethically (*Totality and Infinity*, p. 173). Moreover, he understood our face-to-face encounters as important for ethics because they cannot be evaded: they demand responsibility from us to act other than in our own interests (*Totality and* Infinity, p. 87). Indeed, he saw our captivation with face-to-face encounters as so strong as to speak of us being obsessed, in a state of insomnia, held hostage or traumatised, albeit without violence (*Totality and* Infinity, p. 219; *Otherwise than Being*, pp. 10–11, 15, 54, 84, 87, 156). In some of his writings, he describes the human face as anarchic, but he also talks of it as an infinite phenomenon ('Humanism and An-Archy'; *Totality and Infinity*, pp. 103–104). It is both within and not from our world of finite assumptions about the world, overflowing it, and captured by the 'in' of infinite (*Totality and Infinity*, p. 195).

In *Totality and Infinity* (pp. 110, 114, 187), Levinas thus describes ethics as a 'first morality' in which our openness to others means an acceptance of vulnerability, of a lack of control. We are open in mind and feeling to the possibility that we do not understand the world, that it can shake and shape us. We are surprised, shocked, horrified but also responsible. Even as we see faces more than once, or see them in customary social settings, he does not want us to leave the idea of ethics as a 'first morality' behind (*Totality and* Infinity, pp. 51, 57). The practical dilemma of coping with the responsibility of this 'first morality' is the focus of this chapter, and also Chapter 8, which looks to big histories.

Slicing through mass violence and genocide

As this book as emphasised, history making is an old activity, and we still follow some of its ancient traditions today. Written histories date back a couple of thousand years, but oral histories arguably take us back many tens of thousands of years

122 Slice histories and infinite ethics

before that. Despite the age of history making, it has a good claim to be interested in the kinds of fresh, close, face-to-face encounters that Levinas would describe as 'first morality'. Thucydides' (c. 460–c. 400 BCE) *History of the Peloponnesian War*, for example, includes an in-depth account of the *stasis* or civil strife that ripped Corcyra apart in 427 BCE. People, he tells us, abandoned social and ethical conventions and acted out of self-interest; officials were detained and executed; fathers killed their sons; bodies were left unburied; people were murdered in and near temples; promises and oaths were broken.[8] Notions of the good, the fair and the just were upended, as he explains, 'He that got ahead of another who intended to do something evil and he that prompted to evil one who had never thought of it were alike commended'.[9] Arguably, Thucydides homed in on Corcyra because he wanted us to understand his claim at the opening of his *History* that the Peloponnesian wars were unprecedented in the carnage, suffering and displacement that they caused. A close encounter with the horror of Corcyra might make us more inclined to forethought in our interactions with one another.[10]

These days we understand stasis to mean standstill as much as strife, and that captures well the detailed movement through very short time frames in slice histories of mass murder and genocide. Time seems to slow, or even to stand still, as we consider violent and murderous acts. History makers refer to time being broken or not being relevant in their recounting of frenetic acts of violence, as we shall see in some of the examples discussed next. We can also credit Thucydides for inviting us to think more carefully about the upending of promises, oaths and notions of the good, the fair and the just in those moments of frenetic violence. He did so not only by stepping through what happened in Corcyra in detail. He also made clear that events might be sometimes better understood via speeches and words recounted in gist rather than word for word. In short, he used the power of fiction and, more importantly, the tension created by juxtaposing history and fiction to convey to his readers just how cataclysmic the Peloponnesian wars had been. The term that is used to describe Thucydides' recounting in gist is *oratio obliqua*. Traditionally, this has been contrasted with *oratio recta*, which is understood as the direct recounting of what someone has said. When thinking about histories, it is understandable that we might prefer a record of what people have actually said rather than an account of what a history maker thinks was said. As the work of François Recanti has shown, though, our accounts of what is said are often a mixture of the two. He suggests that we think of *oratio obliqua* not as a secondary option when we do not have the facts that we need but as involving meta-representation.[11] On this view, Thucydides' use of *oratio obliqua* signals his analysis of what happened at Corcyra and his deployment of terms and categories to indicate its significance as an event. This is very interesting for our account of the ethics of history, for meta-representation might be seen as the explanation of phenomena under existing or conventional ideas. In this sense, it is a conservative act: explaining horror through what we know.

The idea that we might explain events of mass violence through what we know seems odd. After all, Thucydides wanted to emphasise how conventional understandings broke down in Corcyra. It is my view that Thucydides used *oratio obliqua* in order to draw attention to the conventional ways in which we think about the ethics of history. When he took that approach to his account of Corcyra, he foregrounded the limitations of our ways of thinking about the violence that occurred there. He wanted to emphasise how people abandoned customary notions of ethics. Importantly, he did that by focusing in and considering horror at close range. I hold that he laid the groundwork for histories of mass murder and genocide which use close encounters with individuals to challenge the ways in which we make histories and respond to them.

I am going to look at two groups of examples to unpack this idea. The first group is the histories made by writers from eight different African countries for the project *Rwanda: écrire par devoir de mémoire* (1998–2000). Regrettably, not all of these works have been translated into English, so I have had to reduce the scope of this group to Boubacar Boris Diop's (1946–), *Murambi, The Book of Bones* (2006); Tierno Monénembo's (1947–), *The Oldest Orphan* (2004); Véronique Tadjo's (1955–), *The Shadow of Imana: Travels in the Heart of Rwanda* (2002); and Abdourahman Waberi's (1965–), *Harvest of Skulls* (2016) for reasons of accessibility. This reduced selection is a powerful reminder that language and assumptions about translational markets play a role in the ethics of history. This group of texts explores the events of 1994 through poetry, fiction, essays, travel writing and reportage. The use of fiction in these texts reflects neither the absence of historical evidence nor archives in Rwanda nor some simple pan-African notion of oral history making or historiography. Rather, these writers interrupt our expectations about how histories can be told and which histories are acknowledged and which are forgotten or even ignored. They draw upon the power of *oratio obliqua* to highlight the silences, inadequacies and even culpability of those who made histories of Rwanda *oratio recta* ahead of 1998. They do so in the knowledge of coming from 'outside' of Rwanda and against any expectation that they would hold to a unified understanding of 'duty to memory'.

The second group is histories of the 9/11 attacks on the US, with a particular focus on Garrett Graff's (1981–) and Michael Zuckoff's (1962–) oral histories *The Only Plane in the Sky* (2019) and *Fall and Rise* (2019); Henry Singer's (1957–) documentary *9/11: The Falling Man* (2006), which was based on a photographic sequence called *The Falling Man* (2001) by Richard Drew (1946–); and David Hein (fl. 2015) and Irene Sankoff's (fl. 2015) musical *Come from Away* (2015). The archival record for 9/11 is rich—even overwhelming—with over 2,000 oral interviews available via the 9/11 Memorial and Museum and over 150,000 items captured in the City University of New York's and Roy Rosenzweig Center for History and New Media at George Mason University's September 11 Digital Archive, to name just two examples.[12] The report of the National Commission on Terrorist Attacks on the United States (2004) also provides a detailed analysis of the broader scale contexts and actions that led to the attacks, as well as of the attacks themselves.[13] These histories reflect those sources but are not simple aggregations or reflections of them. Rather, they home in on relatively small groups of people—including children—to remind us how fraught and confusing that day was and more or less effectively challenge our attempts to make sense of its violence.

124 Slice histories and infinite ethics

The subtitle of the project, *Rwanda: écrire par devoir de mémoire* is customarily translated as 'writing from the duty of memory', but *mémoire* also describes a genre of argumentative or assertive writing. The texts produced in this project were not the recollections or testimonies of those who experienced the Rwandan genocide first-hand. In this sense, they are unlike the first-hand accounts of writers like Scholastica Mukasonga or Yolanda Mukagasana, who wrote from a sense that all that they had left were words.[14] Nor are they like the collections of oral histories by Philip Gourevitch and Jean Hatzfield, which look in-depth at the experiences of survivors and perpetrators through well-established oral history research methodologies.[15] The project texts are, in my view, arguments against a unified history and invitations to a 'first morality' in the experiential sense presented by Levinas.

Two of the four texts I have selected are novels. The Senegalese writer Diop's *Murambi* unravels the main character Cornelius Uvimana's expectation that he could write about the genocide after returning to Rwanda. The Guinean writer Monénembo's *The Oldest Orphan* narrates the struggles and flaws in the child narrator Faustin's attempts to reconstruct what happened to him and his family. Contrary to Audrey Small's view, I do not see Monénembo's *The Oldest Orphan* as an unproblematic, cathartic or therapeutic reconstruction which generates an '*un*distressing' reading experience.[16] I understand that we might expect as much from a close—even face-to-face—encounter with a child. Monénembo's textual face-to-face encounter, though, drives home Levinas' point about our vulnerability in his 'first morality'. We might start *The Oldest Orphan* with the expectation that its child narrator is innocent and needs our protection, but the novel drives us to see that we might not have understood Faustin because we have not acknowledged the Rwandan genocide by its local name: *advents*. The *advents* is the *beginning* of the destruction of notions of the good, the fair and the just, and it continues on account of our failure to see it. Early on in the novel, for example, Faustin asks, 'After hiding in so many places as I had been doing, how could I remember?' (p. 7). This is not just the claim of someone who cannot remember the past and, specifically, the murder of most of his family. It is also an invitation for us to see the *advents*. The *advents*, like Thucydides' account of the *stasis* at Corcyra, saw time—as Faustin expresses it— 'put on the scrap heap', with no one thinking to count or to rearrange it' (p. 52). Everything in Faustin's world, he tells us 'works upside down…[e]veryone strives to break the rules' (p. 55). This culminates in his question, 'You really think I'm a *genocidaire*?' and the chilling answer:

> Everyone is! Children have killed children, priests have killed priests, women have killed pregnant women, beggars have killed other beggars, and so on. There are no innocents left here.
>
> (p. 23)

Faustin's survival by theft and violence after the murder of his family ends with his realisation that 'I had just turned ten for nothing' (p. 6); his confession to acts that we are never told about in the novel; his execution. It makes us wonder whether the genocide was an all-encompassing beginning without an end, expressed in a life in which the annual milestone of a birthday means nothing. Moreover, the labelling of everyone a *genocidaire* raises the question of whether we too are culpable by virtue of not understanding how our acts of attention, telling and granting of significance have not addressed the violence. The Rwanda of Monénembo's *The Oldest Orphan* is not over, and it has not gone away.

Diop also undercuts our expectations about how a history can be told. *Murambi* is a complex argument for two Wolof proverbs, as Diop tells us. The first instructs us that '[i]f someone lends you their eyes, don't be surprised if they see only what [they want] you to see', the second that '[w]hen memory goes to collect dead wood, she brings back the bundle that pleases her' (pp. 186, 189). The novel opens with us understanding Cornelius to be a returning refugee who wishes to write a play about the genocide. It is only when he notices the silences of those around him that he comes to understand himself as the son of a mass murderer. He then takes upon himself a role 'more modest than a survivor':

> He would tirelessly recount the horror. With machete words, club words, words studded with nails, naked words and… words covered with blood and shit. That he could do, because he saw in the genocide of the Rwandan Tutsis a great lesson in simplicity. Every chronicler could at least learn—something essential to his art—to call a monster by its name.
>
> (p. 179)

This would not be the 'same old story of blacks beating up on each other' (p. 9) but one in which we might discover—like Cornelius—that we see what we want to see and see what pleases us. History making is implicated; it is accused of selective vision and a search for ethical comfort. Moreover, in not noticing, responding to, and accepting responsibility for the genocide, it is likely that we too are implicated. Indeed, at its most extreme reading, this close—face-to-face—encounter with Cornelius names us as monster, as needing to confront the fact that 'the country on the other side of the world is mine' (p. 11). The Rwanda of Diop's *Murambi* is too close for historiographical comfort, and it is all of our responsibility.

Véronique Tadjo's *The Shadow of Imana* and Abdourahman A. Waberi's *Harvest of Skulls* signal their challenges to history making through the fragmentary and multi-genre nature of their texts. Tadjo, a writer, artist and poet from Côte d'Ivoire, highlights the voices, gaps and fragments of history making through a combination of short travelogue records ('The First Journey' and 'Those Who Were Not There'), *retours* or journeys back in which she addresses us through the use second-person plural 'you' in the didactic manner we explored in Chapter 4 ('The First Journey'; 'The Second Journey'), fable or fairy tale ('His Voice'), and short story ('Anastase and Anastasie'). In one sense, *The Shadow of Imana* is a ring narrative in the manner of Herodotus, opening and returning to second-person plural address to remind us that the genocide has not gone away and that humanity is in peril (*The Shadow of Imana*, p. 118). What complicates the path of that ring narrative is her use of different

126 Slice histories and infinite ethics

genres: we are never sure whether hers is a factual summary or an account told in gist or *oratio obliqua*. Her genre shifts, which also entail moving from accounts of groups to accounts of individuals, are designed to unsettle us. Moreover, when she addresses us in the second person, she emphasises the power of coming face-to-face with the other in the discomforting sense explored by Levinas. Hers is an invitation to the ethics of history before customary assumptions about humanity and the other take hold. Consider this passage from 'The First Journey':

> We have to remember that time of endless night, return to that time of great terror, the time when humans, face to face with the destiny, had not yet discovered their humanity. Their steps were guided by obscure fears. We must remember the physical fear of the Other.… Are you prepared for this incredible encounter with death distorted by cruelty? For one day we must stop in our tracks to look ourselves in the face, set off in search of our own fears buried beneath apparent serenity.
>
> (pp. 9–10)

Looking ourselves and destiny in the face are needed to unearth the fears which lurk behind serenity. This will bring an 'incredible'—one might even say wondrous in the sense of terrible—encounter with death and the Other in ways that might even generate physical fear.

Tadjo's call for us to stop in our customary history-making tracks and to face others is deeply discomforting. She drives home Levinas' argument that ethics begins with our admission that we are vulnerable and that no events are distant from us. The Djiboutian writer Waberi also recognises the power of ethical encounters in *Harvest of Skulls*. He, like Tadjo, does so through the use of textual fragments in which subjects and modes of address vary. In distinction from Tadjo, though, he also departs from punctuation conventions. Sentences are left open or seem to lack beginnings. His disjointed text drives home his confrontation with history as dynamite, as he explains in 'Return to Kigali':

> History in these parts is a barrel of dynamite, used abusively, and where only a fine line exists between overt falsification and minimum objectivity. However, deeply entrenched hatred between Tutsis and Hutus did not really exist prior to 1959…a few decades earlier, missionaries had succeeded with their pernicious teachings in irrevocably damaging ancestral religious beliefs and in altering both the temporal and eternal balance of power. Shifting power dynamics in which events that have previously been trivial…can take a tragic turn in the blink of an eye.
>
> (*Harvest of Skulls*, pp. 36–7)

His argument, put most baldly, is that Western historiography laid the fuse for the genocide. In his eyes, missionaries created the categories of Hutu and Tutsi in their histories and thereby fuelled social division. Elsewhere, he notes that while violin music can be made through the use of animal tendons, historiographical music might also be made from the severed Achilles tendons of Tutsis (p. 3). His text, by contrast, emphasises the power of the word *ariko*, which means roughly 'but' or 'however' in the Rwandan language Kinyarwanda. His account of Rwanda, he tells us, bumps and jerks along like a bus on a poorly maintained Rwandan road, with the changes in the line of argument facilitated through the twisting grammatical functions of 'but' and 'however'. His aim is to drive home the point that each textual fragment, to use his own words, 'is just a little grain of sand in an otherwise well-oiled machine' (p. 30).

Where Waberi's grains of sand sharpen is through his varying use of personal pronouns. Parts of *Harvest of Skulls* are told in first-person address, as acts of recounting. Some of the most confronting parts, though, are told in an implicating first-person plural. Consider this passage on the machetes used to murder Tutsis, who were dehumanised through the label of 'cockroaches':

> Shipments of gleaming machetes, purchased cheaply in China, are arriving every day at Kanombe Airport. We start unloading them, promising the cockroaches unprecedented levels of violence…. The scoundrels will be completely exterminated. Never again will we hear stories about yesterday, or bygone days, or of tomorrow. Never again will we have to listen to someone spinning a yarn that opens with the naïve or arrogant words "Once upon a time".
>
> (pp. 11–12; see also pp. 16–21)

'We' signals that we are implicated. 'Never again' reminds us that we broke a promise about not allowing another Holocaust. We are the dog, Waberi implies in another part of the book, who feasted on the corpses of family members and who now bears the name Minuar in honour of the UN peacekeeping mission that failed to staunch the violence (p. 24). The past is sharp sand in Waberi's hands, and its abrasiveness is used to scratch away the sense of history as a single story that can be told dispassionately about a faraway place and another time. His message is for us to stop telling customary stories and to confront the pain that we—globally—caused through colonialism and the deft use of a blind eye in past approaches to history making (p. xi). Quoting Denis Hirston's interview with the South African poet Antjie Krog, he notes in the manner of Levinas that to be vulnerable is to be human, for it 'is the only way you can bleed into other people' (p. 33). To acknowledge Rwanda, we need to be open to the idea that it is our monstrous global creation.

At first sight, the small but growing corpus of written histories about September 11, 2001, are very different to those made for *Rwanda: écrire par devoir de mémoire*. Neither Garrett Graff's *The Only Plane in the Sky* (2019) nor Mitchell Zuckoff's *Fall and Rise* (2019), for example, read like argumentive *mémoires* against history making. Rather, they foreground audio, audiovisual and written archival materials and oral histories to lay out hour by hour and even minute by minute accounts of the actions that led to the deaths of just under 3,000 people in 102 minutes. Each

128 Slice histories and infinite ethics

book is copiously referenced, source names and transcripts are signalled through the use of different fonts and events are described in meticulous detail. Their collective intent is deeply respectful towards the victims and driven by the idea of creating a memorial to them in words. Yet both are discomforting texts, and not just because of their subject matter.

Zuckoff tells us somewhat naively in the introduction to *Fall and Rise* that his intent is one of transparent memorial. 'Speaking of truth', he tells us,

> this book follows strict rules of narrative nonfiction. It takes no licence with facts, quotes, characters, or chronologies.
>
> (*Fall and Rise*, p. xx)

He also sets out a simple, linear narrative schematic to account for what 'fell' after the point the planes impacted: '[a]fter the paper came the people. After the people came the buildings. After the buildings came the wars' (p. xviii). This appears to be well buttressed through his detailed chronological, moment-by-moment 'slice' retelling. Yet his history is not so simple, and Zuckoff knows that. First, *Fall and Rise* does not play out as a linear story of cause and effect, with one thing clearly preceding another. Picking up on a key theme from the 9/11 Commission Report, he notes the murderous intent of the hijackers was not thwarted in part because of a lack of information, communication and coordination. His narrative emphasises missed intelligence and opportunities to act, delays in communication, confusion and sheer 'bad luck and timing' (see, for example, pp. xxi, 125, 126, 406). Zuckoff's detailed chronological recounting highlights, for example, how the hijackers were able to board planes with weapons, how the various first responder groups in New York operated with different radio frequencies and communication equipment and how the mass media was the first to inform the world about the impact of American Airlines Flight 11 with the North Tower of the World Trade Center. What collapsed or fell on 9/11 therefore also included knowing, recognition and communication. It is hard not to connect this back to Thucydides' account of Corcyra. By implication, we wonder what else we might have missed, failed to recognise and communicate. Even more disturbingly, we wonder what we continue to miss. We navigate through a mass of information every day through selection, recognition and communication with others. Every decision we make is not making another decision, every act of recognition is not recognising another, every act of communication is a choice not to communicate about other things. How can we bear the weight of this 'first morality', as Levinas would call it?

Zuckoff answers this question in part via an ethical thought experiment we call the trolley problem. In its simplest form, the trolley problem explores whether we might consider sacrificing a smaller group of people to save a larger one. In one trolley problem scenario, for example, we are asked whether we would direct a trolley or tram away from hitting a group of people and into the path of one other person. As ethicists like Francis Kamm have emphasised, dozens of trolley problem scenarios have been developed to highlight the difference between directly harming a person and letting them be harmed.[17] Perhaps more importantly for our purposes,

Slice histories and infinite ethics **129**

they have also highlighted the practical difficulties we might have in accepting the 'most good' arguments of utilitarians that were explored in Chapter 3 of this book. It is not simply the case that we will accept that larger groups of people are worth more than individuals. Slice histories of the Rwandan genocide and 9/11 show us this through their focus on a small number of individuals.

In *Fall and Rise*, Zuckoff notes that US fighter pilots confronted—but did not have to follow through on—the trolley problem of whether to shoot down a passenger jet in order to avoid a potentially larger number of impact fatalities (p. 173). None of us would wish to make a decision of that kind. Yet there is another—unannounced—trolley problem at play in *Fall and Rise* which is commonplace in history making and which tends to go without saying: should a history maker tell the story of 3,000 people killed, or should they tell the story of a handful of people who were killed? Zuckoff opts for the latter, focusing in on the experiences of around two dozen people, including the youngest victim, toddler Christine Lee Hanson. Garrett Graff makes a similar decision in *The Only Plane in the Sky*. They, in turn, are in alignment with the smaller-scale focus of Diop, Monénembo, Tadjo and Waberi in their various texts, as well as Gourevitch's and Hatzfield's oral histories of the genocide.

Graff, like Zuckoff and the 9/11 Commissioners, emphasises missed intelligence opportunities and the challenges that lack of effective coordination and communication posed for responders (*The Only Plane in the Sky*, p. 63, 101). Like Zuckoff, too, he recounts events minute by minute, moving between New York; Washington, DC; and Shanksville, Pennsylvania. What his selection of a slightly larger scale of telling allows—approximately 200 people, as against Zuckoff's couple of dozen—is for the contingency of many people's experiences to be appreciated. People lived, died or were injured by virtue of where they worked in a building, whether they forgot a security pass, the shoes they wore, whether they left a meeting to iron a shirt. They did not know on the day that these things would matter. In this way, Graff emphasises their innocence in an act of mass murder and by implication our daily vulnerability to harm.

Yet for all its slightly larger scale focus, *The Only Plane in the Sky* is also a lament at not being close enough to the people who were killed. Consider, for example, Graff's use of the three following testimonies, from NYPD officers Steven Bienkowski and James Luongo, and Mary Matalin, aide to Vice President Dick Cheney, respectively:

> People saw the helicopter, and I'm sure many of them were thinking that we were going to be able to save them. In fact, we weren't able to do anything. We were as close as you could possibly be, and still we were helpless, totally helpless.
>
> (p. 112)

130 Slice histories and infinite ethics

> With all the things I saw that day, that, to me, was the worst because those people were so close, yet they didn't make it [because they were killed by falling building debris].
>
> (p. 114)

> That was truly emotional, when we learned that Barbara Olson, a friend of all of us and the wife of the solicitor general, was on the plane that hit the Pentagon. The horror of seeing buildings collapse and seeing planes go into buildings, that didn't jibe with any experience anybody had had. But to isolate it to a person—terrified obviously—sitting on that plane, brought it home to everybody. That was a moment of real terror and emotion for all of us.
>
> (p. 301)

You can fly a helicopter close enough to see the faces of people and yet not be able to save them. You can evacuate a person from a building and watch them be killed by falling debris. You can work to save as many people as you can but only really understand the terror of a moment when you know one victim personally. Graff's history of 9/11, I believe, underscores our practical difficulties with 'most good' options in trolley problem ethical dilemmas, including the telling of history. History, it is argued, needs to be told closely for us to understand its hurts and harms.

Graff's last extract above is particularly instructive, for it highlights how knowing the name of one victim can drive home the horror of particular events. This is akin to acknowledging that knowing the name of one of the potential victims in a trolley problem scenario may skew our response. In that sense, a named person may trigger the experience of 'first morality'. Not knowing the name of one person, or the exact circumstances of their death, though, can also kindle an understanding of Levinas' notion of a first morality in powerful ways. Richard Drew's photographic sequence *The Falling Man*, which became the focus of Henry Singer's documentary film *9/11: The Falling Man*, emphasise this point for us. At 9:41:15 a.m. on 9/11, Drew captured around nine images of an individual mid-air, next to the façade of the North Tower. When one of the photographs was selected for the *New York Times* on September 12, 2001, it was accompanied by the caption, 'A person falls headfirst'.[18] Running the image caused distress and anger, and generated complaints.[19] Why? At one level, understanding the image is simple: the individual was a victim of the 9/11 attacks, along with close to 3,000 other people who were murdered. My recounting in gist, at a higher level of analysis, is surely right. What torments us is that we do not know the name of the person or the particular circumstances by which they came to be in that place, at such an exactly captured time. Singer's documentary follows multiple leads and is as archivally rich as Zuckoff's and Graff's histories, but it does not resolve these questions for us. It is disturbing because we have to acknowledge the shortcomings of what we assume to be an information-rich age. How can we capture so much information and not know who this is? Is our duty to memory, and by implication our duty to the living relatives of the falling man, therefore deficient?

Moreover, it is disturbing because the picture is compelling—beautiful even in its composition—in its depiction of one of 3,000 deaths *about to happen*. Our vulnerability is not being able to look away, being engrossed with the horrifying wonder of something we cannot pinpoint to particulars—name, reason for being there, relatives—and not being able to stop this one death. At this moment, Levinas leads us to see—as with that in which we see the unnamed remains of Rwandans that so often grace the covers of books on the genocide—we apprehend the obsessive effort we need to make in ethics. There are no archival details or markers, categories, narrative types, customary approaches to history making there to comfort us. Virtues, rules or calculations of the 'most good' will not help us to know the unnamed dead. Nor will the approaches to the ethics of history canvassed in this book so far help us.

Even our faith in the ability of the trolley problem to highlight the value of individual lives may collapse in cases where we fail to know who those individuals are. This is because it is one thing to think about trolley problems as abstract thought experiments; it is another to think about them when choosing a course of action involves a face that we cannot recognise. How can we pull the lever to direct the trolley when we have not ascertained who we may be about to harm? It could be a friend, a relative, a loved one. Someone whose story could be so significant as to change the way that we think about the world. *The Falling Man* images overflow our ability to deal with them, and we may be repulsed by our own obsession with wanting to know, to sort the details out. To stop the trolley if you like. To focus in even further on the details of the past, hoping to see something new. To zoom in on an image with the hope that we might have missed something critical in our previous viewings. I hold that history is what it is by virtue of these painful gaps. The gaps in the archival record guarantee that we will never answer all the questions that we need to in order to understand what it means to act in ways that are good, fair and just. The ethics of history is a beginning—an *advent*—without end. When we realise this, Levinas argues, our ethical work begins.

Overflow is not just a matter of the who of history making, it is the how. At first sight, David Hein and Irene Sankoff's musical *Come from Away* illuminates this point in a way that appears to be less confronting than *The Falling Man*. It is tempting to use the words 'feel good' to describe the show and that is potentially what makes it fertile ground for exploring Levinas' idea of 'first morality'. *Come from Away* uses musical numbers and comedy to explore how residents from the small town of Gander, Newfoundland, Canada, welcomed over 7,000 passengers that were cleared from US airspace on 9/11. On one reading, *Come from Away* can be seen as shifting the history of 9/11 away from the US and from confronting what happened to individuals like the falling man. Laughing at its jokes or singing along with its lyrics might even be seen as acts of avoidance. As Hannah Gadsby's *Nanette* (2017) shows us, though, comedy often works because it breaks the tension of—or overflows—moments that we do not know how to navigate.[20] It might appear to release us from those moments, but we might also find ourselves dealing with the unease of laughing at things that we do not on reflection find funny and unpacking why they are not funny. We may even be appalled at the self-deprecation of much comedy, as Gadsby pointedly reminds us. In comedy, we come face-to-face with others who may have experienced hurts and harms and wonder whether we are laughing with them or at them. What is instructive about *Come from Away* is that we do not know how every individual who has seen it has responded to it. Some will have enjoyed it; some will have been shocked and some people will have experienced both of those responses. Some people will have decided not to see it because of any or all of those responses. As with Roberto Benigni's film *La Vita è Bella* (*Life Is Beautiful*, 1997) and the texts of Diop, Monénembo, Tadjo and Waberi discussed earlier in this chapter, it breaks our expectations of how histories of mass murder and genocide *ought* to be told and could lead us to question the conventions of history making.[21] Or it might not. Not knowing the answer to this is an admission of vulnerability: we believe that history making has a role in ethics, but we cannot be sure. Moreover, we might be vulnerable to obsessing about this, making statements about history making that buttress its certainty in ways that we cannot guarantee. History is something we all have to figure out for ourselves, and we do not have in place universal or timeless protections to prevent individuals from using it to hate or to harm. This is one of the consequences of Aristotle's explanation of ethics as imprecise, and this is the very point of Levinas' infinite ethics.

Extending the logic of this point to the particulars of this chapter, we cannot be certain that histories of a small number of individuals help us to understand wider histories of mass murder or genocide. We assume, thinking about my exploration of the trolley problem above, that they help us to come face-to-face with individuals; to acknowledge that their experiences are beyond our own and that we will have to take responsibility for treating them in ways that are good, fair and just. We assume that we will not be able to outsource those decisions to convention. We cannot be sure of these things, however, because the making of a history is not the same thing as being an audience to it. Some people loved *La Vita è Bella*, others thought it avoided talking about the reasons for, the scale and the ongoing impact of the Holocaust. Similar criticisms could be made about Stephen Spielberg's *Band of Brothers* and Ridley Scott's *Blackhawk Down*, which both date from 2001.[22] They can be seen as poignant depictions of the D-Day landing in 1942 and the shooting down of a US military helicopter in Mogadishu in 1993 or not talking about the reasons why those conflicts—and even 9/11—happened. What these examples show us—like my selection of some histories in this book and not others—is that not knowing these things about histories is an admission that we have work to do in the ethics of history. Jacques Derrida captures these points well in his reflections on 9/11. Our use of particular scales of telling and even labels to describe the event feel necessary, as we want to signal its significance to the world. On the other hand, our scales of telling and labels—like the label '9/11' itself, for example—may mask the fact that we 'do not really know what is being named in this way' and that repeated use of them may protect us by 'neutralising, deadening, distancing a traumatism'.[23] We cannot settle history, even if we wanted to.

Back to New York

Levinas' use of the word 'infinite' captures both our being enthralled *in* the *finite* particulars of histories—our desire to pin down all the details at smaller scales that we can manage—and our being acutely aware that they can overrun or overwhelm us. Levinas reminds us of the decisions that shape histories and thereby the decisions of exclusion and silence. It is a deeply personal way of thinking about ethics which expects you and me to be open to the experiences of others.

Levinas' vision for the ethics of history, however, is also practically overwhelming and, conversely and somewhat paradoxically, circumscribed. On the first of these points, it is important to note that we make decisions and use shortcuts and conventions in order to manage life. We select in order to live. This is not just a point about ethics; this is also an acknowledgement of our biology and physiology and our need for survival. As I noted in the opening of this chapter, we do not always have the luxury of dwelling on our decisions. I chose to go to Central Park rather than to Ground Zero, but Ground Zero came to me in Central Park, and I could not avoid it. I chose to look at *The Falling Man* photographic sequence, and I noticed even more acutely that unidentified human remains tended to be on the covers of the books I was reading on the Rwandan genocide. The ethics of history is not entirely mine. We see others, and we realise that our understandings of the past are more fragile than we would wish them to be. Yet we use labels and abstractions, Derrida highlights, even when we know that their repeated use might dull us to the trauma experienced in events such as the Rwandan genocide or 9/11. Talking about those abstracting and navigating experiences, therefore, seems important, as the next chapter on big histories will highlight. They may even help us to question the logic that small-scale stories are more ethical than large-scale ones.

Moreover, the invitation to scale up in big history highlights Levinas' apparent circumscription of ethics to human relations. Chapter 10 will unpick this point further, highlighting Levinas' writing on the importance of a particular dog—Bobby— in his experiences of the Holocaust. It will question why this experience did not lead him to include animal faces in ethics. I am aware that I have also paid little heed to animals in this chapter. We recall Waberi's suggestion that we are akin to the dog Minaur, named in honour of the UN's failure to keep peace in Rwanda. It is a deeply confronting thought. I also need to tell you, though, that Waberi also asks whether the world worried more about the fate of the mountain gorillas during the genocide than they did about the Tutsis (*Harvest of Skulls*, p. 34). Tadjo flips the question over and asks whether the gorillas knew what happened at the foot of their mountains (*The Shadow of Imana*, p. 83). By asking these questions, Waberi and Tadjo—like Jacques Derrida in *The Animal That Therefore I Am* (2008)—highlight the paradox of setting limits to infinite ethics and show that it also cannot be settled once and for all.[24]

Notes

1 John Safran Foer, *Extremely Loud and Incredibly Close*, New York, NY: Houghton Mifflin, 2005.
2 Martin Heidegger, *Off the Beaten Track*, trans Julian Young and Kenneth Haynes, Cambridge: Cambridge University Press, 2002, p. v.

134 Slice histories and infinite ethics

3 Martin Heidegger, *Aristotle's Metaphysics* Θ *1–3* [1931], trans Walter Brogan and Peter Warnek, Bloomington, IL: Indiana University Press, 1995, p. 69; and id., *Introduction to Metaphysics* [1935], trans Gregory Fried and Richard Polt, 2/e, New Haven, CT: Yale University Press, 2014, p. 191.

4 Martin Heidegger, *Being and Time* [1953], trans Joan Stambaugh, New York, NY: State University of New York Press, 2010, §§6, 26.

5 This distinction has been applied to ancient historiography, as with J. E. Powell, *The History of Herodotus*, Cambridge: Cambridge University Press, 1939.

6 Steven Crowell, 'Why is Ethics First Philosophy?', *European Journal of Philosophy*, vol. 23(3), 2015, pp. 564–88.

7 M. Hughes-Warrington, *History as Wonder: Beginning with Historiography*, Abingdon: Routledge, 2019.

8 *Thucydides: History of the Peloponnesian War*, 4 vols, trans. C. F. Smith, Loeb Classical Library, London: Heinemann, 1969, 3.81.

9 *Thucydides: History of the Peloponnesian War*, 3.82.6

10 *Thucydides: History of the Peloponnesian War*, 1.23.2 and 4.62.4.

11 François Recanati, *Oratio Obliqua, Oratio Recta: An Essay on Metarepresentation*, Cambridge, MA: MIT Press, 2000.

12 9/11 Memorial and Museum Oral Histories, online at: https://www.911memorial.org/learn/resources/oral-histories <accessed January 2021>; and The September 11 Digital Archive, online at: https://911digitalarchive.org/about <accessed January 2021>.

13 The National Commission on Terrorist Attacks Upon the United States, *The 9/11 Commission Report*, online at: https://9-11commission.gov/report/ <accessed January 2021>.

14 Yolanda Mukagasana, *Not My Time to Die*, trans Z. Norridge, Kigali: Huza Press, 2019; and Scholastique Mukasonga, *The Barefoot Woman*, trans J. Stump, Brooklyn, NY: Archipelago Books, 2018.

15 Philip Gourevitch, *We Wish to Inform You That Tomorrow We Will Be Killed with Our Families*, New York: Farrar, Straus and Giroux, 1998; Jean Hatzfeld, *Life Laid Bare: The Survivors in Rwanda Speak*, trans L. Coverdale, New York: Farrar, Straus and Giroux, 2006; *Machete Season: The Killers in Rwanda Speak*, trans L. Coverdale, New York: Farrar, Straus and Giroux, 2005; and *The Antelope's Strategy: Living in Rwanda after the Genocide*, trans L. Coverdale, New York: Farrar, Straus and Giroux, 2009.

16 Audrey Small, 'The Duty of Memory: A Solidarity of Voices after the Rwandan Genocide,' *Paragraph*, vol. 30(1), 2007, p. 90 [85–100].

17 Frances M. Kamm, *The Trolley Problem Mysteries*, Oxford: Oxford University Press, 2016.

18 *The New York Times*, September 12, 2001, p. 7.

19 Peter Howe, 'Richard Drew', *The Digital Journalist*, 2001, online at: http://digitaljournalist.org/issue0110/drew.htm <accessed January 2021>.

20 Hannah Gadsby, *Nanette* [recording of a live performance], Netflix, 2018.

21 *La Vita è Bella* [*Life is Beautiful*, film], director Roberto Benigni, Melampo Cinematografica, 1997.

22 *Band of Brothers*, directors David Frankel, Tom Hanks, David Nutter, David Leland, Richard Loncraine, Phil Alden Robinson, Mikael Solomon, Tony To [miniseries], HBO, September 9, 2001; and *Blackhawk Down*, director Ridley Scott, Columbia Pictures, December 28, 2001.

23 Jacques Derrida, 'Autoimmunity: Real and Symbolic Suicides,' in *Philosophy in a Time of Terror: Dialogues with Jürgen Habermas and Jacques Derrida*, Chicago, IL: University of Chicago Press, 2003, p. 87.

24 Jacques Derrida, *The Animal That Therefore I Am*, trans D. Wills, New York: Fordham University Press, 2008.

Primary texts

9/11: The Falling Man [documentary], director Henry Singer, Reel Truth Documentaries, 2006, online at: https://www.youtube.com/watch?v=ME7oToyD9QE <accessed January 2021>.

Boubacar Boris Diop, *Murambi, The Book of Bones*, trans F. McLaughlin, Bloomington, IN: Indiana University Press, 2006.

Richard Drew, *The Falling Man* [photographic sequence], Associated Press, 2001, online at: https://www.esquire.com/news-politics/a48031/the-falling-man-tom-junod/ <accessed January 2021>.

Garrett M. Graff, *The Only Plane in the Sky: The Oral History of 9/11*, London: Hatchette, 2019.

David Hein and Irene Sankoff, *Come from Away* [musical], La Jolla Playhouse and Seattle Repertory Company, 2015, official site online at: https://comefromaway.com/about.php <accessed January 2021>.

Emmanuel Levinas, *Basic Philosophical Writings*, eds A.T. Peperzak, S. Critchley and R. Bernasconi, Bloomington, IN: Indiana University Press, 1996.

Emmanuel Levinas, 'Humanism and An-Archy,' in *Collected Philosophical Papers*. trans A. Lingis. Dordrecht: Martinus Nijhoff, 1987, 127–40.

Emmanuel Levinas, *Totality and Infinity: An Essay on Exteriority*. trans. A. Linguis. Pittsburgh: Duquesnue University Press, 1998.

Emmanuel Levinas, *Otherwise than Being, or Beyond Essence*. trans A. Lingis, Pittsburgh, NJ: Duquesne University Press, 1998.

Tierno Monénembo, *The Oldest Orphan*, trans M. F. Nagem, Lincoln, NE: University of Nebraska Press, 2004.

Véronique Tadjo, *The Shadow of Imana: Travels in the Heart of Rwanda*, trans V. Wakerley, Harlow: Heinemann, 2002.

Abdourahman A. Waberi, *Harvest of Skulls*, trans D. Thomas, Bloomington, IN: University of Indiana Press, 2016.

Mitchell Zuckoff, *Fall and Rise: The Story of 9/11*, New York: Harper Collins, 2019.

9
BIG HISTORIES AND INFORMATION ETHICS

Fernand Braudel | David Christian | Jared Diamond | John R. McNeill | William H. McNeill | Luciano Floridi | Katherine Bode

MUNICH, GERMANY. 'Environmental protection does not have borders'. 'Join the protest for a free internet by modernizing copyright'. Two billboards herald the half-way point on my walk to the *Universität*. A few minutes later, I will pass Geschwister-Scholl-Platz, named for Sophie (1921–43) and Hans Scholl (1918–43), who were executed for speaking out against the Nazis. The ethical call on me in a simple commute seems overwhelming in the senses I talked about in the last chapter. What should I notice, recognise, write about? David Christian's (1946–) three big histories—*Maps of Time* (2004, 2011), *This Fleeting World* (2006, 2019) and *Origin Story* (2018)—are sitting on the desk when I get there. You can make sense of what you see in life as you have always done, Christian seems to write in understanding, or you can catch '[t]he idea of a modern origin story [that] is in the air' and pull what you experience into a 'unified history of humanity' that helps you to re-gear and respond to the unprecedented challenges of a global world (*Origin Story*, pp. vii, viii). It is a simple yet bold claim: you need a big sense of history in order to address big ethical issues. Another way of saying it is that the scale of the history making should match the scale of the ethical demand. They are inextricably coupled. On this logic, we need the biggest scale to tackle the biggest problems, and that means understanding the history of humanity in the context of everything we know, right back to the big bang 13.8 billion years ago. What you get from big history, therefore, is a new sense of history, and of ethics, and we need both, Christian argues, for '[c]hanging definitions of what make a good life may turn out to be one of the crucial steps toward a more sustainable relationship with the environment' (*Maps of Time*, 2011, p. 480). Contra the arguments of the last chapter, history making needs to go big, not small.

The idea that you need to make history big in order to address big problems is not new. The universal histories described in Chapter 1 proposed a similar scope of ambition, but the idea of ethics at play was different. Diodorus Siculus, Orosius, Atâ-Malek Juvayni and Rashīd al-Dīn Ṭabīb wrote human, agent-oriented ethics into

DOI: 10.4324/9780429399992-9

their histories. Their focus was on the character, dispositions—virtues—and responsibility of humans in the achievement of the good, the fair and the just. Moreover, as I have argued, they built dynamic worlds by treating the virtues of individuals and groups as interchangeable and by shifting between them across space and time. Liu Xiang, Fan Ye, Mary Hays, Lucy Aikin, Sarah Strickney Ellis and Mary Cowden Clarke, on the other hand, treated virtuous individuals as more discrete entities who could be aggregated up to calculate and judge the 'most good' for human history. The cosmopolitan global historians of Chapter 6 and their microhistorical twins in Chapter 7 reversed that computability and again assumed the interchangeability of individual and social virtue in order to write personalised histories of humanity. That model was challenged in turn by the confronting and unrelenting request for personal responsibility by the historians of mass murder and genocide canvassed in Chapter 8. On their view, the ethics of history is overwhelming and unrelenting. We are called to make good histories every moment of our lives.

Yet not everything we have read in this book has treated the ethics of history as agent—and more specifically human—oriented. In the writings of the Kyoto School of philosophical world history—outlined in Chapter 4—and in the little world histories of Chapter 5, we saw intimations of what might be called entity-oriented ethics, as distinct from agent-oriented ethics. Entity-oriented ethics broadens out the discussion of the good, the fair and the just to include all organisms, and even non-living entities.

This chapter teases out the idea of an entity-oriented ethics further and highlights how a range of macro-scale writers from the late-twentieth and early twenty-first century such as Christian, Fernand Braudel (1902–85), Jared Diamond (1937–), John McNeill (1954–) and William H. McNeill (1917–2016), Luciano Floridi (1964–) and Katherine Bode (1971–) position this approach to ethics as necessary for the enhancement of agent-oriented—and human-centred—ethics. This necessity, on their view, stems from the acknowledgement of what is called the tragedy of the commons, or multi-agent problems such as environmental degradation, resources depletion, inequality and cyberattacks in which no one and everyone seems responsible. Moreover, information ethicists like Floridi identify a pressing need to grapple with the idea of histories made about, or even by non-human actors such as bots. How their creation of ethics for the commons and all entities unfold is through step logic in which first, the acceleration, 'hyperhistory'—as Floridi puts it—or flood of information or human technologies is acknowledged; second, a change in scales or levels of abstraction or even a call for 'total' or unified history is promoted as a viable response; and third, the organisation of information is treated as the basis for ethical decisions. The result is a distinctive, entity-oriented ethics that covers humans, other living and non-living entities and artificial agents alike. We'll notice that entity-oriented ethics remains a goal rather than a realised idea by virtue of the fact that humans make histories for humans. At the same time, though, I will acknowledge the possibility of artificial agents making histories and that the timing for this might be sooner than we think or even want.

138 Big histories and information ethics

Just as importantly, I will argue that Christian's and Floridi's thoughts on organisation and entropy apply to the ethics of histories, as well as to the phenomena that they write about. This will lead me to say—and this is the core argument of this book—that the ethics of history is plural as a result of Aristotle's guiding idea of imprecision. As people think through ethics for themselves, they are bound to adapt or transform existing ideas of ethics, and even to think of new ones. Another way of saying this is that *ethos* is generative rather than replicative. This generation is not towards any end, goal or single approach to the ethics of history. Consequently, our frameworks for history need to recognise and appreciate the effort and the imprecision of *ethos*, even when they cannot guarantee for certain that histories will not hurt or harm. This entails being open to approaches to the ethics of history that encompass non-human organisms and non-living entities, including the powerful place-driven approaches to history education in Indigenous histories that I will look to in Chapter 11.

Information ethics

As with previous chapters, I would like to provide some introductory thoughts on information ethics. These thoughts will be at more length in this chapter on account of this approach being less established than the others described so far in this book. Luciano Floridi argues that we are living in a 'hyperhistorical' moment and that the only way that we can respond to it is through an ethics of information (*The Ethics of Information*, pp. 12–13). He argues that we arrive at an ethics of information via three steps. His first step is to argue—much as was suggested in the previous chapter—that the world of information we live in is overwhelming. In contrast to those writers, however, he notes that our 'hyperhistorical predicament' *diminishes* rather than accentuates our sense of responsibility because we have lost the defence of ignorance. Whenever or wherever we are in the world, we are expected to know what is going on and to respond for the good. The burden of needing to know places an impossible demand upon us and consequently cripples us as ethical agents ('Hyperhistory and the Philosophy of Information Policies, p. 130; *The Ethics of Information*, p. 7).

Floridi's second step is to acknowledge that our 'hyperhistorical predicament' stems from assessing information *at one or a small range* of level(s) of abstraction. He observes, importantly, that other levels of abstraction are available (*The Philosophy of Information*, pp. 36–7; *The Ethics of Information*, p. 27).[1] We saw this at play in Derrida's argument in the last chapter that abstractions help to signal significance. Abstraction is an everyday term, but it also has more particular meanings in philosophical logic and computing, particularly object-oriented computing. Object-oriented computing treats data fields as having distinct attributes. Floridi has object-oriented computing in mind when he characterises abstraction, and in particular, programmer Edsger Dijkstra's idea of abstraction:

> It has been suggested that there is some kind of law of nature telling us that the amount of intellectual effort needed grows with the square of program

length. But, thank goodness, no one has been able to prove this law. And this is because it need not be true. We all know that the only mental tool by means of which a very finite piece of reasoning can cover a myriad cases is called 'abstraction'; as a result the effective exploitation of his powers of abstraction must be regarded as one of the most vital activities of a competent programmer. In this connection it might be worthwhile to point out that the purpose of abstracting is *not* to be vague, but to create a new semantic level in which one can be absolutely precise.[2]

Dijkstra's characterisation of abstraction is that it saves work and that it generates *precise* novelty. This is interesting for our purposes because it suggests that Floridi's information ethics is more than just an aggregate of smaller abstractions and that it does not lack novelty or detail. Abstractions may be built from treating smaller-scale observables as data in a new set and related in what Floridi calls 'gradients of abstraction' (*The Philosophy of Information*, p. 55), but it is also feasible to think of distinct abstractions that are generated from observables that do not overlap at all. Whether that building implies that the logical rules and methodologies used in one abstraction are carried in higher-level abstractions, though, is not specified. We might want to say that they are, but it is not the case that a big historian such as Christian uses the methodologies—and in particular the documentary archival approaches—of smaller-scale historians. Rather, he looks to histories and to the insights of the sciences to inform his arguments, and the resulting text does not lack detail or novelty. Yet Christian also abides by the rules of English grammar, mathematical logic and the use of conventions such as endnotes. This might lead us to say that the logic of abstractions needs to be consistent but that the methodologies we use to arrive at them do not.

Levels of abstraction in hand, Floridi moves to 're-ontologise' ethics via a third step. This involves him suggesting a new level of abstraction for ethics: one that assumes that all informational objects—including humans—have intrinsic moral value and that they can be agents. He then unfurls three theses to explain this object-oriented ethics:

> The first thesis states that all entities *qua* informational entities have an intrinsic moral value, although possibly quite minimal) and overridable, and hence that they qualify as moral patients subject to some (possibly equally minimal degree of moral respect. The second thesis states that *artificial* informational entities, insofar as they can be agents, can also be accountable *moral* agents. This means…showing that an artificial agent *A*, such as a webbot, a company or a tank, can be correctly *interpreted* as an information system that can play the role of a moral agent accountable for its actions…. In short, all entities are informational entities, some informational entities are agents, some agents are artificial, some artificial agents are moral, and moral artificial agents are accountable but not necessarily responsible.
>
> (*The Ethics of Information*, p. 110)

140 Big histories and information ethics

On this view, any body of information—informational entity—is worthy of respect; some informational entities are accountable for actions (for example a house falling down is accounted to an earthquake), and some informational entities are responsible in that they are 'aware of the situation and capable of planning, withholding, and implementing their interactions with the infosphere with some degree of freedom and according to their evaluations' (*The Ethics of Information*, p. 68). To give a simple example: a star is worthy of respect; the element iron is accountable for the death of a star in a supernova, and humans are responsible for writing about stellar evolution. Ethics, in his view, is therefore interested in entities other than—but also including—humans.

In this infospheric sense of ethics, harm is defined as any action that threatens or harms the being of an entity and which leads to 'metaphysical entropy' or 'metaphysical nothingness' (*The Ethics of Information*, pp. 65, 67). It does not require intent, virtues, rules or notions of the 'most good'. On that basis, he proposes four cardinally ranked ethical principles:

0 entropy ought not be caused in the infosphere (null law);
1 entropy ought to be prevented in the infosphere;
2 entropy ought to be removed from the infosphere;
3 the flourishing of informational entities as well of the whole infosphere ought to be promoted by preserving, cultivating, and enriching their well-being (*The Ethics of Information*, p. 71)

On the face of it, these principles do have the potential to help us to think about non-human phenomena, including artificial agents. He notes that the need for us to come to terms with artificial agents in ethics is pressing. It is hard to argue with this when we think of examples such as !Mediengruppe Bitnik's 'Random Darknet Shopper', a bot which was arrested and then released without charge for purchasing illicit drugs from the darknet; Microsoft's chatbot Tay, which condoned Holocaust denial and racist, sexist and even genocidal statements; and the delivery of terminal patient diagnoses via medical telepresent robots.[3] Potentially, in a forum such as a big history, the ethics of information can help us to think of organic and artificial entities, as well as humans. In the case of humans, it can also include children and those with impaired cognitive abilities. Moreover, it can include hominids and our 'kindred', as Rebecca Wragg Sykes calls Neanderthals.[4] Potentially, then, the ethics of information can help us to navigate the responsibilities of ethics by thinking more explicitly about the different levels of abstraction we can use to define and address problems.

Big informational histories

Across 13.8 billion years, we have seen eight threshold shifts in information organisation and complexity. This is David Christian's summary of big history in his most recent articulation of the field, *Origin Story*, and it signals the potential application of the ethics of information. The first threshold is passed when something emerged from nothing in the big bang (13.8 BYO, pp. 17–38; *Maps of Time* pp. 17–38), the second when stars were formed from the reaction of atoms of hydrogen and helium (c. 13.2 BYO, pp. 39–48; *Maps of Time*, pp. 39–56), the third when the endothermic fusion of iron atoms triggered supernovae and the creation thereby of most of the rest of the fundamental atomic elements (c. 13.2 BYO, pp. 49–55; *Maps of Time*, pp. 48–56), the fourth when these elements accreted to form objects like planets (4.5 BYO, pp. 57–74; *Maps of Time*, pp. 57–79), the fifth when life resulted from the combination of intricate molecular combinations (3.8 BYO, pp. 75–157; *Maps of Time*, pp. 79–138), the sixth when some forms of life adopted bipedal posture and harnessed the energy of fire and of language (200,000 before the present, hereafter BP, pp. 157–87; *Maps of Time*, pp. 139–206), the seventh when humans improved their energy intakes through the intensification of farming (10,000 BP, pp. 188–258; *Maps of Time*, pp. 207–334) and the eighth when humans harnessed the power of fossil fuels (200 BP, pp. 259–86; *Maps of Time*, pp. 335–466). We perhaps now sit on the brink of a ninth threshold, which will be realised when humanity takes on the responsibility of planetary energy manager (pp. 287–306; *Maps of Time*, pp. 467–92), and further changes are anticipated when the sun swallows the earth and the universe becomes more and more disordered as a result of entropy.

In combination, Christian's thresholds suggest the narrative arc of order and complexity, followed by disorder and entropy (*Origin Story*, p. 12). He is agnostic about whether this complexity is necessarily good, as we will see later in the chapter. An account of thresholds six to eight is also presented in the human-focused version of big history for younger readers, *This Fleeting World*, and their combination highlights the importance of information transference through human collective learning. When framed as a story of at least eight information or organisation thresholds, it is possible to see how Christian can present a history of the world in his 18-minute TED talk.

It is worth pausing to think through three elements of Christian's approach, for they help us to get a glimpse of the views of knowledge and of ethics that shape the summary that I have just given. This will help us to assess whether big history demonstrates the ethics of information. They are, first, his ideas of a history of everything, or 'total history'; second of 'mapping' history, and third, his choice of organisation and complexity as the focal point of his mapping. The first, the idea of a history of everything, a complete or 'total' history, is bound to jar the ears of many a history maker. After all, it will be argued, a history maker's selection of evidence says a lot about their understanding of ethics. Indeed, I have said much about history makers' choices throughout this book. In response, it is important to note that Christian does not have a literal total history of reality in mind. His choice of wording reflects a push to challenge the limits of history as the discipline understands it and offers a distant echo of the approach of the *Annales* school and, more particularly, the mid-twentieth-century writings of Fernand Braudel.

For Braudel as for Christian, histories tend to illuminate the past as much as fireflies illuminate the night ('The Situation of History in 1950', *On History*, pp. 10–11; *Origin Story*, p. 3). This is because contemporary historians typically focus

142 Big histories and information ethics

on events, human actions and short-term developments. It does not have to be this way, Braudel suggests, and, indeed, he argues that a different approach is needed if we are to appreciate the interrelation of living and non-living entities in the world. That different approach begins with the acknowledgement that the temporal frame used to make histories is not natural and therefore that it is not fixed. Moving on from this acknowledgement, Braudel argues for three broad groupings in historical time that can be used as frames for analysis: geographical time *(la longue durée)*, social time and individual time *(histoire événementielle)*. These three timescales provide the structure for his best-known work, *The Mediterranean and the Mediterranean World in the Age of Philip II* (1949). Braudel first explores the history of the relationship of people to the physical environment in a geohistory

> in which all change is slow, a history of constant repetition, ever-recurring cycles. I could not neglect this almost timeless history, the story of man's contact with the inanimate, neither could I be satisfied with the traditional geographical introduction to history that often figures to little purpose at the beginning of so many books, with its descriptions of the mineral deposits, types of agriculture, and typical flora, briefly listed and never mentioned again, as if the flowers did not come back every spring, the flocks of sheep migrate every year, or the ships sail on a real sea that changes with the seasons.
>
> (*The Mediterranean*, vol. 1, p. 20)

Second, he outlines a history of the rhythms and forces at work in economic systems, scientific and technological developments, political institutions, conceptual changes, states, societies, civilisations and forms of warfare (p. 21). It is only the third part that

> gives a hearing to traditional history…the history of events: surface disturbances, crests of foam that the tides of history carry on their strong backs. A history of brief, rapid, nervous fluctuations, by definition ultrasensitive; the least tremor sets all its antennae quivering.
>
> (p. 21)

While Braudel does not want to dismiss the history of individuals, he makes it clear that history makes people more than people make history ('The Situation of History in 1950', p. 11). So too he wants us to think about the potential spatial scales of history, as he does in characterising the 'webs' that enmesh objects and people in his global history of the Industrial Revolution and capitalism, the three-volume *Civilization and Capitalism 15th–18th Century*. Knowing what we are affected by, as well as what we can bring into effect, can help the historian to disentangle the ethics of history in terms of human responsibility.

Braudel was not the first historian to write about long-term geological or environmental history: it is not uncommon for even the oldest universal histories to begin with comments on natural phenomena and the nature of the known universe or for the environment to feature in a variety of histories. What is distinctive about Braudel's approach is his explicit invitation for us to think about the possibility of different spatial and temporal scales generating different knowledge and that the simultaneous use of multiple scales might generate a more comprehensive or total knowledge than the use of a single one.

Christian acknowledges the influence of Braudel on his thinking, and particularly the idea of time as a social convention that can be shifted to help us to deal 'collectively with real aspects of our world'.[5] I will return to Christian's call for collective action in due course, but for the moment, I want to note that he sees the potential to shift spatio-temporal frames as more open than the three broad groupings suggested by Braudel. To explain this, he uses the analogy of a map, noting that maps come in a variety of different scales and that they represent objects in accordance with the mapmaker's beliefs about what the map user needs (*Maps of Time*, pp. 3, 11). This is the second key element of Christian's approach and another analogy to add to the various ones we have already considered in this book. As he explains,

> We can never see the world directly in all its detail; that would require a brain as big as the universe. But we can create simple maps of a fantastically complicated reality, and we know that those maps correspond to important aspects of the real world. The conventional diagram of the London Underground ignores most of the twists and turns, but it still helps millions of travellers get around the city. This book offers a sort of London Underground map of the universe.
>
> (*Origin Story*, p. 4)

Again, his works are not literal maps, for temporal rather than spatial scale is the organiser of the various charts that are used to provide an overview of big history, as with the chart in the introduction to *Origin Story* (p. 13).[6] What interests him most about maps is that they can be made in different scales and that while some details thin out at scale, some new things come into view that can be extremely helpful for their users (*Maps of Time*, p. 8). This is akin to Floridi's point that abstraction does not necessarily come at the cost of detail or of novel insight. Part of what comes into view is due to the evidence that the sciences can bring to history beyond humanity, but Christian also holds that you can see things differently too. His point is about the nature of knowledge, as well as domain or disciplinary knowledge. In this way, he accords with Braudel's view that the use of different scales leads to different insights and that the use of multiple scales can foster more comprehensive knowledge than that afforded through the use of a single scale.

Christian acknowledges a multiplicity of scale options in history making, but he prioritises large-scale analysis in order to counterbalance the more common use of smaller scales by history makers. In this way, he appears to be in alignment with other contemporary large-scale history makers like John McNeill and Jared Diamond. Their telling of a longer or larger history—global or stretching back to

144 Big histories and information ethics

the appearance of humans—supports their intent to illuminate the interrelation of humans to the environment and the tragedy of the commons when people do not cross economic, political or intellectual borders to see the consequences of their actions. McNeill's *Something New Under the Sun: An Environmental History of the Twentieth-Century World* (2000), for example, opens with the portrayal of humanity as a gambler:

> Asteroids and volcanoes, among other astronomical and geological forces, have probably produced more radical environmental changes than we have yet witnessed in our time. But humanity has not. This is the first time in human history that we have altered ecosystems with such intensity, on such scale and with such speed. It is one of the few times in the earth's history to see changes of this scope and pace. Albert Einstein famously refused to 'believe that God plays dice with the world.' But in the twentieth century, humankind has begun to place dice with the planet, without knowing all the rules of the game.
>
> (*Something New Under the Sun*, p. 3)

McNeill's work can be described as judgemental and even eschatological, but he is under no allusion that this eschatology is the result of anything other than human action. Similar themes echo in Diamond's eighth century history *Collapse* (2005), which opens with the tale of two farms 500 years apart to signal 'that even the richest, technologically most advanced societies today face growing environmental and economic problems that should not be underestimated' (p. 2).

McNeill and Diamond foreground environmental history, but arguably they see human environmental actions as symptomatic of, or as ancillary to, other features of humanity. This leads them on a search for the distinctive features of humanity. Diamond's history of the last 11,000 years in *Guns, Germs and Steel*, for example, opens with a New Guinean—Yali's—question as to why some people have so much 'cargo' or goods, wealth and power, and others so little and whether more cargo is necessarily better. For Indigenous societies at the receiving end of guns, germs and steel, Diamond tells us, the 'so-called blessings of civilization are mixed', and they are peculiar to humanity (p. 18; see also 13–17). In this way, Diamond builds upon the insights of earlier environmental historians such as Alfred Crosby, whose *The Columbian Exchange* locates the significant biological and cultural consequences of the reconnection of the Americas with Europe after 1492 as part of a 50-million-year history of increasing biological homogeneity.[7] Crosby is almost apologetic for the brevity and disciplinary incursions needed to write a book at that scale but notes that it was needed to shift knowledge:

> I am the first to appreciate that historians, geologists, anthropologists, zoologists, botanists, and demographers will see me as an amateur in their particular fields. I anticipate their criticism by agreeing with them in part and replying that, although the Renaissance is long past, there is great need for

Renaissance-style attempts at pulling together the discoveries of the specialists to learn what we know, in general, about life on this planet.[8]

Diamond is less apologetic and interested in the shorter timescale of five million years across his works, noting that humans are obviously different from other animals but that we do have a strong historical appreciation of why that is the case. John McNeill is also pragmatic, writing with his father William in *The Human Web* that keeping on top of specific disciplinary knowledge is challenging and that there are recent large-scale historiographical precedents in the form of Stephen Hawking's *A Brief History of Time* (1998) and Bill McNeill's *The Rise of the West* (1966).[9] As they explain,

> This book is written for people who would like to know how the world got to be the way it is but don't have time to read a shelf or two of history books. It is written by a father and son who wanted to know as well, and had the chance to read several shelves of books. The project began when the son had the erroneous idea that if Stephen Hawking could compress the history of the universe into 198 pages, then he ought to be able to squeeze the history of humankind into 200 pages. He soon realised he couldn't, but recruited his father, who had already written a history of humankind (at 829 pages) as co-author. Thus began a collaboration between two stubborn historians.
>
> (*The Human Web*, p. xvii)

The language of compression, squeezing and stubbornness are used to reinforce the impression of the difficulty of—and perhaps even their discomfort at—the task but also the necessity of doing so for time-poor and non-specialist readers. Re-scaling means managing a mountain of information but also managing the potential criticisms of researchers who work at smaller scales.

Diamond and the McNeills manage that shift with less anticipated crossfire than Crosby because humanity is always firmly in their sights. Yali's question is important to Diamond because it is the preface to his history of humanity. That history points to human bipedalism, sexuality and semantic abilities as explanations as to why humans treat living and non-living entities in the way that they do, with resulting cultural and biological consequences, including inequality and extermination (*The Third Chimpanzee*, p. 13; *Why Is Sex Fun?*, p. 9). The McNeills start *The Human Web* four million years ago for similar reasons, but they draw out one feature as explaining a globally dominant humanity: symbolic semantic ability and the transmission of information. As they write of the 'extraordinary career' of humanity, for example, they note,

> Marked improvements in the web of human communication and cooperation were what allowed roving *Homo sapiens* bands to colonize the habitable globe and to establish themselves everywhere as a dominant species. The key innovation was probably the full deployment of language to create symbolic

146 Big histories and information ethics

> meanings.... Thus, in turn, allowed social behaviour to attain increasingly precise coordination. For, as with tools and with fire, agreed-upon meanings could be changed and improved whenever experience disappointed expectation.
>
> (*The Human Web*, p. 12)

The organisational frame of their history is therefore found in human communicative and organisational webs, as told through the five levels of ever-thickening web-weaving that bound small groups and then civilisations individually (11,000 to 500 years ago, pp. 9–155); the weaving, re-weaving and strengthening of a worldwide web (500 to 130 years ago, pp. 156–267); and then the strains and potential rents to that web (130 years ago to the future, pp. 268–328). Their simple point is that the world wide web is an example from the deep and broad history of the human—communication—web.

More recently, John McNeill has reasserted the important of large-scale approaches to the history of humanity through his interdisciplinary collaborative work on the Anthropocene. The biologist Eugene Stoermer and chemist Paul Crutzen are credited with starting the now burgeoning field of anthropocenic history with a paper published in the *Global Change Newsletter* in 2000 with the title 'The Anthropocene.' In this paper and a follow up by Crutzen in *Nature* in 2002, the case is made for it as a distinctive period of history on the grounds that the human impact on the earth system is unprecedented, that the range of that impact—from climate to biodiversity and biogeochemical cycles—is broad and that there is an imminent shift in the functioning of our planet that warrants attention and action.[10] John McNeill's contribution, in conjunction with Crutzen, the environmental scientist Will Steffen and development studies researcher Jacques Grinevald, is to make a case for the Anthropocene starting with the Industrial Revolution and for it being a distinctive and better approach to history than those focused on the biosphere or the realm of living entities, or the noösphere or the realm of knowledge. Their grounds, quite simply, are that these previous approaches do not give sufficient attention to the interaction of humans with living *and* non-living entities and the biochemical and geo-engineering impacts that follow from those interactions ('The Anthropocene: Cultural and Historical Perspective', pp. 843–5).[11] The combined fields of history, paleontology, biology, archaeology, linguistics and anthropology in 'deep history'—which is younger than the term 'Anthropocene' and which I will explore in connection with Indigenous histories in Chapter 10—would likely also attract a similar assessment by John McNeill.

Yet anthropocenic histories are ultimately histories of human action, and the cases made for them do not necessarily explain why Christian might choose to write about the universe and the earth before and after humans or why indeed John McNeill stretches back to the big bang in his postscript to *The Human Web*. The organisational frame of John McNeill's mini (postscript) history is expansive, suggesting a place for the history of humanity within a broader universal history of organisation and complexity:

Human history, like the history of the universe and the history of life, shows an evolution towards complex structures, created and maintained by energy flows, the sizes of which correspond to the degree of complexity and structure in question.

(*The Human Web*, p. 320)

This echoes Christian's interest in human semantics and collective learning as the sixth threshold of organisation in big history. This is because learning allowed for access to greater management of energy, and this, in turn, supported greater organisational complexity. It is the analytic frame of organised information that Christian uses to locate anthropocenic history within the history of the universe. This is the third key element of Christian's approach. This frame makes it possible to read Christian's call for us to deal collectively with the 'real aspects of our world', which I noted earlier in this chapter, as a call for action in response to anthropocenic impacts. His inclusion of phenomena pre- and post- humanity, however, also makes it possible to read this as a reminder that we are one organism on one planet in a universe that is tending towards entropy. Human organisation may be global now, but we cannot escape the longer-term tendency towards disorganisation. The question is, does big history support both of these readings and the more or less human focus of the ethics that they imply?

More than one level of abstraction

To figure out whether Christian's big history turns on human, or a wider object-oriented, ethics, it is instructive to look at how he and Floridi use the word 'flourishing' and 'entropy'. Indeed, I hold their uses of these terms to be diagnostic. We recall Floridi's four ethical principles which I provided at the beginning of this chapter. Zero to three present entropy as needing not to be caused, to be prevented and to be removed. The fourth principle suggests, by contrast, that flourishing needs to be promoted. Floridi's only other description of flourishing occurs in a footnote in *The Ethics of Information* in which an Aristotelian connection is drawn. He writes,

> For example, in Aristotle courage is having just the right amount of concern for safety, neither too much nor too little, implying a willingness to take risks always and only for the right sorts of things in the right ways and the right times, and this is just one part of flourishing, which requires having all the virtues (exactly the right amount of concern for every good) and having the right amount of those goods as a result (which requires good fortune and not just virtue).

(*The Ethics of Information*, p. 73 n.6)

What he might be referring to here, as with Terrell Bynum in his paper 'Flourishing Ethics,' is Aristotle's notion of *eudemonia* or living well as the aim of ethics, which we met in the introduction to this book.[12] This seems a regression back to

148 Big histories and information ethics

human-focused virtue ethics, and this impression is not helped by the absence of illustrative non-human examples in either Floridi's or Bynum's writings.

Christian's uses of the terms 'flourishing' and 'entropy' are more frequent and expansive than those of Floridi: for example, he refers to entities flourishing on more than forty occasions in *Maps of Time* and over 20 in *Origin Story*. He uses the idea of flourishing to suggest the possibility of humanity achieving a more sustainable relationship with the biosphere (*Origin Story*, p. 301), but the majority of his uses are for non-human organisms, and there is also one case where its use is linked to his theme of complexity to look at life and stars at what Floridi would call a different level of abstraction:

> As for the *rules* of complexity in living organisms, these are different from those that dominate at the astronomical scale. Individual organisms (as least as we know them) flourish at much smaller scales than stars or planets. At those smaller scales, gravity counts; but other forces count for more. Life is shaped largely by electromagnetism and the nuclear forces that control how atoms work.
>
> (*Maps of Time*, p. 81)

The sense we build up from Christian's collection of uses is of entities not just existing but also achieving greater complexity. That greater complexity might be internal—as with an organism evolving or the fusion of elements in a supernova—or external as entities accrete, come together in various kinds of relationship and thereby expand. In a way, Christian's big history is a casebook in information ethics through time, but his use of the terms 'complexity' or 'organisation' signals a much stronger interest than Floridi in organic entities and in entities that pre- and potentially post-date humans.

Moreover, Christian does not consistently present entropy as absolutely bad or as evil. Like Aristotle, he holds that context and outcomes matter. A critical example is his discussion of Lynn Margulis' idea of an 'oxygen holocaust' in *Microcosmos*—a text we will explore in more depth in the next chapter—which happened around 2.5 billion years ago. Christian neither treats the event in which the biological production of oxygen led to many species perishing, nor Margulis' description of it as 'holocaust', as evil actions in Floridi's terms:

> One or more negative messages, initiated by *A*, that brings about a transformation of states that (can) damage *P's* well-being severely and unnecessarily; or more briefly, any patient-unfriendly message.
>
> (*The Ethics of Information*, p. 183)

This is because Christian sees thermodynamic entropy as a necessary part of complexity and, therefore, of big history but also because humanity would arguably not have evolved without this event. An event can be to the detriment of some entities and the benefit of others, and this can be the case within and across time and space.

Put bluntly, the rise of eukaryotes and the extinction of the dinosaurs was good for humans but evil for some prokaryotes and the dinosaurs. This is also the point of Yuval Harari's history of humans in *Sapiens*: human flourishing was at the expense of other hominids and living organisms.[13] Lest, however, we jump to the horrifying conclusion that all holocausts are good—including the Holocaust in which the Scholls were executed—the detail of Christian's argument is worth remembering: *humans* benefitted.

This example raises the important question of whether Christian, like Floridi, is ultimately interested in human ethics rather than a broader ethics of information. The simple response to this point is that while Christian and Floridi write of informational entities, they do not write *for* informational entities. Christian does not write for the universe any more than Floridi writes for earthquakes. Christian writes for humans, the 'you' of the various origin stories he introduces:

> *This* is what you are; *this* is where you came from; *this* is who existed before you were born; *this* is the whole thing of which you are a small part; *these* are the responsibilities and challenges of living in a community of others like yourself.
>
> (*Origin Story*, p. 8)

This 'you' is a responsible agent. They thus circumscribe their approach on account of who they see as causing and as able to address significant global challenges. As Onora O'Neill put it in Chapter 5, to address global problems, you need agents who have the responsibility and capability to address them. If we recall Floridi's ethical principles, only humans are capable of responsibility at present. Importantly, however, Christian's and Floridi's views open our minds to the possibility that other entities might make histories. Arguably, this the point of Christian's focus on oxygen-producing organisms. I have to entertain the idea that bacteria might make history. It might also be argued that computing recommendation systems are an example of artificial agents writing history. In short, we need the ethics of information because the age of informational entities acting in ways that harm or benefit humans has already arrived.

How do we know that Christian and Floridi are open to this broader notion of ethics? I hold that Christian's signals on this question are slightly stronger in the affirmative than they are for Floridi. This is because he describes a universe in which informational entities arise, are sustained and disappear. The engine for that is entropy, which Floridi presents as something to be avoided. His 'plurality of ontologies' is very much in the present (*The Ethics of Information*, p. 70). A universe without entropy is a universe without change in Christian's view. Some changes break information down in ways that might be seen as deleterious (*Origin Story*, pp. 26–7), but some changes generate novelty. Consider, for example, the ways in which Christian describes the role of RNA as the potential predecessor to DNA:

> Unfortunately, RNA copies itself less accurately than DNA, and this creates real problems. A system of replication that is good but not quite good enough

150 Big histories and information ethics

> may be the worst of all possible worlds, because it may be bad enough to accumulate errors and good enough to transmit those errors faithfully to later generations. It has been shown that such a system may lead to breakdown more rapidly than the sloppier forms of replication required in 'metabolism first' models of the origins of life.
>
> (*Maps of Time*, p. 103)

The flip side of the 'unfortunate' inaccuracy of RNA relative to DNA, as Christian notes in *Maps of Time*, is that it can drive evolution and diversity. Sometimes those inaccuracies are 'just right' for the creation of new informational entities, like humans. Christian sees these 'goldilocks' moments as particularly important drivers in the threshold informational changes he sees at play in the history of the universe.

It is also important to remember that Christian's universe of informational entities includes histories and understandings of the ethics of history. Aristotle's notion of ethics as imprecise might be read, on Christian's terms, as saying that history making, including the ethics of history, is akin to RNA rather than DNA transcription. Histories are not exact replicants. History makers adapt, transform and reject previous approaches, and they do not work to a single, timeless or highly specific template. Regardless of their intentions, there will be a constellation of histories that is never static and a constellation of approaches to the ethics of history that is never static. Indeed, we may expect multiple, even conflicting, notions of history and the ethics of history to arise, be sustained over varying spatial and temporal scales and disappear. Some will benefit some informational entities; others will generate harm. On this view, we cannot expect big history to be the only approach to history making, and Christian acknowledges as much in *Origin Story*:

> It is different, of course, from most traditional origin stories. This is partly because it has been built not by a particular region or culture but by a global community of more than seven billion people, so it pools knowledge from all parts of the world. This is an origin story for all modern humans, and it builds on the global traditions of modern science.
>
> (*Origin Story*, p. 9)

We should expect, therefore, that big history is not the only approach to history making that is available to us now and in the future.

Back to Munich

This is an important point because the informational foundations of both Christian's and Floridi's worlds are arguably not fair. This point is driven home beautifully in Katherine Bode's argument in *A World of Fiction* (2018) for a combination of 'distant' or abstracting and 'close' reading in what is now called computational literary studies. Much has been said about the potential to analyse literature at a distance through the use of computational techniques. Such approaches have been lauded as potentially illuminating the gaps in our knowledge of world literature that have resulted from the suppression of writing from the world's economic and social periphery rather than core. The incomplete translation of the *Rwanda* project texts I noted in the previous chapter, for instance, illuminates this point.

We can quibble about the specific statistical approaches at play in distant techniques, but Bode's point is that they rest upon the naïve assumption that information is generated, coded and curated in ways that are fair. Not all texts are digitised because not all texts are valued equally. I may hope that Google Books, for example, will deliver something different to the 'classics' shelf in a bookshop, but it may simply magnify it and broadcast it to an even wider audience. Floridi's infosphere is not objective, and it is not fair: he arguably relies on what is coded in computer science. The same can be said about the historical and scientific research that underpins Christian's approach to an origin story. Arguably, his book celebrates the achievements and publications of individual scientists and small scientific teams that require no more celebration. Indeed, you could even argue that his vision of the universe is simply another Western history of science in which history making plays an ancillary part. I do not see that intent in Christian's descriptions of what he is trying to achieve, but arguably the greatest test of his informational approach will be the acceptance of other big histories that are made with different informational sources and which range over spatial and temporal scales differently. Can we, for example, treat Peter Sloterdijk's bubbles, Brian Greene's strings or Manuel de Landa's self-organised meshworks as plausible frameworks for thinking about big history?[14] That is, can we talk of big histories rather than a single origin story in big history?

Moreover, signalling that we expect such diversity can be an important invitation for others to make history. Bode, for example, undertakes both large-scale analyses of digital text corpuses and fine-scaled readings of individual texts. More importantly, she openly acknowledges the sources, purposes and gaps in the information that she uses and publishes the data sets and codes that she uses for analysis. As a result of this work, she has produced both a macroscopic mapping of the currents and interconnections of global literature in Australia, for example, and identified over a thousand individual authors that we did not know about before. As she shows us, you can combine macro- and micro-approaches and see both large-scale trends and problems and the lives of individuals such as Sophie and Hans Scholl.

As Kwame Anthony Appiah notes in *As If*, we live lives in which multiple, and sometimes even conflicting, idealisations or abstraction heuristics apply. He sees that as ethically preferable to totalising theories that mask their unfairness and metaphysical incompleteness.[15] Yet Appiah does not have an answer here to our notion of an ethical overburdening. Indeed, he, like Floridi and Christian, might have made the burden heavier by noting that more than one level of abstraction is available to history makers. The same is true of historiographers like me. I can tell the story of the ethics of history using one history maker at a particular point in time. I can tell another story using a small range of thinkers over the timeframe of a couple of thousand years. Or I can treat histories as informational entities that arose thousands of years ago and which will disappear when the earth is swallowed by the sun. All of these—and more—are plausible options, but I have chosen the middle one. I have done so because I want

152 Big histories and information ethics

you—whether you are a human or an artificial agent reading this—to see that the ethics of history was shaped by Aristotle in ways that we are yet to fully appreciate.

Notes

1 See also Luciano Floridi, 'The Method of Levels of Abstraction,' *Minds and Machines*, vol. 18(3), 2008, pp. 303–29.

2 Edsger W. Dijkstra, 'The Humble Programmer', 1972 ACM Turing Award Lecture, *Communications of the ACM*, vol. 15(10), p. 864, online at: https://amturing.acm.org/award_winners/dijkstra_1053701.cfm <accessed 10 April 2019>. For a shorter extract of Dijkstra's speech, see Jan van Leeuwen, 'On Floridi's Method of Levels of Abstraction,' *Minds and Machines*, vol. 24(5), 2014, p. 7.

3 !Mediengruppe Bitnik, 'Random Darknet Shopper,' online at: https://wwwwwwwww-wwwwwwwwwwwww.bitnik.org/r/2/ <accessed 10 April 2019>; Max Read, 'It Only Took a Day for Microsoft's "Teen" Chatbot to Become a Racist, Misogynist Holocaust Denier', *New York Intelligencer*, 24 March 2016, online at: http://nymag.com/intelligencer/2016/03/microsofts-teen-bot-is-denying-the-holocaust.html <accessed 10 April 2019>; and Julia Jacobs, 'Doctor on Video Screen Told a Man He Was near Death, Leaving Relatives Aghast,' *New York Times*, 9 March 2019 <accessed 10 April 2019>.

4 Rebecca Wragg Sykes, *Kindred: Neanderthal Life, Love, Death and Art*, London: Bloomsbury Books, 2020.

5 David Christian, 'History and Time', *Australian Journal of Politics and History*, vol. 57(3), 2011, pp. 353–4.

6 See also the big history project website, https://www.bighistoryproject.com/home <accessed 8 April 2019>.

7 Alfred W. Crosby, *The Columbian Exchange: Biological and Cultural Consequences of 1492*, New York: Praeger, 1972; see also *Ecological Imperialism: The Biological Expansion of Europe, 900–1900*, Cambridge: Cambridge University Press, 1986; *Germs, Seeds and Animals: Studies in Ecological World History*, London: M. E. Sharpe, 1994; and *Children of the Sun: A History of Humanity's Unappeasable Appetite for Energy*, New York: W. W. Norton, 2007.

8 Alfred W. Crosby, *The Columbian Exchange*, p. xxvi.

9 Stephen Hawking, *A Brief History of Time: From the Big Bang to Black Holes*, London: Bantam, 1988; and William H. McNeill, *The Rise of the West: A History of the Human Community*, Chicago, IL: University of Chicago Press, 1963.

10 Paul J. Crutzen and Eugene F. Stoermer, 'The Anthropocene,' *Global Change Newsletter*, no. 41, 2000, pp. 17–18; and Paul J. Crutzen, 'Geology of Mankind,' *Nature*, no. 415 (January), 2002, p. 23.

11 See also Clive Hamilton and Jacques Grinevald, 'Was the Anthropocene Anticipated?' *The Anthropocene Review*, vol. 2(1), 2015, pp. 59–72; and David Lowenthal, 'Origins of Anthropocene Awareness,' *The Anthropocene Review*, vol. 3(1), 2016, pp. 52–63.

12 Terrell Ward Bynum, 'Flourishing Ethics,' *Ethics and Information Technology*, vol. 8(4), 2006, pp. 157–73.

13 Yuval Noah Harari, *Sapiens: A Brief History of Mankind*, London: Harvill Secker, 2014.

14 Peter Sloterdijk, *Bubbles: Spheres volume 1*, trans. Wieland Hoban, Los Angeles: Semiotext(e), 2011; Brian Greene, *The Elegant Universe: Superstrings, Hidden Dimensions and the Quest for the Ultimate Theory*, New York: Norton, 1999; and Manuel de Landa, *A Thousand Years of Nonlinear History*, Brooklyn, NY: Zone, 1997.

15 Kwame Anthony Appiah, *As If: Idealization and Ideals*, Cambridge, M: Harvard University Press, 2017.

Primary texts

Katherine Bode, *A World of Fiction: Digital Collections and the Future of Literary History*, Ann Arbor: University of Michigan Press, 2018.

Fernand Braudel, *The Mediterranean and the Mediterranean World in the Age of Philip II*, [1949] 2 vols, trans. S. Reynolds, Glasgow: William Collins, 1972–73.

Fernand Braudel, *Capitalism and Material Life 1400-1800*, trans. M. Kochan, Glasgow: Fontana, 1974, revised edn, *Civilization and Capitalism 15th–18th Century*, 3 vols (*The Structures of Everyday Life, The Wheels of Commerce, The Perspective of the World*), trans. S. Reynolds, Glasgow: William Collins, 1981-92.

Fernand Braudel, *On History*, trans. S. Matthews, Chicago, IL: University of Chicago Press, 1980.

David Christian, *Origin Story: A Big History of Everything*, Harmondsworth: Allen Lane, 2018.

David Christian, *Maps of Time: An Introduction to Big History*, 2/e, Berkeley, CA: University of California Press, 2011a.

David Christian, *The History of the World in Eighteen Minutes* [TED Talk], 2011b, online at: https://www.ted.com/talks/david_christian_big_history?language=en <accessed April 3 2019>.

David Christian, *This Fleeting World*, 2/e, Great Barrington, MA: Berkshire, 2019.

Jared Diamond, *Collapse: How Societies Choose to Fail or to Succeed*, New York: Viking, 2005.

Jared Diamond, *Guns, Germs and Steel*, New York: W.W. Norton, 1997a.

Jared Diamond, *The Third Chimpanzee: The Evolution and Future of the Human Animal*, London: Hutchinson, 1991.

Jared Diamond, *Why Is Sex Fun?: The Evolution of Human Sexuality*, New York: Basic Books, 1997b.

Luciano Floridi, *The Philosophy of Information*, Oxford: Oxford University Press, 2011.

Luciano Floridi, 'Hyperhistory and the Philosophy of Information Policies', *Philosophy and Technology*, 2012, vol. 25(2), pp. 129–31.

Luciano Floridi, *The Ethics of Information*, Oxford: Oxford University Press, 2013.

John R. McNeill, *Something New under the Sun: An Environmental History of the Twentieth-Century World*, New York: W.W. Norton, 2000.

John R. McNeill and William H. McNeill, *The Human Web: A Bird's Eye View of World History*, New York: W.W. Norton, 2004.

Will Steffan, Paul J. Crutzen and John R. McNeill, 'The Anthropocene: Are Humans Now Overwhelming the Great Forces of Nature?' *Ambio*, vol. 36(8), 2007, pp. 614–21.

Will Steffan, J. Grinevald, Paul J. Crutzen and John R. McNeill, 'The Anthropocene: Conceptual and Historical Perspective', *Philosophical Transactions of The Royal Society A: Mathematical, Physical and Engineering Sciences*, vol. 369, 2011, pp. 842–67.

10

NON-HUMAN HISTORIES AND ENTANGLEMENT ETHICS

Mark Kurlansky | Lynn Margulis and Dorion Sagan | Sven Beckert | Stephen Budiansky| Donna Haraway | Karen Barad | Gerardo Beni | Jing Wang

HOBART, AUSTRALIA. The barking booms and cracks off the sinuous eucalyptus trunks even before I set foot on the driveway. In the dusk, the barker is grim-like: black, shadowy in motion, ears cocked at acute angles. I start to call his name—Winnie—and before I am even finished, he moves seamlessly from a menacing crouch to lolloping and tail wagging. He will be down the driveway in a shot, singing a range of sounds and walking close to the bag that he knows contains a squeaky toy gift. Within a matter of minutes, we will be playing hide and seek with the squeaky toy around the kitchen island before settling down to watch television with his paw resting on my hand. My sister laughs in her beautiful way, enjoying the moment before Winnie sits at the window looking for me after I leave. I think she also suspects that Winnie and I could be partners in crime, and in that thought, she would be right. We are a fine pair, she jokes, sending photos to my family. When Winnie is gone, I know that I will always look up at the window for him. Kelpie dogs are strong, smart and loyal. Smart enough to break their way into your food cupboard when you are out, to know that you will bring them a gift when you visit them every three to four months and to move livestock with very little instruction. Smart enough to make you loyal to them.

My interactions with animals like Winnie lead me to wonder, like Martha Nussbaum in Chapter 6, Véronique Tadjo and Abdourahman A. Waberi in Chapter 8 and Andrew Cohen in his article 'Contractarianism, Other-Regarding Attitudes, and the Moral Standing of Nonhuman Animals', how we might or even should include them in our thinking about the ethics of history.[1] A search for advice from the profession, however, turns up a blank, as it does for artificial agents and informational entities. Animals are not currently covered in professional codes of conduct for history or in writings on the ethics of history. Ethics is a human concern. This is a blind spot given that animals often feature in histories and are sometimes even the focus of them.

DOI: 10.4324/9780429399992-10

Not all history makers will agree that animals are a priority for the ethics of history or that advice on animal ethics from other disciplines is appropriate or helpful. Like Nussbaum, for example, they may see ethics as a rational human activity. On this view, humans play a special role in advocating for the dignified existence of animals.[2] Alternatively, they may share Peter Singer's view that minimising suffering and maximising happiness—as with the utilitarian view of ethics we covered in Chapter 3—extends to human interactions with animals. Animal ethics is, on both of these views, an activity of human advocacy and care, and therefore, animal ethics is a part of human ethics.[3] Moreover, that activity of advocacy and care can be quite specific, with dignity afforded to chordates—animals with skeletal rods like spines—and particular exceptions made for invertebrates like octopuses. Dragonflies, ants and cell colonies might not get a look in. It is also not evident which ethical frameworks—human or animal—we might use to assess work with hominids, with the recent example of the biofabrication of neanderthal 'minibrains' or organoids in dishes springing to mind.[4]

Neanderthal histories like Rebecca Wragg Sykes' *Kindred* (2020), as well as a broader group of non-human histories, intimate at something more than the need for advocacy or care, or for ethics by extension for non-human entities.[5] Indeed, it turns out that these histories can help us to think about the ethics of history in new—and more historical—ways. This chapter picks up where the last one left off and teases out the idea of a dynamic, porous ethics of history using post-humanist or entanglement philosophies and swarm intelligence research.

This chapter looks at examples of what are variously called animal, commodity or little big histories. These typically look at one kind of entity—living or non-living—over timescales of 1,000 years or more. For ease of reference, I am going to call them non-human histories, though few of their authors would talk of them in this way. My primary reason for doing so is that they contemplate a world beyond, before, after or even without humans. Non-human histories feature regularly on bestseller lists, so there is no shortage of materials for us to consider. As a starting point, I will look to Mark Kurlansky's (1948–) single entity histories—from which I have chosen the examples of cod, salt and paper—and Sven Beckert's (fl. 2015) global history of cotton. Both are well known within and beyond universities. If I were to settle for their works alone, however, then Joshua Specht and Timothy LeCain may appear justified in their argument that non-human histories are simply global human histories with entity lenses.[6] More bluntly, histories are either about humans or about the things we eat, wear or use. This chapter would in their terms provide a rehearsal of the ideas and issues raised in Chapter 5, albeit with works that appear to knock humans off centre stage. There are other non-human histories, however, that hint at a view of the ethics of history that is not easily explained by our understandings of global history. These encourage us to think more about the potential of Kurlansky's and Beckert's ideas. Moreover, they help us to pick up on the tantalising glimpses of an ethics of history which unites the human and non-human that we saw in the writings of the Kyoto philosophers of world history in Chapter 4, the little world histories in Chapter 5 and the big histories in Chapter 9.

156 Non-human histories and entanglement

Stephen Budiansky's (1957–) work on the history of animal domestication and Lynn Margulis (1938–2011) and Dorion Sagan's (1959–) work on the history of bacteria spring to mind as triggers for a re-think on the ethics of history. As we will see, Budiansky asks whether animals domesticated humans as much as we domesticated them, and Margulis and Sagan use the language of a holocaust to frame the rise of cyanobacteria two billion years ago. None of them tell a simple story in which humans advocate or care for non-human entities. Indeed, in the case of Sagan and Margulis, humans simply provide the language needed to open up a history of living entities that are more globally prevalent and persistent than us. Yet neither of these writers articulate the potentially radical implications of their claims for the ethics of history. I will tease out these ideas by looking to the post-humanist philosophies of Donna Haraway (1944–), Karen Barad (1956–), Gerardo Beni (1946–) and Jing Wang's (fl. 1989) idea of swarm intelligence. I will show that theirs are views of the ethics of history as always in motion and not the only option for a dynamic ethics of history. Chapter 11 will suggest that Indigenous histories provide an important alternative.

Entanglement ethics

Donna Haraway and Karen Barad look to the scientific idea of diffraction—traces of the intersection of waves of light after interference—to posit an idea of ethics in which entities are mutually entailed and inseparable. Beni and Wang are interested in the 'intelligent' behaviour that appears to be at play in natural systems like termite colonies and artificial systems in which humans, artificial agents and algorithms are connected. In combination, their diffraction and swarm intelligence theories help us to see the power and potential of entanglement in the ethics of history.

On the view of Haraway and Barad, our universe is not to be understood as made of clearly discrete objects that sit in isolation or which bump into one another. Rather, they see it as defined by the traces, perturbations and ripples that flow from the continuous interaction of entities across time and space. The universe is not constituted by objects but by the echoes of relationships that are in motion. Neither of them denies the existence of persistent forms of interaction or outcomes from interactions, but they ask us to remember that the universe is like an ever-rippling web record of entanglements that is constantly being made and re-made. This includes the world of the ethics of history: our understandings of ethics change as entanglements shift the course of our world this way and that. Their entanglement ethics of history is, therefore, also a metaethics of history: the interactions of entities is dynamic, and the ethics we use to navigate those interactions is also dynamic.

This focus on dynamism is both enticing and challenging. We might ask, for example, whether the entanglements of entities make ethics and even reality. We can also question whether anything persists in ethics and therefore whether we can have an ethics of history at all. I will touch on questions like these in this chapter but note that answers to them are a matter of ongoing philosophical dispute. More pragmatically—and simply—I will note that the dynamism Haraway and Barad argue for is

Non-human histories and entanglement **157**

not just temporal. Both use sub-atomic phenomena to explain macro-level entanglements and the other way around. Their use is not one of analogy: both insist that entanglement is a matter of reality. Furthermore, this idea can be conjoined with Gerardo Beni and Jing Wang's idea of swarm intelligence—the collective behaviour of human, non-human animal and artificial agents in decentralised systems—to provide us with new ways of thinking about history, history making and the ethics of history. To take a simple example, my interactions with a termite can be seen as entangled with a colony of termites, as well as human communities and configurations of non-living entities. I could study the patterns of interactions of termites and use them to train a computer to select historical evidence to make a history. The expectation these writers generate is that the ethics of history will—indeed, must—involve shifts in spatio and temporal scale for us to understand how the world is made and re-made, over and over again. For them, big and little histories, as well as the worlds they describe, are conjunctions of space, time and ethics. As I will note in conclusion, though, this vision of the ethics of history—like that of Chapter 9—has its origins in twentieth-century Western science. Moreover, it can be rightly asked whether the idea of swarm intelligence is simply a revisitation of Hegel's idea of the cunning of reason—outlined in Chapter 4—in the language of computer science. By asking this question, we might find ourselves in established historiographical territory, testing what collective culpability and ethics means in cases such as the Holocaust. As Chapter 11 will show, there are other options available for the consideration of an entangled notion of ethics than those provided by Western science.

Writing the human from the non-human

Fish, milk, salt, oysters. Baseball, paper, cookbooks. Islands and cities. A year, a homecoming, non-violence. Mark Kurlansky's books seem to be on every bookstore shelf and sales list I scan. By the time this book is published and you read it, there will no doubt be more titles to add. He seems the opposite of David Christian, whose push for a total big history suggests a story that can be told only once. Kurlansky has not one but many histories to tell. As many stories as there are entities, it seems. He is prolific, yet he is also singular in his focus on unravelling the histories of particular and even discrete phenomena on local, national and global scales. How these phenomena relate to one another and whether there is a single world that they all constitute are topics that he is yet to tackle. I suspect they might not be on his to-do list. I dive in, looking for traces of an ethics of history that will help us to think about something other than ourselves.

Cod: A Biography of the Fish That Changed the World (1997) opens with two epigraphs. The first captures the foundational question in Thomas Henry Huxley's *Evidence as to Man's Place in Nature* (1863), which concerns the relation of humans to the 'universe of things'. We are all interested, Huxley argues, in how we came to be in our power over nature and the power of nature over us and in the problems and tendencies of our world.[7] The second quote, from Will and Ariel Durant's *The Lessons of History*, proposes competition as the trade of life.[8] Both seem to come together nicely

158 Non-human histories and entanglement

in Kurlansky's prologue, which tracks the fruitless efforts of Newfoundland fishermen to find cod big enough to reverse the Canadian Government's decision in 1992 to close their fishing grounds. The problem, Kurlansky observes, 'is that they are at the wrong end of a 1000-year fishing spree' (*Cod*, p. 14). Cod are also at the wrong end of that fishing spree, as are sardines, herring and various species of whales that have been taken to the brink of extinction in various parts of the world on account of overfishing.[9] It is not clear, however, how much *Cod* is about the fish or other ocean-dwelling entities, as distinct from human uses of them. The book, to take just one example, is punctuated with recipes: it is at its base about humans eating cod. One chapter out of fourteen offers a very brief evolutionary history of the cod over 120 million years, yet it is anchored in observations about how easy it is to catch them and the various ways they can be preserved and cooked. These textual features support Kurlansky's primary argument that if there is one open-mouthed species greedier than the cod, it is humanity (p. 45). From this we glean that cod consume living and non-living entities, but the fate of these entities is out of focus. Humans act; cod are acted upon, and they are thereby denied the dignified existence or care that Nussbaum or Singer would suggest. This history is one of humans developing the technologies, forms of social organisation and laws to increase their catch yields and to deliver fish to dinner tables all over the world. Cod are, therefore, useful not only as food but also as a lens on the development of cities, states and international relations; industrialisation and systems of taxation; democratisation and popular revolt; and environmental change, management and degradation at the hands of people. In short, the story of human interactions with cod is the story of globalisation and thus of global human history.

Salt: A World History (2002) is not about a disappearing resource but about one that is today so ubiquitous that Kurlansky sees himself as needing to remind us of its historical scarcity and thus value (*Salt*, p. 6). His history of salt is—like that told for cod—connected with the development of human communities, technologies and revolts, but we are left in no doubt that the story is not just about an entity found across the globe but a globe-shaping entity. As he writes,

> The search for salt has challenged engineers for millennia and created some of the most bizarre, along with some of the most ingenious, machines. A number of the greatest public works ever conceived were motivated by the need to move salt. Salt has been at the forefront of the development of both chemistry and geology. Trade routes that have remained major thoroughfares were established, alliances built, empires secured, and revolutions provoked.... Almost no place on earth is without salt. But this was not clear until revealed by modern geology, and so for all of history until the twentieth century, salt was desperately searched for, traded for, and fought over. For millennia, salt represented wealth. Caribbean salt merchants stockpiled it in the basements of their homes. The Chinese, the Romans, the French, the Venetians, the Habsburgs, and numerous others governments taxed it to raise money for wars.
>
> (p. 12)

Non-human histories and entanglement **159**

The search for salt prompts human organisation, movement and even violence. Yet there is no argument for salt shaping the story in the manner of some of the histories we canvassed in the last chapter. Manuel de Landa's *A Thousand Years of Nonlinear History* (1997), we recall from Chapter 9, explains global history as a self-organising lattice, whereby it assembled as a structure in the absence of a designer or external controller.[10] *Salt*, like *Cod*, is a human history in which humans are actors and salt is the recipient of that action.

Arguably Kurlansky would see De Landa's *A Thousand Years of Nonlinear History* as falling prey to G. E. Moore's idea of a 'naturalistic fallacy'. This is the argument that just because salt has particular properties, it does not mean that those properties have to be conveyed in our approaches to history making.[11] By way of example, I may write a history by selecting pinches of archival materials and sprinkling them through a story or programme a computer to grow a lattice of documents randomly and treat that lattice as a history. Both 'salt historiographies' are possible, but my use of them may be rejected by other history makers. Where we see Kurlansky argue against this fallacy most clearly is in *Paper: Paging through History* (2016). In this case, the target is what he calls the 'technological fallacy'. As he argues,

> Studying the history of paper exposes a number of historical misconceptions, the most important of which is [the] technological fallacy: the idea that technology changes society. It is exactly the reverse. Society develops technology to address the changes that are taking place within it.... Chroniclers of the role of paper in history are given to extravagant pronouncements: Architecture would not have been possible without paper. Without paper there would have been no Renaissance. If there had been no paper, the Industrial Revolution would not have been possible.
>
> None of these statements is true. These developments came about because society had come to a point where they were needed. This is true of technology, but in the case of paper, it is particularly true.
>
> (*Paper*, p. xiv; see also xviii)

Calling on Martin Heidegger, Kurlansky reasserts that technology is a means to an end and that it serves to reveal the global history of humans.[12] People are the purpose of history making.

The idea of entity histories revealing human history is not isolated to Kurlansky. 'The fluffy white fibre', Sven Beckert reflects in the introduction to *Empire of Cotton: A Global History* (2014), 'is at the centre of this book'. In the next sentence, though, he quickly qualifies that

> [t]he plant itself does not make history, but if we listen carefully, it will tell us of people all over the world who spend their lives with cotton.
>
> (*Empire of Cotton*, p. xix)

Those people built a system of 'war capitalism' in which new production, trade and consumption activities were wrought through slavery, imperial expansion, dispossession and even violence (p. xv; 83–135). This system ushered in a wave of de-industrialisation that consolidated manufacturing in Europe and North America and reduced other parts of the world to the roles of labour-intensive production and the consumption of manufactured goods (p. xvii). Arguably, the patterns of this global economic system remain in place today. Beckert is thus interested in how cotton helps us to understand global human history and the present, which he has characterised—with Dominic Sachsenmaier—as the study of the development of interactive human communities.[13] Yet there may be more to the story of cotton, as Alfred Crosby's various writings on ecological imperialism suggest.

We recall Crosby's apology in the last chapter for the brevity and disciplinary border crossing of his works in large-scale environmental history. Crosby writes of the movement of crops that accompanied globalisation. Yet he also makes the bold and intriguing claim in *Ecological Imperialism* that the sun never sets on the empire of the dandelion.[14] To understand the force of his suggestion, it is worth considering his description of weeds:

> Weeds are combative. They push up through, shade out, and shoulder past rivals…. Direct sun, wind, and rain do not discourage them. They thrive in gravel beside railway tracks, and in niches between slabs of concrete. They grow fast, seed early, and retaliate to injury with awesome power.[15]

Crosby's language suggests that our relationship with weeds is not one of human control or exploitation. Indeed, his descriptions of weeds as combative, retaliative and awesome suggests that humans are not always in the driving seat of global history. Weeds are agents which shift our history this way and that.

Weeds are not the only entities that complicate the notion of global history as a human-led story. Stephen Budiansky positions his account of animal domestication in *The Covenant of the Wild* (1992) as a riposte to the core 'myth' that humans are apart from nature on account of being in control of their destiny (p. 19). The idea of human exceptionalism, he notes, fails to explain why we have not domesticated animals across the globe. This means that we have little choice but to finally recognise that 'domesticated animals chose us as much as we chose them' and that they 'found it in their interest' to associate with us (pp. 24, 43). In unpacking this idea further, though, he comes down against the idea of animal and plant domestication as a matter of planning and choice. The rise of agriculture was not, he makes clear, an 'ideological revolution' (p. 113). Squirrels bury nuts and ants cultivate plants without intention. So too humans threw seeds onto rubbish piles without thinking that they were establishing agriculture (pp. 82–6). On similar lines, we can think through the steps in which animals came to hang around camps without bestowing notions of planning upon them or the humans with which they associated. This is not to deny the ability of humans to invent and to transmit adaptive behaviours, but Budiansky's work serves to remind us that domestication is not explained fully either by human intention or by the lack of it. Understanding this provides the foundation for his conclusion that humans are part of a global history of interdependent entities, some of which have flourished and some of which have been driven to extinction (p. 124). This was Christian's point about entropy in the previous chapter, which we introduced but did not unpack fully.

As Melinda Zeder has noted, Budiansky's work on domestication sits towards the middle of a variety of views on whether humans drove the domestication of other entities or the other way around.[16] On the more extreme end—away from explanations which privilege humans and human intention—she notes the work of David Rindos in arguing that plants had the upper hand in domestication because they tied humans down and reduced their selective fitness.[17] Moreover, it is also possible to write global history in which humans are not even present. This is the territory of Lynne Margulis and Dorion Sagan's *Microcosmos* (1986), which charts the history of bacteria on Earth. It opens with an unforgiving assessment of human appraisals of history that

> strips away the guilded clothing that serves as humanity's self-image to reveal our self-aggrandizing view of ourselves is no more than that of a planetary fool.
>
> Humans have long been the planetary or biospheric equivalent of Freud's ego, which 'plays the ridiculous role of the clown in the circus whose gestures are intended to persuade the audience that all the changes on the stage are brought about by his orders.' We resemble such a clown except that, unlike him, our egotism concerning our own importance for Nature is often humourless.... The human 'emperor,' from the revisionary perspective of *Microcosmos*... is wearing no clothes.
>
> (pp. 13–14)

The revision offered by *Microcosmos* is the telling of global history from the point of view of its biologically simplest and most persistent entities, entities upon whom humans depend for life (p. 28; 235). This is necessary, in Margulis and Sagan's view, to help humans to appreciate the 'ecological carnage' they have wrought upon the earth by not being in symbiotic balance with other living entities (pp. 21–2).

Microcosmos is also radical in style. Terms used by other history makers are selected to tell a story designed to humble humans. This is not benign usage, as the title and opening of Chapter 6 make clear:

> The oxygen holocaust was a worldwide pollution crisis that occurred about 2,000 million years ago. Before this time there was almost no oxygen in the Earth's atmosphere. The Earth's original biosphere was as different from ours as that of an alien planet. But purple and green photosynthetic microbes, frantic for hydrogen, discovered the ultimate resource, water, and its use led to the ultimate toxic waste, oxygen. Our precious oxygen was originally a gaseous poison dumped into the atmosphere.
>
> (p. 99)

Global events from two billion years ago were literally a holocaust—a burning by oxygen—and one that Margulis and Sagan claim 'rivals the nuclear one we fear

162 Non-human histories and entanglement

today' (p. 109). This is not a one-off usage on their part, for later on in the book, the holocaust—and they use lower case 'h' deliberately—they associate with the Second World War is explained as the nuclear bombing of Hiroshima and Nagasaki, which they see as 'unwittingly' ushering in a Japanese-led information revolution in the latter decades of the twentieth century:

> World War II ushered in radar, nuclear weapons, and the electronic age. And the holocaust of Hiroshima and Nagasaki over forty years ago decimated Japanese industry and culture, unwittingly clearing the way for a new beginning in the form of the red rising sun of the Japanese information empire.
>
> (p. 237)

It is hard not to fix on their passing over of the Holocaust and the claim that the nuclear bombings of Hiroshima and Nagasaki were 'revolutions' with broadly positive outcomes. These provocations, though, are part of their wider—very pointed—argument that global changes are simultaneously beneficial and deleterious and therefore that our customary approaches to ethics fall short. Moreover, they make it quite clear that a global history of bacteria does not need humans to feature in it. It is as if they are human envoys that have been sent by bacteria to tell us that we aren't that special.

From entities and abstractions to tangles and swarms

In a way, Margulis' and Sagan's approach is as bold a stroke as Orosius' decision to write a Christian universal history from the perspective of pagans, which we explored in Chapter 2. Their global history of bacteria is designed to unsettle our sense of mastery and to drive home the ethical impacts that have flowed from treating humans as special or as separate from the universe that they inhabit. This is the element of Margulis' work that Donna Haraway magnifies in the opening of 'The Companion Species Manifesto' (*Manifestly Haraway*, 2003). What Margulis and Haraway want us to understand is that the relation of entities is not that of discrete phenomena connecting with other discrete phenomena. In a way, it is a pointed riposte at the notion of abstractions or entities—which we looked at in Chapters 7 and 8—as discrete.

The phrase that Margulis' uses to describe the relation of entities—and which Haraway adopts—is that of symbiogenesis.[18] The best-known example of this in *Microcosmos* is the process by which eukaryotic bacteria emerged when prokaryotic organisms came together in a relation of host and hosted entities (pp. 22–3; 32–3). Margulis promotes symbiogenesis as playing a key role in evolutionary jumps, including the emergence of humans. As she reminds us, '[o]ur bodies contain a veritable history of life on Earth' (p. 32). Haraway pushes this idea further, arguing that the recognition of the 'potent transfections' between living entities makes it difficult to maintain that we are discrete from companion species like dogs and the other way around ('The Companion Species Manifesto', p. 93). A similar point may be made about the traces of Neanderthal DNA in human genomes, and this highlights that past interactions have traces in the present. Haraway does not just want to highlight the mutual benefits derived by companion species in the manner of Stephen Budiansky's *The Covenant of the Wild* or to remind humans that the effects of their actions are not isolated, as is argued in *Microcosmos*. Rather, she sees the intermingling of species as supporting the idea of process philosophy, including process ethics. As she explains,

> Reality is an active verb....Through their reaching into one another, through their 'prehensions' or graspings, beings constitute each other and themselves. Beings do not pre-exist their relatings. 'Prehensions' have consequences. The world is a knot in motion. Biological and cultural determinism are both instances of misplaced concreteness—i.e., the mistake of, first, taking provisional and local category abstractions like 'nature' and 'culture' for the world and, second, mistaking potent consequences to be preexisting foundations. There are no pre-constituted subjects and objects, and no single sources, unitary actors, or final ends.
>
> ('The Companion Species Manifesto', p. 98)

Her point, in simple terms, is that the lack of firm or set boundaries between entities should be reflected in the ways that we think, write and make ethical judgements. If the relation of humans and animals is dynamic, for example, then the ethics we use to think about humans and animals should be dynamic too. The ethics of history will, therefore, focus on relationships rather than entities (p. 99).

In using the word process, Haraway signals her revisitation of dynamic approaches to philosophy which arguably stretch back as far to Heraclitus' claim that everything flows.[19] Moreover, her interest in process philosophy and thereby ethics is arguably as extensive as that of Heraclitus and other thinkers. Our ground for thinking such is her argument for the commingling of human and non-human animals, and human and artificial agents in 'A Cyborg Manifesto' (1985). Haraway is not simply interested in pointing out that tool use by animals confounds our sense of uniqueness or that ubiquitous technologies such as predicative text make it hard to discern where the moves of a writer and a machine begin and end. The artificial agents I introduced in Chapter 8 may also come to mind. She highlights these 'boundary breakdowns' or 'leaky distinction[s]' (pp. 10, 11) in order to argue that we are unduly fixated by creating and holding to abstract concepts and dualisms of abstractions which promulgate patriarchy, racism and speciesism. In short, we keep trying to stop the world and to stop history. She writes,

> certain dualisms have been persistent in Western traditions; they have all been systemic to the logics and practices of domination of women, people of colour, nature, workers, animals—in short, domination of all constituted as others, whose task is to mirror the self. Chief among these troubling dualisms are self/other, mind/body, culture/nature, male/female, civilised/primitive,

reality/appearance, whole/part, agent/resource, maker/made, active/passive, right/wrong, truth/illusion, total/partial, God/man.... To be One is to be autonomous, to be powerful, to be God; but to be One is to be an illusion, and so to be involved in a dialectic of apocalypse with the other. Yet to be other is to be multiple, without clear boundary, frayed, insubstantial. One is too few, but two is too many.

(pp. 59–60)

Acknowledging the distraction of these dualisms is frightening, she admits, because we then have to face up to ideas of existence, knowledge and ethics in which it is never clear who makes and who is made in relations of identity (p. 60). This is not simply Floridi's acknowledgement in the previous chapter that humans and machines can be agents that act upon or with one another. It is, rather, confronting the idea that we and other entities are inseparable and thus that we might be what we have so long labelled as monstrous. We, like a centaur or a cyborg, cannot have integrity in the double sense of its meaning: because we cannot hold fast to unchanging ethical principles, we cannot be whole and undivided (pp. 64–5).

Haraway's manifestos are not destructive interventions so much as invitations to the unravelling of our understanding of the world. Ethics takes shape in the moment, but she also holds that its aftereffects can be usefully understood via the idea of diffraction, which refers to the physical process of the apparent bending and spreading of light as it encounters obstacles. In *Modest_Witness@Second_Millennium. FemaleMan© Meets_OncoMouse™* (1997), Haraway explains that the usefulness of the idea of diffraction is metaphorical or figurative. Diffraction patterns, she advances, '[r]ecord the history of interaction, interference, reinforcement, difference', and 'heterogenous history' (p. 273; Barad, *Meeting the University Halfway*, p. 71). We take this as Haraway reminding us that while ethics is an open process, its traces are historical. What we do not know is whether her metaphorical use of diffraction extends to the acknowledgement of diffraction patterns, which have recognisable peaks of intensity which can be varied through apparatus adjustments. What this might mean in simple terms for a process philosophy and ethics is the acknowledgement that changes in environmental conditions will vary the intensity of specific entity relations, perhaps in predictable patterns. This is an important consideration for this book and for the task of thinking through what an ethics of history might look like. If it holds, we might expect a view of ethics that is historicised and that history makers will have an important role to play in discerning patterns of entity relations, and their environmental triggers.

The question of how diffraction aids our understanding of being, knowing and ethics is explored at some length in Karen Barad's writings, including her major work *Meeting the Universe Halfway* (2007). Karen Barad acknowledges Haraway as the inspiration for her exploration of the role of diffraction in a process philosophy and ethics. In distinction from Haraway, however, Barad's interest in diffraction is not as a metaphorical or figurative tool. This is because she does not hold the behaviour of small—quantum—entities to be other than that for macroscopic entities (*Meeting the Universe Halfway*, p. 85). To her view, knowing and ethics are part of our engagement with the world in what she calls 'agential realism' (*Meeting the Universe Halfway*, p. 56). In crude terms, this means that knowing and ethics are not our *constructions* of the world. Nor are they reflections of the world. Rather, they are touchpoints that show us as much about how the world makes us as we make it. As she explains:

> Experimenting and theorizing are dynamic practices that play a constitutive role in the production of objects and subjects and matter and meaning.... theorizing and experimenting are not about intervening (from outside) but about intra-acting from within, and as part of, the phenomenon produced
>
> (p. 56)

To help us understand both the nature and implications of her claim, Barad offers at least three major examples from physics.

Barad's first example is Neils Bohr's double-slit thought experiment, which posits the idea of matter being both a wave and a particle, even though these characteristics are thought to be mutually exclusive. This has been demonstrated in a succession of experiments in which matter such as light passes through a screen with two slits. If the slits are monitored, light passes through the slits as particles; if not monitored, light goes through both slits and shows the diffraction pattern of a wave. The most likely explanation of this phenomenon is that the particle or wave nature of matter is undefined until a measurement is made (*Meeting the Universe Halfway*, pp. 71–85). Interaction determines the outcome. Another—less likely—explanation is that the matter observed has information from the future, but this would entail matter breaching the rules of relativity and travelling faster than the speed of light.[20] Measurement is not a simple act of seeing, as Barad's second example of the operation of a scanning tunnelling microscope reminds us. In this case, the close positioning of the tip of the conducting microscope allows electrons to tunnel through barriers to form a current which is the result of the tip position, voltage used and the atomic density of the sample being measured. Drawing on the work of Don Eigler, Barad likens this to the tapping of a cane across a surface and thus the building up of knowledge via touch and interaction (*Meeting the Universe Halfway*, p. 52).[21] Touch is also the dominant theme of Barad's exploration of quantum field theory, but in this case, the excited states that define matter involve interactions between entities *and* within themselves, as with an electron exchanging a virtual photon within itself ('When Two Hands Touch, How Close Are They?').

What emerges from Barad's exploration of physics is a shift away from the thought that we interfere with or make the world and towards the idea of us being made by and making a world in which no entity is discrete. We touch, interact with and change the world; it touches, interacts with and changes us. This has far-reaching implications not only for history making, but also for the idea of the ethics of history itself. It will not be the discrete and firm product of philosophy, or history, or science or one scale of ideas or another. Rather, Barad sees it as at play in the ever-changing traces of interactions across and within scales and entities. In physics,

166 Non-human histories and entanglement

the interactions of matter lead to trace patterns, such as the intersecting ripples that characterise diffraction. Barad's talk of ethics is peppered with references to diffraction, but her intent is not to see it used to suggest that our world is all patterns and thereby calculable. Understanding ethics, and any form of theory, she argues, means allowing yourself to be 'lured by curiosity, surprise, and wonder' ('When Two Hands Touch, How Close Are They?'). Life, she explains,

> whether organic or inorganic, animate or inanimate, is not an unfolding algorithm. Electrons, molecules, brittlestars, jellyfish, coral reefs, dogs, rocks, icebergs, plants, asteroids, snowflakes, and bees stray from all calculable paths, making leaps here and there, or rather, making here and there from leaps, shifting familiarly patterned practices, testing the waters of what might yet be/have been/could still have been, doing thought experiments with their very being.… Stepping into the void, opening to possibilities, straying, going out of bounds, off the beaten path—diverging and touching down again, swerving, and returning, not as consecutive moves, but as experiments in indeterminacy. Spinning off in any old direction is neither theorizing nor viable; it loses the thread, the touch of entangled beings (be)coming together-apart.
>
> ('When Two Hands Touch, How Close Are They?')

Barad's approach sees all entities engaged in thought experiments, turning, twisting and perturbating the habitual storylines that we humans like to make, including that in which we feature as the entity that has ethical responsibility for all other entities. Yet the above extract also sets boundaries for those perturbations. Spinning off and out of contact with other entities means a loss of ethics because it is a loss of what she calls 'response-ability' ('When Two Hands Touch, How Close Are They?'). Barad does not unpack the idea further, but we see enough in her claims to know that she would see histories of entities that are used to magnify the achievements and failings of humans as fruitless spinning off and as a spinning out of ethics.

It is possible to write a history of 'response-ability' that focuses on the intersecting ripples cast by the interactions of entities, at all kinds of spatio-temporal scales. This would respect Barad's claim that quantum physics is not just an analogical tool for understanding the world at the smallest of scales. Moreover, it would reinforce that ethics is not a tale once told, but as something that we experience without end. Yet as I noted above, it cannot all be quantum diffraction either, for this would bestow a relatively predictable, calculable plot upon history, the present, and the future. It is not only humans that can spin out from response-ability; subjects like physics can too. Barad is interested in the leaping and twisting of entities—their thought experiments—but how that might be understood highlights the limitations of her almost singular interest in looking to Western science to explain ethics and history.

Non-human histories and entanglement   **167**

Other explanatory options are available, as with the convergence of biological and computational research in studies of swarm intelligence. As Gerardo Beni has explained, the concept of a swarm is useful for understanding the outcomes that result from the activities of groups of both natural and artificial agents—like ants and chatbots—that are decentralised, relatively homogenous, not synchronised and not so large as to be dealt with via statistical averages and not so small as to be idiosyncratic ('From Swarm Intelligence to Swarm Robotics', p. 2). Moreover, they are 'stimergic' or indirectly coordinated through the environment without planning, intent or control. An example of stimergy is seen in ants marking paths with pheromones, with the most commonly taken or 'successful' paths having the strongest signals. This is because pheromones evaporate over time. The use of pheromones in this case supports swarm optimisation, a system which promotes the best way to do something (p. 2). Yet predictable optimisation can also make a group of entities susceptible to predators or—as was the case with the last chapter, entropy—so allowance for novel or unpredictable successes is also important. This would correspond to Barad's interest in entities leaping. When we consider the patterns of swarms, Beni notes, we have the potential, therefore, to see examples of both optimisation and intelligence (pp. 4–5). This is a potentially large area of research, as he explains:

> One group of problems is based on pattern formation: aggregation, self-organisation into a lattice, deployment of distributed antennas or distributed arrays of sensors, covering of areas, mapping of the environment, deployment of maps, creation of gradients, etc. A second group of problems focuses on some specific entity in the environment: goal searching, homing, finding the source of a chemical plume, foraging, prey retrieval, etc. And another group of problems deals with more complex group behaviour: cooperative transport, mining (stick picking), shepherding, flocking, containment of oil spills, etc. This, of course, is not an exhaustive list; other generic robotic tasks, such as obstacle avoidance and all terrain navigation, apply to swarms as well.
>
> (p. 8)

In the decades since Beni and Wang's first description of what the field of swarm robotics research might be, swarm computational research has burgeoned ('Swarm Intelligence in Cellular Robotic Systems'). Algorithms derived from the behaviour of, among other examples, ants, bees, dragonflies and fireflies have been used to design computer systems and to make and manage small groups of artificial agents, such as robots and drones.[22] In ant colony optimisation, for example, algorithms drive artificial ants through mathematical models to find the shortest or best solutions to problems, with those solutions progressively retained or rejected through cycles of comparison. Bee algorithms include the step of evaluating paths through the artificial equivalent of a waggle dance, whereas dragonfly and firefly algorithms model the interaction of these insects when seeking food and avoiding enemies.

Aspects of computational swarm research form part of what is called non-classical computing, which draws upon physical, chemical and biological processes to design algorithms and systems. DNA computing, for example, treats problems and solutions as base strands, and uses ideas of strand splitting, and recombination to design and perform algorithms.[23] So too research in plant growth, evolution, neurology and immunology has inspired the design of algorithms and systems and helped people to understand how systems may emerge or develop over time.[24] The advantages of these approaches, along with quantum computing, is that they provide alternatives to binary logic and to the serial processing of single problems or calculations at one time.[25]

Non-classical computational research is burgeoning, and yet ethics—and more specifically the ethics of history—has arguably not kept pace with its developments. It is not simply that we can cite the naturalistic fallacy and note that just because ants forage in particular ways—to take just one example—that computational processes ought to follow the same design principles. Nor does it mean that histories ought to be made using ant colony optimisation techniques. I say this knowing that it is possible to do this and that history makers may use this technique in the future if they are not doing so already. It is that there are so many naturalistic options available and that there is no relief from decisions about which ones are good, fair or just. This choice is not just one of species or processes but also one of scales: we can focus our attention on one ant, or on the interactions of an ant colony or an ant colony with the wider world.

The beauty of entanglement ethics is that it opens up possibilities for thinking about the world in different ways, including through different scales. Yet if the ethics of entanglement has a blind spot, it is humans, plural. As Mark Moffett has observed, you can use the term 'swarm' to describe human history, even though his use of the term is focused on the emergence of larger human groupings over time and not the ongoing impact of those 'swarms' on the natural environment.[26] That blind spot means that computational researchers may be unaware of the questions that history makers have raised about the collective culpability of humans, particularly in Holocaust histories and in histories of the Anthropocene.

Collective culpability for the Holocaust stands out as a strong example of where questions of scale and ethics intersect. Tim Mason has used the terms 'functionalism' and 'intentionalism' to characterise the tensions in research on the Holocaust.[27] Functionalist accounts seek to describe the social structures and forces and collective processes that explain the actions of individuals and groups. We could interpret this as Hegel's 'cunning of reason'—which we explored in Chapter 4—making a comeback. Intentionalist accounts, by contrast, seek to explore the motivations, decisions and designs of individuals. On first blush, this seems a useful way of thinking about the phenomena described in this chapter, with the functionalist approach better matching the interactions and swarms of entities, and the intentionalist account belonging to older notions of humans as isolated and exceptional entities. What examples of histories such as Christopher Browning's *The Path to Genocide* (1992) and *Ordinary Men* (2001) and Daniel Goldhagen's *Hitler's Willing Executioners* (1996) show us, however, is that functionalism and intentionalism are not dichotomous.[28] This is because while we might see social forces as driving the behaviour of groups of people, it does not excuse them from culpability. Nor are mature, fully formed intentions necessary for humans to act in ways that we would not describe as good, fair or just.

Rather, the distinctiveness of the Holocaust and human histories seems to turn on their *conceptual* nature and the implications that has for ethics. To explain this point, it is worth looking to Jeff Malpas' example of how we might think about a rat and human using a map. He writes,

> An important part of what distinguishes, for instance, my use of a topological survey map in exploring the countryside around my home from the role played by some 'cognitive map' in a rat's navigating a maze is that I grasp the map conceptually, *as* a map, and so *as* a representation of space.... And the map can thereby be used in an 'engaged' fashion, in relation to action, as well as in a more detached and even "theoretical" mode.[29]

On this account, abstraction is an important feature of humanity, and by extension, ethics, which we noted in the previous two chapters. Conversely, as Darren Chitty, Elizabeth Wanner, Rakhi Parmar and Peter Lewis argue, the performance of swarm computing improves when the decision making required by artificial ants is reduced heavily.[30] Humans possess conceptual capabilities like no other known entity. We use those capabilities as a gift to either to separate ourselves from the rest of the universe, or to such an extent that we create abstractions and categories that seem to halt time and history. More dangerously, it can blind us to the ongoing impacts of our actions as a swarm in the Anthropocene. Many of the writers in this chapter want us to let go of this sense of giftedness for two reasons. First, ants can show us how to write histories differently, and the age of histories made by artificial agents is arguably already with us. We are not the only history makers in town and thereby not the only makers of the ethics of history. Second, we are not that special as entities. Bacteria obliterated other entities long before us, and our blindness to our interconnections with the planet means that we do not understand it or our interactions with it.

Returning to Hobart

This brings me back to a dog. Not Winnie the kelpie in this case, but Bobby, as named in Emmanuel Levinas' 'The Name of a Dog, or Natural Rights', in *Difficult Freedom*. Levinas characterises Bobby as 'the last Kantian in Nazi Germany, without the brain needed to universalise maxims and drives.'[31] Bobby was incapable of abstraction, and thus of conceptualising ethics in the form of virtues, rules, maximal benefits or being humbled by others. Yet he came into Levinas' life when he was interned as a prisoner of war and reminded him that he was a delight. As Levinas writes, rather poignantly,

> And then, about halfway through our long captivity, for a few short weeks, before the sentinels chased him away, a wandering dog entered our lives. One day he came to meet this rabble as we returned under guard from work. He survived in some wild patch in the region of the camp. But we called him

Bobby, an exotic name, as one does with a cherished dog. He would appear at morning assembly and was waiting for us as we returned, jumping up and down and barking in delight. For him, there was no doubt that we were men.[32]

Bobby's interaction with the prisoners—his jumping up and down and barking in delight—showed Levinas that he was not the subhuman or part of a 'gang of apes' that his captors took him to be.[33] He was accorded dignity through joy. On one reading of the story, it seems logical to extend Levinas' infinite ethics to non-human animals' faces. It is as if Bobby has earned the right to be included in 'our' ethics. On another reading, however, we wonder how Levinas came to be in that camp and how it took a dog to show us the destructiveness wrought by our special sense of separation and its consequent categories.

In a similar vein, Deborah Bird Rose asks whether the angel of history is a dog.[34] In asking this question, Rose has in mind the Australian dingo, which is both protected and treated as a killer, and the philosopher Walter Benjamin, who took his own life when trying to escape from the Nazis. In the ninth thesis of his 'Philosophy of History', Benjamin writes,

A Klee painting named 'Angelus Novus' shows an angel looking as though he is about to move away from something he is fixedly contemplating. His eyes are staring, his mouth is open, his wings are spread. This is how one pictures the angel of history. His face is turned towards the past. Where we perceive a chain of events, he sees one single catastrophe which keeps piling wreckage upon wreckage and hurls it in front of his feet. The angel would like to stay, awaken the dead, and make whole what has been smashed. But a storm is blowing from Paradise; it has got caught in his wings with such violence that the angel can no longer close them. This storm irresistibly propels him into the future, to which his back is turned, while the pile of debris before him grows skyward. This storm is what we call progress.[35]

The dingo angel reveals history as our 'narcissistic mirror', a planetary colonising mission based on an 'utterly delusional *as if: as if* the others don't matter, *as if* there are no limits'. The planet is not ours to reject or to destroy because we are never apart from it. We are entangled with other entities, big and small. Rose imagines the dingo howling with grief at the relentless pain and destruction we have caused ourselves and our planet and as calling us back to a dynamic, living world of connectivity. We have lost history, but we have the chance to get it back.

Notes

1 Andrew Cohen, 'Contractarianism, Other-Regarding Attitudes, and the Moral Standing of Nonhuman Animals', *Journal of Applied Philosophy*, vol. 24(2), 2007, pp. 188–201.
2 See, for example, Martha Nussbaum, 'Beyond Compassion and Humanity: Justice for Nonhuman Animals', in *Frontiers of Justice: Disability, Nationality, Species Membership*, Cambridge, MA: Harvard University Press, 2006, pp. 325–407.

3 Peter Singer, *Animal Liberation*, 2/e, New York: New York Review of Books, 1990; and Peter Singer, *Practical Ethics*, Cambridge: Cambridge University Press, 1979, pp. 48–71.

4 Sedeer el-Showk, 'Neanderthal Clues to Brain Evolution', *Nature*, no. 571, 2019, pp. S10–11.

5 Rebecca Wragg Sykes, *Kindred: Neanderthal Life, Love, Death and Art*, London: Bloomsbury, 2020.

6 Joshua Specht, 'Commodity History and the Nature of Global Connection: Recent Developments', *Journal of Global History*, vol. 14(1), 2019, pp. 145–50. See also Timothy LeCain, *The Matter of History: How Things Create the Past*, Cambridge: Cambridge University Press, 2017.

7 Thomas Henry Huxley, *Evidence as to Man's Place in Nature*, London: Williams and Norgate, 1863, p. 57.

8 Will Durant and Ariel Durant, *The Lessons of History*, New York: Simon and Schuster, 1968, p. 17.

9 Joy McCann, *Wild Sea: A History of the Southern Ocean*, Kensington: NewSouth, 2018, p. 185.

10 Manuel De Landa, *A Thousand Years of Nonlinear History*, Cambridge, MA: MIT Press, 1997.

11 G. E. Moore, *Principa Ethica*, Cambridge: Cambridge University Press, 1993, §10.3

12 Martin Heidegger, *The Question Concerning Technology and Other Essays*, trans W. Lovitt, New York: Harper, 1977.

13 Sven Beckert and Dominic Sachsenmaier (eds), *Global History, Globally*, London: Bloomsbury, 2018, p. 5.

14 Alfred W. Crosby, *Ecological Imperialism: The Biological Expansion of Europe, 900–1900*, Cambridge: Cambridge University Press, 1986, p. 7.

15 Alfred W. Crosby, *Ecological Imperialism*, pp. 168–9. See also *The Columbian Exchange: Biological and Cultural Consequence of 1492*, Westport, CT: Greenwood, 1972, p. 73.

16 Melinda A. Zeder, 'The Domestication of Animals', *Journal of Anthropological Research*, 2012, vol. 68(2), pp. 161–90.

17 David Rindos, *The Origins of Agriculture: An Evolutionary Perspective*, Orlando, FL: Academic Press, 1984.

18 Lynn Sagan (née Margulis), 'On the Origin of Mitosing Cells', Journal of Theoretical Biology, vol. 14(3), 1967, pp. 225–74.

19 Heraclitus, *The Cosmic Fragments: A Critical Study*, trans. G. S. Kirk, Cambridge: Cambridge University Press, 1954.

20 See for example A. G. Manning, R. I. Khamikov, R. G. Dall and A. G. Truscott, 'Wheeler's Delayed-Choice Gedanken Experiment with a Single Atom', *Nature Physics*, vol. 11(7), 2015, pp. 539–42.

21 Don Eigler, 'From the Bottom Up: Building Things with Atoms', in *Nanotechnology*, G. Timp ed, New York: Springer, 1999, pp. 425–36.

22 For recent examples, see Aleem Akhtar, 'Evolution of Ant Colony Optimization: A Brief Literature Review', online at https://arxiv.org/abs/1908.08007, <accessed 17 December 2019>; Lydia Taw, Nishant Gurrapadi, Mariana Macedo, Marcos Oliveira, Diego Pinheiro, Carmelo Bastos-Filho and Ronaldo Menezes, 'Characterizing the Social Interactions in the Artificial Bee Colony Algorithm', online at https://arxiv.org/abs/1904.04203, <accessed 17 December 2019>; Bestoun S. Ahmed, 'Generating Pairwise Combinatorial Interaction Test Suites Using Single Objective Dragonfly Optimisation Algorithm', https://arxiv.org/abs/1905.06734, <accessed 19 December 2019>; and Nazeeh Ghatasheh, Hossam Faris, Ibrahim Aljarah, Rizik M. H. Al-Sayyed, 'Optimising Software Effort Estimation Models Using Firefly Algorithm', *Journal of Software Engineering and Applications*, vol. 8(3), 2015, pp. 133–42.

23 See for example Leonard M. Adelman, 'Molecular Computation of Solutions to Combinatorial Problems', *Science*, no. 266, 1994, pp. 1021–4.
24 See for example, Leandro de Castro and Jonathan Timmis, *Artificial Immune Systems and their Applications*, Berlin: Springer, 2002, Dipankar Dasgupta and Fernando Nino, *Immunological Computation: Theory and Applications*, Boca Raton, FL: Auerbach, 2008; David Goldberg, *Genetic Algorithms in Search, Optimisation and Machine Learning*, Boston, MA: Addison Wesley, 1998; Christopher Bishop, *Neural Networks for Pattern Recognition*, Oxford: Oxford University Press, 1995; John Koza, *Genetic Programming: On the Programming of Computers by Means of Natural Selection*, 2 vols, Cambridge, MA: MIT Press, 1992–4; Melanie Mitchell, *An Introduction to Genetic Algorithms*, Cambridge, MA: MIT Press, 1996; Przemyslaw Prusinkiewicz and Aristid Lindenmayer, *The Algorithmic Beauty of Plants*, Berlin: Springer, 1990; and David Rumelhart and James McClelland, *Parallel Distributed Processing*, Cambridge, MA: MIT Press, 1986.
25 On quantum computing, see, for example, Michael Nielson and Isaac Chuang, *Quantum Computation and Quantum Information*, Cambridge: Cambridge University Press, 2000.
26 Mark Moffatt, *The Human Swarm: How Our Societies Arise, Thrive, and Fall*, London: Head of Zeus, 2019.
27 Tim Mason, 'Intention and Explanation: A Current Controversy about the Interpretation of National Socialism', in *Nazism, Fascism and the Working Class*, ed. Jane Caplan, Cambridge: Cambridge University Press, 1995, pp. 212–30.
28 Christopher Browning, *The Path to Genocide: Essays on Launching the Final Solution*, Cambridge: Cambridge University Press, 1992; id., *Ordinary Men: Reserve Battalion 101 and the Final Solution in Poland*, New York: Harper, 1998; and Daniel Goldhagen, *Hitler's Willing Executioners: Ordinary Germans and the Holocaust*, New York: Vintage, 1996.
29 Jeff Malpas, *Place and Experience: A Philosophical Topography*, 2/e, Abingdon: Routledge, 2018, p. 59.
30 Darren Chitty, Elizabeth Warner, Rakhi Parmar and Peter Lewis, 'Can Bio-Inspired Swarm Algorithms Scale to Societal Problems?' preprint available at https://arxiv.org/abs/1905.08126v1 <accessed 2 January 2020>.
31 Emmanuel Levinas, 'The Name of a Dog, or Natural Rights', in *Difficult Freedom: Essays on Judaism*, Baltimore, MD: Johns Hopkins University Press, 1997, p. 153.
32 Emmanuel Levinas, 'The Name of a Dog, or Natural Rights', p. 153.
33 Emmanuel Levinas, 'The Name of a Dog, or Natural Rights', p. 153.
34 Deborah Bird Rose, *Wild Dog Dreaming: Love and Extinction*, Charlottesville: University of Virginia Press, 2011, pp. 81–95.
35 Walter Benjamin, 'Theses on the Philosophy of History', *Illuminations*, trans Harry Zohn, New York: Schocken Books, 1969, pp. 257–8.

Primary Texts

Karen Barad, *Meeting the Universe Halfway: Quantum Physics and the Entanglement of Matter and Meaning*, Durham, NC: Duke University Press, 2007.
Karen Barad, 'When Two Hands Touch, How Close Are They?: On Touching—The Inhuman That I Therefore Am', in *Power of Material/Politics of Materiality*, eds K. Stakemeier and S. Witzgall, Zurich: Diaphones, 2012, online at: https://www.diaphanes.de/titel/when-two-hands-touch-how-close-are-they-3075 <accessed October 11 2019>.
Sven Beckert, *Empire of Cotton: A Global History*, London: Vintage, New York, 2014.
Gerardo Beni, 'From Swarm Intelligence to Swarm Robotics', in *Swarm Robotics: Lecture Notes in Computer Science*, vol. 3342, eds E. Şahin and W. M. Spears, Springer, Berlin, Heidelberg, 2004, pp. 1–9.

Gerardo Beni and Jing Wang, 'Swarm Intelligence in Cellular Robotic Systems', in *Robots and Biological Systems: Towards a New Bionics?*, NATO ASI Series vol. 102, eds P. Dario, G. Sandini and P. Aebischer, Berlin: Springer, 1992, pp. 703–12.

Stephen Budiansky, *The Covenant of the Wild: Why Animals Chose Domestication*, New York: William Morrow, 1992a.

Stephen Budiansky, *The Covenant of the Wild: Why Animals Chose Domestication*, New York: William Morrow and Co., 1992b.

Donna J. Haraway, *Manifestly Haraway*, Minneapolis, MN: University of Minnesota Press, 2016.

Donna J. Haraway, *Modest_Witness@Second_Millennium. FemaleMan© Meets_OncoMouse™: Feminism and Technoscience*, New York: Routledge, 1997.

Mark Kurlansky, *Cod: A Biography of the Fish That Changed the World [1997]*, New York: Vintage, 1999.

Mark Kurlansky, *Paper: Paging through History*, New York: W. W. Norton, 2016.

Mark Kurlansky, *Salt: A World History [2002]*, London: Vintage, 2003.

Lynn Margulis and Dorion Sagan, *Microcosmos*, Berkeley, CA: University of California Press, 1986.

11

INDIGENOUS HISTORIES AND PLACE ETHICS

Written with Aunty Anne Martin

Jakelin Troy | Linda Tuhiwai Smith | Karin Amimoto Ingersoll | Sandra D. Styres | Deborah Bird Rose

NGUNNAWAL COUNTRY, CANBERRA, AUSTRALIA. Aunty Anne talks in circles. Big and little ones, beautiful and incomplete. They intersect and encircle past, present, herself and the world and me. They also leap, weave and ripple, sometimes plunging with the force of a muttonfish (Abalone) diver and sometimes dancing like fingers tracing the surface of tidal sands. The first time I heard her speak, I struggled to make sense. I searched for a linear order, a spatio-temporal scale to slide up and down, a before and an after, a cause, and its ethical effects. The shortest point between two lines. All the while, her laughing eyes and enfolding stories looped history around me, and she reeled me in. At this point, I began to see why she was called 'Aunty', a term of deep respect in Aboriginal Australia.

'Look down', she once told me as we flew over the landscape near Alice Springs. Scrubby bush, hills and rocks that bore the patterns of Australian Aboriginal dot paintings that I had looked at side on, on walls, for years. Dots telling dreaming stories of what it means to be a part of, and to nourish, Country—the place of an Aboriginal people—in ways that know no boundaries between past, present and future and between entities. Doing what is good, fair and just has no singular timestamp in Aboriginal Australia and no place for authority derived from distance or objective detachment. 'Look down', I remind myself every time I fly over the Country where she was raised—Gameygal, La Perouse on Gamay (Botany Bay) just south of Sydney, home of Anne, proud Yuin descendent, 'saltwater girl'—and I see the Bay this way and that, wind-whipped waves or none at all, curly sandy fringes, salty scrub and industrial parks, big skies that shimmer from blue to grey and back again. I begin to understand that I cannot see or hear Country once.

I do not speak with the authority of a teacher in this chapter. It is not just a matter of *daraya*, or making mistakes with my words, as might be said in one of the many Sydney languages that Jakelin Tory and so many others are working hard to nurture back to life (*The Sydney Language*, 1993, p. 74).[1] It is that I have so much yet to learn, and I know

DOI: 10.4324/9780429399992-11

Indigenous histories and place ethics **175**

that my learning is not a right. Knowing is not a matter of possession or dispossession. My hope is that, as Bruce Pascoe puts it in *Dark Emu*, you and I might tilt our heads just a little and see a new way of thinking about history and the ethics of history.[2]

Hello, my brother

As a school student, I was taught that there were no Aboriginal people where I lived. The Tasmanian Aborigines were past tense—history—the regrettable victims of the British 'colonisers' 'black line' from the 1820s which scooped the survivors of violence and disease up to Oyster Bay where they withered away like plants lacking the right soil. A few years later, when the story was overturned with the news that they were not history and that they had never gone away, I sensed deeply, for the first time, the hurt that my chosen discipline could inflict.

William E. H. Stanner called it a 'cult of disremembering' in a series of radio lectures from 1968.[3] He suggested that we needed to look out of a different historical window to appreciate Aboriginal experiences. It is not uncommon for people to use the analogy of a house or houses when they speak of history making or historiography, as Stanner did.[4] It is a handy analogy, but like the others in this book, it might hold back our understanding of the ethics of history. This is because inserting a window, like adding a room, does not generally rock a house to its foundations.

Aboriginal peoples do not organise history by time or chronology. Rather, as Aunty Anne tells it, history is about knowing the paths that will take you to the cockles or to the muttonfish. Sometimes you get there via shortcuts—cutting through the corner of the local school—and sometimes you take the long way round. Country, and more specifically care for Country by all of its connected entities, organises that history. I use the word 'history' because the stories told are neither timeless nor abstract. They are historical in at least two important senses, as I will explain in this chapter.

First, Aboriginal histories can include named historical figures. Some of these figures may be known to global audiences, but the manner in which they appear can breach conventional understandings of when and where they lived. Put in simple terms, individuals from different times and places can appear in the same history—and interact with one another—to underscore the knowledge that is needed to live well in a particular place. Two well-documented examples help to illuminate this point. The first is Paddy Wainburranga Fordham's painting and telling in Rembarrnga language of 'Too Many Captain Cooks'.[5] As he paints, Paddy tells the story of *Badaparr*, whom he tells us is Captain Cook. This Captain Cook lived millions of years ago and was a good custodian of Country. He fought the devil *Ngayang Lunji* and won. *Badaparr*/Cook threw the body of *Ngayang Lunji* down and created Sydney Harbour. Then, he tells us, millions of years later, other captain cooks turned up. These captain cooks were, and are, no good for Country, and there are too many of them. The story ends with us being told that 'we know only one Captain Cook', the one who cares for Country. By implication, the 'captain cooks'—European settlers—do not.

176 Indigenous histories and place ethics

The second example is the Ned Kelly/Captain Cook stories told by Mudburra man Hobbles Danayari and Kuwang man Big Mick Kankinang, which were recorded by Deborah Bird Rose (1946–2018) in the early 1980s. We recall Rose from the last chapter as asking us whether the angel of history is a dingo. Here is her transcript of Big Mick Kankinang's account of Ned Kelly and Captain Cook in English and Kriol from c.1983–4:

> This world been covered up. All the salt water every way. Two men came down from sky. Ned Kelly and Angelo [an angel]. Come down, get a boat, travel round that sea, salt water. Can't findem any bank. Those fellows travelling. This leaf been fall down. 'Hello! Green leaf here!' Twofellow still travelling la boat. They hit a high ridge. 'Hello! Pull up here.' Put em anchor. Go down [out of the boat] and stand up. 'What me and you gotta do?' 'We'll have to do something.' They been makem river, and salt water been go right back. That's for Ned Kelly and Angelo. Dry now, every way. Twofellow just walking now. Some bush blackfellow been go longa business [doing ceremony]. They come down. 'Hello! Some blackfellows there!'… Wyndham people look those two whitefellows: 'Oh, really different men. Different to we. We'll have to get em policemen.' Four policemen been come…. Twofellow get a gun and shoot four policemen la Wyndham…. Captain Cook been come down to Mendora [beach, in Darwin], gotta boat, from England they been come. Captain Cook come longa this land, longa Sydney Harbour. Good country him been look. Captain Cook shot and broke a leg for one fellow belonging to that country Sydney Harbour. Get a boat and going back again. Bring longa this country now horse and cattle. Captain Cook got a revolver…. Ned Kelly going back to England, Ned Kelly by himself now, he lose his mate. Ned Kelly got his throat cut. They bury him. Leave him. Sun go down, little bit dark now, he left this world. BOOOOOOOMMMMM! Go longa top. This world shaking. All the white men been shaking. They all been frightened!… He's not here now. He's finished from that salt water time. Him blackfellow, first blackfellow….
>
> ('Ned Kelly Died for Our Sins', p. 182)

In this blend of biblical, historical and Country sources, Ned Kelly—whom is more commonly known as an Australian bushranger who was hanged for killing policemen—appears as a Noah-like figure. He and his angel or angels engage in a shoot-out with the police, and he is taken back to England, where he has his throat cut. He is buried but rises up into the sky and is recognised as 'having law' or the ethics of knowing the relationships that connect and sustain Country. In the 1981 telling by Hobbles Daniari, Ned Kelly also teaches Aboriginal people how to cook damper, and he feeds the multitude ('Ned Kelly Died for Our Sins', p. 178).[6] Captain Cook, by contrast, is described as looking for good Country, possessing a weapon and shooting a man in the Country of Eora (Sydney Harbour). He does not have law.

Indigenous histories and place ethics **177**

The Ned Kelly and Captain Cook stories emphasise the synchronous, placemaking nature of Aboriginal histories. Aunty Anne's histories bear some of these features too: she moves between times and places as she recounts important things that she has learned. In one story she told me in early 2019, for example, she moved effortlessly from an account of the time when her grandfather was refused service when he went to buy her a fizzy drink, to her roamings over the beaches of the Bay to find cockles to eat. Discrimination separated her grandfather and her out and denied them access to food; being on Country brings the freedom to move and to seek nourishment and to nourish the environment in turn. The moment her grandfather told her he could not buy her a drink made her acutely aware of her identity and that her identity might mean not being treated fairly or justly. This was despite him being recognised as a dignified stalwart of the community. European notions of identity and colonising history separated her and her family out and broke her moving relationship to the places that nourish her.

Stanner describes histories of these kinds as taking place 'everywhen'.[7] Rose affirms this description, citing Tony Swain's work in documenting how the Walpiri people of the Northern Territory treated Adam, Moses and Jesus as contemporaneous ('Ned Kelly Died for Our Sins', p. 180).[8] I do not agree with this characterisation of Aboriginal histories entirely. Aboriginal histories are not told once. This is the second sense in which Aboriginal stories are histories. This second quality is not on account of a methodological or theoretical deficit. Rather, as Elizabeth Povinelli explains in her account of the history making of the Belyuen people,

> they are constantly finding 'stories'…during everyday hunting trips…. One such story recounts how a deceased man left five bright coloured pebbles lined up on a log for his widow to find while she was hunting sugarbag…. He put the five stones to let her know his desire that she and her five children continue camping at a nearby site. A story may be made up of more mundane origins, such as the antics of a day's fishing trip. But people muster all such events when evaluating 'who has the stories' for a place.[9]

History cannot be told once, secured, pinned down or possessed because the environment in which it is made is not static. The relationships of Country shift like the tidal sands of Gamay. Nor are these stories told by one person, although some people will be recognised for their wisdom. Moreover, they are told more than once because their listeners may need to learn different things about Country at different times. And they may not be listening, and they may not hear the first or even second time around. They are dynamic, personalised tellings which emphasise the importance of relationships between entities. Some knowledge is secret to some groups of tellers and listeners on account of its importance to Country; other knowledge is not shared because the auditor is not trusted. Different ethical principles move in and out of view in these tellings, but respect for all entities and the nourishing of Country persist as imperatives. I have never heard the same Aboriginal history told twice because the ethical message about caring for Country was adapted for me by its teller.

178 Indigenous histories and place ethics

Aboriginal histories are personalised considerations of Country, and they have been so for a long time. Long before we even contemplated ideas such as 'industry 5.0', which aim to usher in an age of personalisation across sectors such as healthcare, financial services, and education.[10] More specifically, Aboriginal histories are personalised considerations of *a* Country. The Australian Institute of Aboriginal and Torres Strait Islander Map of Indigenous Australia provides a powerful reminder that there are hundreds of larger-scale groups of people living on a patchwork of Countries.[11] Countries are not simple dotted lines on a map. This is because crossing into a Country is not a right; you have to be welcomed and offered protection on account of your perturbation of the relationships between entities.

I, like many Australians, have been welcomed into multiple Countries. Sometimes these take the form of ceremonies at the start of meetings or events. They are offered in accordance with a protocol framework, but they are never the same twice. They often include historical reflections on those who have cared for Country and taught their families to do the same. On other occasions, they take the form of seemingly more informal conversational exchanges. Once, for example, as Aunty Anne and I walked on to the shore of the Arafura Sea near Darwin, a group of Larrakia People walked down from the sand dunes. They saw us and stopped. A 'Hello, my brother' from Aunty Anne elicited a smile, a laugh and a welcome. I had no right to be there without that welcome, and I still recognise how important Aunty was in asking for us to have protection and how generously that gift of protection was given.

Aboriginal histories are also not 'everywhen' because they are articulated through around 120 living languages and hundreds of associated dialects. The structure and nature of those languages vary, some in ways that generate distinctive forms of history making. Directional term systems are a case in point. In languages such as Arrernte, Guugu Yimidhirr, Murrinhpatha and Kayardild, for example, you refer to objects using the equivalent of compass points—north, south-east and west—rather than relative terms such as left or right, or in front of or behind. Consequently, you do not, for example, talk of the past being behind you.[12] Rather, in the Dyirbal language, for example, you would speak of the past as vertically up and the future as vertically down. Languages may also suggest varying senses of tense: some talk of past, present and future; others of the future and the non-future; and still others of the past and the non-past.[13] Generally, these tenses are not assumed to have a figuratively linear relation to one another. Place and Country are the organisers. This can have the effect of it seeming that past, present and future phenomena are all synchronously present in a particular location, but the linguistic expression of that will be subtly different in different Countries. If you work to concepts of the future and the non-future, for example, your history making will not be the same as if you work to the past and the non-past. These approaches to knowledge challenge the idea that linear chronology is the one thing that history can hang its definitional hat upon.

The language of expressing care for Country is critical because it is also seen as part of the interconnected web of entities. Language does not sit on top of knowledge of the environment but is one with it. This holistic view of the role of language in Country is seen most acutely in the idea of 'singing up'. Singing up, as

Rose notes, is designed to give life in a particular Country 'a charge, a boost, a call of care and connection' (*Wild Dog Dreaming*, 2011, p. 62). This can be a literal boost to Country, as Walpiri and Anmatayerr women's songs about the collection and dispersion of edible seeds show.[14] But language is also seen as promoting health across an integrated range of medical, economic, social, expressive and environmental forms, for living and non-living entities.

Singing up the ethics of history

Stop a people from speaking their language, and you not only break their connection to Country; you also break history making and Country itself. What is good, fair and just cannot flourish. Aunty shares a photo of her brother playing the Australian musical instrument, the didgeridoo. Rainbow lorikeets sit on his head, his arms, his shoulders. They perch at his feet, some with tucked wings and some leaning into flight. The image is luminous, the sonorous breathing song captured in the ripple of feathers across the colour spectrum. He is gone now, one of too many young Aboriginal people who have taken their lives. Not seen, not heard—recognised as the subject but not the maker of histories.

I just want our children to live longer lives than us, a Ngunnawal Elder once told me and Aunty. He sounded so tired when he said it, as if it had been said so many times before. Yet he talked to me not as a doctor, or an economist or a policy maker. He knew I was a history maker, and he knew I had both capability and responsibility. He was not the Yali of Jared Diamond's *Guns, Germs and Steel*, who ushers in a tale of global inequality told on the terms of those who have the historiographical resources to make it.[15] Nor was he asking me to make a place for Aboriginal histories via archaeological, genetic or scientific extension, as might be read into Daniel Lord Smail's *On Deep History and the Brain* (2007) or David Christian's *Origin Story*.[16] The depth and richness of Aboriginal experiences over time can be seen with more focus in deep and big history, but we also have to question their 'housing' of history to ensure that ways Aboriginal history making are also seen.[17]

His words told me that recognition and respect are not just about health clinics, housing, meaningful work and public policy. They are about histories and about history makers. They are about teaching about Aboriginal history making in the same classes in which we speak of, for instance, Herodotus, Hegel, Noah Harari and Natalie Zemon Davis. They are about having the comfort and even courage to recognise that Aboriginal histories offer distinctive approaches to knowledge and that the views of ethics that they nurture might help us to think through the barriers that writers canvassed in this book put up between human and non-human animals, living and non-living entities and even organic and artificial entities.

A feather ruffles, the wind sends ripples over the tidal flats. Jakelin Troy, Ngarigu woman from the Snowy Mountains of New South Wales, flies across the world to accelerate the rematriation of the Sydney languages, including the language of Aunty Anne's family, as well as those stretching west and north of the central business district. Languages thought long dead. Her sources are the word lists, dictionaries and

180 Indigenous histories and place ethics

manuscripts of colonisers like Lieutenant William Dawes, which remain possessions in basements, shelves and displays of libraries, museums and institutes in places like London (*The Sydney Language*, p. 8). She also acknowledges, critically, that Aboriginal languages have death taboos which generate new vocabulary. When a person dies, you cannot use their name, and a new word must be found to express any item, place or concept their name expressed (*The Sydney Language*, p. 3). This means that the words—and thus the nature—of Aboriginal histories keep changing. History making is historicised. Troy, therefore, connects with Country to generate new words; she sings up language, history making and new senses of the holistic ethics of history. Troy is one of many people now singing up, hunting out word lists to restore the speaking links to Countries all across the Sydney region and thus to restore the health of all the region's entities.

When Aboriginal scholars put breath back into the Sydney languages, they do not just add a new form of history making to the 'house' or 'houses' of history. As Māori scholar Linda Tuhiwai also argues, they expose 'history', like the wider activity of 'research', as a process of knowledge making that too often exploits Indigenous peoples, their knowledges and their resources. Neither history nor research are innocent, distant academic exercises (*Decolonizing Methodologies*, pp. xi, 1). Each is an activity, she writes, 'that has something at stake and that occurs in a set of political and social conditions' (p. 5). More specifically, history is a word 'of emotion which draws attention to the thousands of ways in which [I]ndigenous languages, knowledges and cultures have been silenced or misrepresented, ridiculed or condemned in academic and popular discourses' (p. 21). History making thus has to be decolonised to be rewritten and re-righted (p. 29). That means, on her terms, critiquing at least nine assumptions made about history, including that it

- can be total, including all knowledge in a coherent whole;
- can be universal in expressing values for the globe;
- refers to one large chronology;
- tells the story of development;
- is about a self-actualising human subject;
- can be told in one coherent narrative;
- is an innocent discipline;
- is made from binary categories; and
- is patriarchal (pp. 31–2).

In sum, it means acknowledging that many of the ideas expressed in the name of the ethics of history in this book have played out in silencing, misrepresentation, ridicule and even condemnation (p. 21). We have to let go of the idea of an ethics of history, told for all space and time, if we are to return to the idea of a practical ethics. The ethics of history is embodied, spoken, in place and interconnected with all the entities of that place.

We might also need to challenge the idea of us writing the ethics of history through the linear movement up and down or across spatio-temporal scales. Writing on the land of the Six Nations of the Grand River Territory in Ontario, Canada, for example, Sandra Styres asks us to think of remembering, history, education and ethics as interconnected parts of a world that derives its power from circles (*Pathways for Remembering and Recognising Indigenous Thought in Education*, p. 30). Big ones and little ones that loop in a vision for the future, relationships, knowledge and action in time and place (p. 87). History is made and remade again and again to educate ourselves and the auditors of our stories. Circularity, in sum,

> allows for a research or curricular design that is culturally and epistemologically responsive and emergent according to shared themes and place-specific epistemologies.
>
> (p. 31)

In this dynamic vision of history, ethics is never completed, simple or of someone else's making. It is our responsibility, over and over again.

Styres looks to circular petrographs, to trees and to leaves to explain her argument for a dynamic vision of history and history education. On a different track of thought, Karin Amimoto Ingersoll argues that as a Kanaka Maoli (Hawaiian), she is more agile in the waves than on land (*Waves of Knowing*, p. 1). In the movement of water, she acknowledges a

> [s]eascape epistemology [that] organizes events and thoughts according to how they move and interact, while emphasizing the importance of knowing one's roots, one's centre, and where one is located in the constant movement…. The power of seascape epistemology lies in its organic nature, its inability to be mapped absolutely, and its required interaction with the intangible sea.
>
> (p. 6)

This means moving through theories, approaches to history making and understandings of the ethics of history, even when they feel like solid ground (p. 15). Movement is working through for yourself what you think the good, the fair and the just are, and therefore, movement is ethics (pp. 18, 3). The domain of seascape ethics is always shifting: tranquil and tumultuous, nurturing and deadly (p. 21). And you are always in it.

Niina Marni?

I can keep going and cite other examples from around the world of how Indigenous peoples have explained their ways of knowing and how the idea of history might be rewritten and re-righted as part of that. I can explain and theorise Aunty Anne's stories as radical, decolonising challenges to history making and ground her in an epistemology that follows the curves of shells, sand ripples and the gentle waves of Gamay. She is a magical history maker. But she calls me back and asks me to come and look at the fairy-wrens that live outside of her office. Their singing travels through me, leaving me unsure about where they are singing from, where I stop and where they begin. She is right there with the wrens and with me, not the subject of history, or an ethics framework, or an abstraction or a stereotype of an Aboriginal person living far away, talking in another language and producing cultural works for me to put on display. Hers is an ethics that pulls me back to histories that we make together, in circles, in the places where we are, where the boundary of 'we' is not prescribed.

The pandemic has broken my face-to-face connection with Aunty Anne, but we stay in touch using social media. Yet the ethics of history is still being made. I am now living in the Country of the Kaurna People of the Adelaide Plains, thousands of kilometres from Ngunnawal Country—the Country where Aunty taught me to think about history differently—and from her Gameygal birthplace and the Country of her Yuin ancestors. This Country is different: its language, trees, landscape, animals and organic forms are not the same. My understanding is shifting slowly, the fumblings of a learner finding my way.

In Kaurna, the greeting 'Niina marni' not only means 'How are you going?' It also means 'Where are you going?' The first time I meet the Elder Uncle Lewis, I tell him that I hear my name every time the greeting is used. Maybe the Country is calling you he says. It is, over and over again.

Notes

1 On the Sydney peoples, see http://visitsydneyaustralia.com.au/heritage-aboriginal-clans.html <accessed 20 February 2021>.
2 Bruce Pascoe, *Dark Emu*, Broome: Magabala Books, 2014.
3 W. E. H. Stanner, 'The Boyer Lectures: After the Dreaming', in *The Dreaming and Other Essays*, Collingwood: Black Inc, 2009, pp. 172–224.
4 See, for example, Anna Green and Kathleen Troup (eds), *The Houses of History: A Critical Reader in Twentieth-Century History and Theory*, New York: New York University Press, 1999; David Punter, Arundhati Roy and the House of History', in *Empire and the Gothic*, eds A. Smith and W. Hughes, Basingstoke: Palgrave, 2003, pp. 192–207; Patrick Joyce, 'The End of Social History?' *Social History*, vol. 20(1), 1995, pp. 73–91; and Ethan Kleinberg, *Haunting History: For a Deconstructive Approach to the Past*, Stanford: Stanford University Press, 2017, p. 27.
5 Paddy Wainburranga Fordham, *Too Many Captain Cooks* [painting], c.1989, which can be viewed online at: http://collections.anmm.gov.au/en/objects/details/31547/too-many-captain-cooks;jsessionid=398F9ABB3127794F11B204D6E65878B4 <accessed January 2021>; and *Too Many Captain Cooks* [film], director Penny McDonald, Ronin Films, 1989.
6 See also Deborah Bird Rose, 'Jesus and the Dingo', in *Aboriginal Australians and Christian Missions*, eds T. Swain and D. Rose, Bedford Park: Australian Association for the Study of Religions, 1988, pp. 370–1.
7 W. E. H. Stanner, *The Dreaming and Other Essays*.
8 See also Tony Swain, 'The Ghost of Space', Reflections on Walpiri Christian Iconography and Ritual', in *Aboriginal Australians and Christian Missions*, pp. 452–69.
9 Elizabeth Povinelli, *Labor's Lot: The Power, History and Culture of Aboriginal Action*, Chicago, IL: University of Chicago Press, 1993, p. 33.

10 See for example, Bruce Salgues, *Society 5.0: Industry of the Future, Technologies, Methods and Tools*, New York: Wiley, 2018.
11 The AIATSIS map of Indigenous Australia is available online at: https://aiatsis.gov.au/explore/map-indigenous-australia <accessed January 2021>.
12 Joe Blythe, Kinngirri Carmelita Mardigan, Mawurt Ernest Perdjert and Hwyel Stoakes, 'Pointing out Directions in Murrinhpatha', *Open Linguistics*, vo1 2(1), 2016, pp. 132–59; and Nicholas Evans, *Dying Words: Endangered Languages and What they Have to Tell Us*, New York: Wiley, 2010, p. 27.
13 Nicholas Evans, *Dying Words*, p. 41.
14 Georgia Curran, Linda Barwick, Myfany Turpin, Fiona Walsh and Mary Laughren, 'Central Australian Aboriginal Songs and Biocultural Knowledge: Evidence from Women's Ceremonies Relating to Edible Seeds', *Journal of Ethnobiology*, vol. 39(3), 2019, pp. 354–70.
15 Jared Diamond, *Guns, Germs and Steel*, New York: W. W. Norton, 1997.
16 Daniel Lord Smail, *On Deep History and the Brain*, Oakland: University of California Press, 2007; and David Christian, *Origin Story*, Harmondsworth: Penguin 2018.
17 The Research Centre for Deep History at the Australian National University, for example, is working to ensure that ways of Aboriginal history making are captured in a broader understanding of the past. See https://re.anu.edu.au/, <accessed 20 February 2021>.

Primary Texts

Karin Amimoto Ingersoll, *Waves of Knowing: A Seascape Epistemology*, Durham, NC: Duke University Press, 2016.
Deborah Bird Rose, 'Ned Kelly Died for Our Sins', *Oceania*, vol. 65(2), 1994, pp. 175–86.
Deborah Bird Rose, *Wild Dog Dreaming: Love and Extinction*, Charlottesville, VA: University of Virginia Press, 2011.
Linda Tuhiwai Smith, *Decolonizing Methodologies: Research and Indigenous Peoples*, London: Zed, 2012.
Sandra D. Styres, *Pathways for Remembering and Recognising Indigenous Thought in Education: Philosophies of Iethi'nihsténha Ohwentsia'kékha (Land)*, Toronto: University of Toronto Press, 2017.
Jakelin Troy, *The Sydney Language*, Canberra: Aboriginal Studies Press, 2019.

12

ONE ANGEL? SCALING THE ETHICS OF HISTORY

Does it take just one angel—Walter Benjamin's—to see human history as the shards of a single catastrophe? Or do we need Emmanuel Levinas' encounter with a single dog in a concentration camp to understand our inhumanity? Conversely, do we need to look back to the big bang—as David Christian implores us—to accept our role as planetary energy managers? Or should we split the idea of responsibility apart from that of accountability to make room for artificial agent history makers in the world imagined by Luciano Floridi?

Look to the codes of conduct for professional historical peak bodies for answers to these questions, and you will likely draw a blank.[1] These codes present the ethics of history as a matter of individual and professional responsibility to treat the past and other colleagues with honesty, care, fairness and dignity. Codes for the conduct of responsible research and ethics application protocols canvas much the same points, with a particular focus on the treatment of living persons with fairness and dignity.[2] These are all important points for practice, but as this book has shown, the ethics of history is a much broader, and bigger, matter than this.

Codes of conduct tend not to tell us whether they are unique ethical statements or whether they are adaptations or challenges to established ethical theories. As this book have suggested, there are multiple ethical theories for us to consider, not the one that Peter Singer argued for in *Practical Ethics*.[3] This point will come as no surprise to those who have a deep understanding of ethics, but it is new to suggest that the breadth and variety of views of the ethics of history might contribute to our understanding of ethics.

The argument of this book is that histories—plural—help us to understand Aristotle's important idea of ethics as developed through *ethos* and that *ethos* historicises ethics. Ethics, Aristotle tells us in the *Eudemian Ethics* and the *Nicomachean Ethics*, is practical, of our own making and imprecise.[4] Conversely, it is not abstract, not someone else's making and not precise. You cannot produce a theory or an ethics of history checklist to tell you what to do for all situations. You can take guidance

DOI: 10.4324/9780429399992-12

from a focus on virtues, maximising the good, or nourishing the interconnections between the human and the non-human world, for example, but you have to work through the ethical dilemmas and challenges of history making for yourself. And you will not always feel that you have succeeded in your attempts to act ethically. This idea of working through ethical questions is captured well in Aristotle's notion of *ethos*, the never-ending work of trying to live well. This is far from the idea of ethics as a subjective anything goes. Aristotle was interested in reasoning as the means of engaging in ethos, but it is also possible to understand that reasoning as Buddhist reflection or as singing up in Aboriginal Australia. Ethics is effort in and over time to live well. In order to understand ethics better, we can look at our own efforts in and over time and to the effort of others in and over time. Ethics as effort implies a temporal scale, but no particular temporal scale. Ethics implies history, without the temporal scale of that history set. It is not prescribed or precise.

Aristotle also offered the interesting idea of little and big goods. His argument is that the *you* engaged in *ethos* is both singular and plural. This means that the ethics of history concerns both the individual and collective effort of history makers in society. It is not personalist in the individual sense, and it is not restricted to those with professional training in history. In order to understand ethics better, we can look at our own efforts in or across space and to the efforts of others in or across space. Ethics as effort implies a spatial scale but no particular spatial scale. Ethics implies history, without the spatial scale of that history set. Like the temporal scales of history, the spatial scales of history are not prescribed or precise.

The implications of these seemingly simple ideas are profound for the ethics of history. They teach us not to expect a set size or scale for a history in or across time. We ought not expect that of the past of history making or the future of history making. The variety of histories within and across time indicates a sense of *ethos*. This is a diagnostic of the ethical health of history making. This is far from the world of hate history makers or deniers, whom I see as wanting to fix the past to a particular view or to denigrate or silence the efforts of particular groups who wish to explain the experiences of, say, the victims or survivors of acts of mass harm or genocide. It also means that we have to let go of the insistence that any one kind of history is best for understanding the past, including the insistence on particular models of historical training or forms of public expression. Microhistory, big history, national history or Netflix alone do not speak for the ethics of history. As the examples provided throughout this book have shown, you can see different ethical dilemmas and challenges at different scales, using different sources and different media. What you see with each of these kinds of histories does not lack for detail; they bring different issues into view. Moreover, as we have seen throughout this book, history makers switch scales. It is not as if history making is akin to a trolley problem in which we travel only one spatio-temporal track in order to do good by others. History making is far more nimble than that.

There is also no reason to exclude the possibility of histories made by artificial agents or to turn our back on the idea that we are just one part of an entangled universe. It is in the nature of *ethos* that we grapple with these possibilities. They are

186 Scaling the ethics of history

not future possibilities. They are with us now, and it is critical that history makers play a role in the design of policies, commercial decisions and digital systems that can shape the lived experiences and health of both human and non-human actors in the short and longer terms.

Not appreciating or explaining the ethics of history as *ethos* can make it hard for the audiences of histories to understand the nature and purposes of history making. I took it for granted ahead of writing this book that a world history can be either 44 volumes, or 29 pages long, or that a history can be about 13.8 billion years or one minute, or about the universe or one kind of bacterium. I now realise that I ought not have taken the varying sizes and scales of histories for granted. Without explanation, varying scales, like revisiting and revising, can be mistaken for a lack of rigour or a susceptibility towards capriciousness. Reading a code of conduct can make this confusion even worse: if history makers are so committed to the truth, it may be asked, why are there so many histories? The audiences of histories should know that working through the same body of sources can lead to different explanations on ethical grounds. Yes, Hayden White was right to highlight the idea of histories as stories, but he also saw those stories as shaped by ethical decisions.[5] I am concerned that our foregrounding of his ideas on narrative has meant that his views of the ethics of history have not garnered the attention they deserve. The same is true for so many other history makers. With attention, codes of conduct can reflect the importance of *ethos*, ethics permissions protocols might better fit with history making practices and history makers might understand even more how they contribute to making a better world.

These practical outcomes matter because the ethics of history—like ethics itself—is practical. The ethics of history is a wide field that deserves exploration. That exploration will not be apart from our daily lives. As the opening and ending of each of the chapters in this book have shown, everyday ethical decisions and challenges shape and are shaped by our understandings of history. This contributes to the dynamism of history making as *ethos*. I have not attempted to tell the story of the ethics of history for all times and places because I do not see that as possible. Like the history makers in this book, I have skipped, leapt and switched scales. I have engaged in the practice of *ethos*, and I am still working to understand how histories are connected to living well. I started with an understanding that histories often explain why other people are reluctant to speak, have no living relatives or engage in acts of violence. I am still learning—thanks to Aunty Anne Martin, that I have a role in nurturing the interconnections of Country. That work will not stop until I do, but others will continue on.

One angel, one dog, one death can make histories. But it also takes one universe, one swarm, one song, one endless cycle of retelling to appreciate that the size of history is no more and no less than every moment in which we decide and act for what is good, fair and just.

Notes

1 American Historical Association, 'Statement on Standards of Professional Conduct (2019)', online at: https://www.historians.org/jobs-and-professional-development/statements-standards-and-guidelines-of-the-discipline/statement-on-standards-of-professional-conduct <accessed 20 February, 2021>; Australian Historical Association, 'Code of Ethics', n.d., online at https://www.theaha.org.au/about-the-aha/aha-code-of-ethics/#:~:text=The%20Australian%20Historical%20Association%20(AHA,sexual%20orientation%2C%20and%20physical%20abilities <accessed 20 February, 2021>; Canadian Historical Association, 'Statement on Research Ethics', n.d., online at: https://cha-shc.ca/english/about-the-cha/statement-on-research-ethics.html <accessed 20 February, 2021>; and Royal Historical Society, 'Statement on Ethics', online at: https://royalhistsoc.org/rhs-statement-ethics/ <accessed 20 February 2021>.

2 See, for example, UK Research Integrity Office, *Code of Practice for Research*, September 2009, online at: http://ukrio.org/wp-content/uploads/UKRIO-Code-of-Practice-for-Research.pdf <accessed 27 February 2021>; European Science Foundation, *The European Code of Conduct for Research Integrity*, March 2011, online at: http://archives.esf.org/index.php?eID=tx_nawsecuredl&u=0&g=0&t=1614502500&hash=c9c6557043a3b6b869094975466f1a8698036897&file=/fileadmin/be_user/CEO_Unit/MO_FORA/MOFORUM_ResearchIntegrity/Code_Conduct_ResearchIntegrity.pdf <accessed 27 February 2021>; and The Australian Research Council, National Health and Medical Research Council and Universities Australia, *Australian Code for the Responsible Conduct of Research*, 2018, online at: <https://www.arc.gov.au/policies-strategies/policy/codes-and-guidelines>, accessed 27 February 2021.

3 Peter Singer, *Practical Ethics*, 3/e, Cambridge: Cambridge University Press, 2011.

4 Aristotle, *Eudemian Ethics*, trans B. Inwood and R. Woolf, Cambridge: Cambridge University Press, 2013; and id., *Nicomachean Ethics*, trans R. Crisp, Cambridge: Cambridge University Press, 2012.

5 See, for example, Hayden White, *The Content of the Form: Narrative Discourse and Historical Representation*, Baltimore, MD: Johns Hopkins University Press, 1990; and id., *Metahistory: The Historical Imagination in Nineteenth-Century Europe*, Baltimore, MD: Johns Hopkins University Press, 1975.

BIBLIOGRAPHY

!Mediengruppe Bitnik, 'Random Darknet Shopper', online at: https://www.bitnik.org/r/2/ <accessed 10 April 2019>.

9/11 Memorial and Museum Oral Histories, online at: https://www.911memorial.org/learn/resources/oral-histories <accessed January 2021>

9/11: The Falling Man [documentary], director Henry Singer, Reel Truth Documentaries, 2006, online at: https://www.youtube.com/watch?v=ME7oToyD9QE <accessed January 2021>.

Adelman, Leonard M., 'Molecular Computation of Solutions to Combinatorial Problems', *Science*, vol. 266, 1994, pp. 1021–4.

Ahmed, Bestoun S., 'Generating Pairwise Combinatorial Interaction Test Suites Using Single Objective Dragonfly Optimisation Algorithm', https://arxiv.org/abs/1905.06734, <accessed 19 December 2019>.

AIATSIS map of Indigenous Australia is available online at: https://aiatsis.gov.au/explore/map-indigenous-australia <accessed January 2021>.

Aikin, Lucy, *Epistles on Women, Exemplifying Their Character and Condition in Various Ages and Nations*, Boston: W. Wells and T. B. Wait, 1810.

Akhtar, Aleem, 'Evolution of Ant Colony Optimization: A Brief Literature Review', online at https://arxiv.org/abs/1908.08007, <accessed 17 December 2019>.

Allerdyce, Gilbert, 'Toward World History: American Historians and the Coming of the World History Course', in Ross E. Dunn, Laura J. Mitchell and Kerry Ward (eds), *The New World History: A Field Guide for Teachers and Researchers*, Berkeley: University of California Press, 2016, pp. 48–77.

Alonso-Núñez, Jonathan M., 'The Emergence of Universal Historiography from the 4th to the 2nd Centuries BC', in eds H. Verdin, G. Schepens and E. de Keyser, *Purposes of History in Greek Historiography from the Fourth to the Second Centuries BC*, Leuven: Orientaliste, 1990, pp. 173–92.

American Historical Association, 'Statement on Standards of Professional Conduct (2019)', online at: https://www.historians.org/jobs-and-professional-development/statements-standards-and-guidelines-of-the-discipline/statement-on-standards-of-professional-conduct <accessed 20 February 2021>.

Antonova, Kate Pickering, *The Essential Guide to Writing History Essays*, Oxford: Oxford University Press, 2020.

Appiah, Kwame Anthony, *As If: Ideals and Idealization*, Cambridge, MA: Harvard University Press, 2017.

Appiah, Kwame Anthony, *Cosmopolitanism: Ethics in a World of Strangers*, New York: W. W. Norton, 2007.

Appiah, Kwame Anthony, *The Lies That Bind: Rethinking Identity*, London: Profile, 2018.

Aristotle, *Categories*, in *The Complete Works of Aristotle* trans. J. L. Ackrill and ed. J. Barnes, Princeton, NJ: Princeton University Press, vol. 1, 2014a.

Aristotle, *Eudemian Ethics*, trans B. Inwood and R. Woolf, Cambridge: Cambridge University Press, 2013.

Aristotle, *Nicomachean Ethics*, 2/e, Cambridge: Cambridge University, 2014b.

Australian Historical Association, 'Code of Ethics', n.d., online at https://www.theaha.org. au/about-the-aha/aha-code-of-ethics/#:~:text=The%20Australian%20Historical%20 Association%20(AHA,sexual%20orientation%2C%20and%20physical%20abilities <accessed February 20 2021>.

Australian Research Council, National Health and Medical Research Council and Universities Australia, *Australian Code for the Responsible Conduct of Research*, 2018, online at: <https://www.arc.gov.au/policies-strategies/policy/codes-and-guidelines> accessed February 27 2021.

Azzouna, Nourane Ben, 'Rashīd al-Dīn Faḍl Allāh al-Hamadhānī's Manuscript Production Project in Tabriz Reconsidered', in *Politics, Patronage and the Transmission of Knowledge in 13th–15th Century Tabriz*, Leiden: Brill, pp. 187–200.

Band of Brothers, [miniseries], directors David Frankel, Tom Hanks, David Nutter, David Leland, Richard Loncraine, Phil Alden Robinson, Mikael Solomon, Tony To, HBO, 9 September 2001.

Band, D. C., 'The Critical Reception of English Neo-Hegelianism in Britain and America, 1914–1960', *Australian Journal of Politics and History*, vol. 26(2), 1980, pp. 228–41.

Barad, Karen, 'When Two Hands Touch, How Close Are They? On Touching—The Inhuman That I Therefore Am', in *Power of Material/Politics of Materiality*, eds K. Stakemeier and S. Witzgall, Zurich: Diaphones, 2012, online at: https://www.diaphanes.de/titel/when-two-hands-touch-how-close-are-they-3075 <accessed October 11 2019>.

Barad, Karen, *Meeting the Universe Halfway: Quantum Physics and the Entanglement of Matter and Meaning*, Durham, NC: Duke University Press, 2007.

Barclay, Linda, *Disability with Dignity: Justice, Human Rights and Equal Status*, Abingdon: Routledge, 2018.

Bartky, Elliot, 'Aristotle and the Politics of Herodotus's "History"', *The Review of Politics*, vol. 62(3), 2002, pp. 445–68.

Beck, Ingrid, *Die Ringkomposition bei Herodot und ihre Bedeutung für die Beweistechnik*, Hildesheim: Georg Olms, 1971.

Beckert, Sven and Sachsenmaier, Dominic (eds), *Global History, Globally*, London: Bloomsbury, 2018.

Beckert, Sven, *Empire of Cotton: A Global History*, London: Vintage, New York, 2014.

Beni, Gerardo and Wang, Jing, 'Swarm Intelligence in Cellular Robotic Systems', in *Robots and Biological Systems: Towards a New Bionics?*, NATO ASI Series vol. 102, eds P. Dario, G. Sandini and P. Aebischer, Berlin: Springer, 1992, pp. 703–12.

Beni, Gerardo, 'From Swarm Intelligence to Swarm Robotics', in *Swarm Robotics: Lecture Notes in Computer Science*, vol. 3342, eds E. Şahin and W. M. Spears, Springer, Berlin, Heidelberg, 2004, pp. 1–9.

Benjamin, Walter, '*Theses on the Philosophy of History', Illuminations*, trans Harry Zohn, New York: Schocken Books, 1969, pp. 253–64.

190 Bibliography

Bentham, Jeremy, *An Introduction to the Principles of Morals and Legislation [1823]*, Mineola, NY: Dover, 2007.

Bielenstein, Hans, *The Restoration of the Han Dynasty, with Prolegomena on the Historiography of the Hou Han Shu*, 2 vols, Göteborg: Elanders Boktryckeri Aktiebolag, vol. 1, 1953.

Bishop, Christopher, *Neural Networks for Pattern Recognition*, Oxford: Oxford University Press, 1995.

Blackhawk Down, [film], director Ridley Scott, Columbia Pictures, December 28, 2001.

Blythe, Joe, Mardigan, Kinngirri Carmelita, Perdjert, Mawurt Ernest and Stoakes, Hwyel, 'Pointing out Directions in Murrinhpatha', *Open Linguistics*, vol. 2(1), 2016, pp. 132–59.

Bode, Katherine, *A World of Fiction: Digital Collections and the Future of Literary History*, Ann Arbor: University of Michigan Press, 2018.

Boudonivia, *De vita santtae Radegundis liber II*, in *Sainted Women of the Dark Ages*, eds and trans Jo Ann McNamara, John E Halborg and E. Whatley, Durham, NC: Duke University Press, 1992, pp. 60–106.

Braudel, Fernand, *Capitalism and Material Life 1400–1800*, trans. M. Kochan, Glasgow: Fontana, 1974, revised edn, *Civilization and Capitalism 15th–18th Century*, 3 vols (*The Structures of Everyday Life, The Wheels of Commerce, The Perspective of the World*), trans. S. Reynolds, Glasgow: William Collins, 1981–92.

Braudel, Fernand, *On History*, trans. S. Matthews, Chicago, IL: University of Chicago Press, 1980.

Braudel, Fernand, *The Mediterranean and the Mediterranean World in the Age of Philip II*, [1949] 2 vols, trans. S. Reynolds, Glasgow: William Collins, 1972–3.

Brown, Tom, *Breaking the Fourth Wall: Direct Address in the Cinema*, Edinburgh: Edinburgh University Press, 2012.

Browning, Christopher, *Ordinary Men: Reserve Battalion 101 and the Final Solution in Poland*, New York: Harper, 1998.

Browning, Christopher, *The Path to Genocide: Essays on Launching the Final Solution*, Cambridge: Cambridge University Press, 1992.

Budiansky, Stephen, *The Covenant of the Wild: Why Animals Chose Domestication*, New York: William Morrow, 1992.

Bynum, Terrell Ward, 'Flourishing Ethics', *Ethics and Information Technology*, vol. 8(4), 2006, pp. 157–73.

Canadian Historical Association, 'Statement on Research Ethics', n.d., online at: https://cha-shc.ca/english/about-the-cha/statement-on-research-ethics.html <accessed February 20, 2021>.

Carr, David, and Makreel, Rudolf (eds), *The Ethics of History*, Evanston, IL: Northwestern University Press, 2004.

Cato and Varro, *On Agriculture*, Loeb Classical Library, Cambridge, MA: Harvard University Press, 1934.

Cherkasova, Evgenia, 'On the Boundary of Intelligibility: Kant's Conception of Radical Evil and the Limits of Ethical Discourse', *The Review of Metaphysics*, vol. 58(3), 2005, pp. 571–84.

Child, Arthur, 'Moral Judgement in History', *Ethics*, vol. 61(4), 1951, pp. 297–308.

Child, Lydia Maria, *Good Wives*, Boston: Carter, Hendee and Co, 1833.

Chitty, Darren, Warner, Elizabeth, Parmar, Rakhi and Lewis, Peter, 'Can Bio-Inspired Swarm Algorithms Scale to Societal Problems?' preprint available at https://arxiv.org/abs/1905.08126v1 <accessed 2 January 2020>.

Christian, David, 'History and Time', *Australian Journal of Politics and History*, vol. 57(3), 2011a, pp. 353–4.

Christian, David, *Maps of Time: An Introduction to Big History*, 2/e, Berkeley, CA: University of California Press, 2011b.

Christian, David, *Origin Story: A Big History of Everything*, Harmondsworth: Allen Lane, 2018.

Christian, David, *The History of the World in Eighteen Minutes* [TED Talk], 2011c, online at: https://www.ted.com/talks/david_christian_big_history?language=en <accessed April 3 2019>.

Christian, David, *This Fleeting World*, 2/e, Great Barrington, MA: Berkshire, 2019.

Chua, Lynnette J., *Mobilizing Gay Singapore*, Philadelphia, PA, 2014.

Clark, George Kitson, *The Critical Historian*, London: Routledge, 1967.

Clarke, Mary Cowden, *World-Noted Women; or Types of Womanly Attributes of All Lands and Ages*, New York: D. Appleton, 1858.

Cohen, Andrew, 'Contractarianism, Other-Regarding Attitudes, and the Moral Standing of Nonhuman Animals', *Journal of Applied Philosophy*, vol. 24(2), 2007, pp. 188–201.

Cohen, Thomas V., *Roman Tales: A Reader's Guide to the Art of Microhistory*, Abingdon: Routledge, 2019.

Collingwood, Robin George, 'The Rules of Life', in *Essays in Political Philosophy*, ed. David Boucher, Oxford: Oxford University Press, 1989, p. 174.

Collingwood, Robin George, *An Essay on Philosophical Method*, Oxford: Oxford University Press (1933), rev. edn, eds James Connelly and Giuseppina D'Oro, 2005.

Collingwood, Robin George, *Speculum Mentis*, Oxford: Oxford University Press, 1924.

Collingwood, Robin George, *The Idea of History*, rev. edn., ed. W. J. Van Der Dussen, Oxford: Oxford University Press, 1993.

Collingwood, Robin George, *The Idea of Nature*, Oxford: Oxford University Press, 1945.

Collingwood, Robin George, The New Leviathan, rev. edn., ed. David Boucher, Oxford: Oxford University Press, 1992.

Conrad, Sebastian, 'Enlightenment in World History: A Historiographical Critique', *American Historical Review*, vol. 117(4), 2012, pp. 999–1027.

Conrad, Sebastian and Osterhammel, Jürgen (eds), *A History of the World: An Emerging Modern World 1750–1870*, volume 4 of *A History of the World*, eds Jürgen Osterhammel and Akira Iriye, Cambridge, MA: Harvard University Press, 2018.

Conrad, *Sebastian Global Geschichte: Eine Einführung*, Munich: C. H. Beck, 2013.

Conrad, *Sebastian Globalisation and the Nation in Germany*, Cambridge: Cambridge University Press, 2010.

Conrad, Sebastian *What is Global History?*, Princeton, NJ: Princeton University Press, 2016.

Cooper, Anthony Ashley (Third Earl of Shaftsbury), *An Inquiry Into Virtue and Merit* [1699], in *Characteristicks of Men, Manners, Opinions, Times*, vol. 2, ed. Douglas den Uyl, Indianapolis, IN: Liberty Fund, 2001.

Crosby, Alfred W., *Children of the Sun: A History of Humanity's Unappeasable Appetite for Energy*, New York: W. W. Norton, 2007.

Crosby, Alfred W., *Ecological Imperialism: The Biological Expansion of Europe, 900–1900*, Cambridge: Cambridge University Press, 1986.

Crosby, Alfred W., *Germs, Seeds and Animals: Studies in Ecological World History*, London: M. E. Sharpe, 1994.

Crosby, Alfred W., *The Columbian Exchange: Biological and Cultural Consequences of 1492*, New York: Praeger, 1972.

Crossman, Samuel, *The young man's calling: or the whole duty of youth. In A serious and compassionate address to all young persons to remember their creator in the days of their youth. Together withrRemarks upon the lives of several excellent young persons of both sexes, as well ancient as modern, noble and others, who have been famous for piety and virtue in their generations. With twelve*

192 Bibliography

curious pictures, illustrating the several histories. Also Divine Poems, 7/e, London: Nathaniel Crouch, 1713.

Crouch, Nathaniel (pseud. Robert Burton), *The vanity of the life of man. Representing the seven several stages thereof, from his birth to his death. With pictures and poems, exposing the follies of every age. To which are added, several other poems upon divers subjects and occasions*, 5/e, London: A. Bettesworth and J. Batley, 1729.

Crouch, Nathaniel (pseud. Robert Burton), *Youth's divine pastime. In Two parts. Part I. Containing forty remarkable scripture histories, turn'd into English verse. With forty pictures proper to each story; very delightful for young persons, and to prevent vain and vicious divertisements. Also several scripture hymns upon various occasions*, 15/e, London: A. Battersworth and C. Hitch, 1732.

Crowell, Steven, 'Why Is Ethics First Philosophy?' *European Journal of Philosophy*, vol. 23(3), 2015, pp. 564–88.

Crutzen, Paul J. and Stoermer, Eugene F., 'The Anthropocene', *Global Change Newsletter*, vol. 41, 2000, pp. 17–18.

Crutzen, Paul J., 'Geology of Mankind', *Nature*, vol. 415 (January), 2002, p. 23.

Curran, Georgia, Barwick, Linda, Turpin, Myfany, Walsh, Fiona and Laughren, Mary, 'Central Australian Aboriginal Songs and Biocultural Knowledge: Evidence from Women's Ceremonies Relating to Edible Seeds', *Journal of Ethnobiology*, vol. 39(3), 2019, pp. 354–70.

Dasgupta, Dipankar and Nino, Fernando, *Immunological Computation: Theory and Applications*, Boca Raton, FL: Auerbach, 2008.

Davis, Bret, 'The Step Back through Nihilism: The Radical Orientation of Nishitani Keiji's Philosophy of Zen', *Synthesis Philosophica*, vol. 37, 2004, pp. 139–59.

Davis, Natalie Zemon, 'On the Lame', *American Historical Review*, vol. 93(3), 1988, pp. 572–603.

Davis, Natalie Zemon, *The Return of Martin Guerre*, Cambridge, MA: Harvard University Press, 1983.

Davis, Natalie Zemon, *Trickster Travels: In Search of Leo Africanus A Sixteenth-Century Muslim Between Worlds*, New York: Faber, 2006.

Davis, Natalie Zemon, *Women on the Margins: Three Seventeenth-Century Lives*, Cambridge, MA: Harvard University Press, 1995.

de Baets, Antoon, *Responsible History*, Oxford: Berghahn, 2009.

de Castro, Leandro and Timmis, Jonathan, *Artificial Immune Systems and their Applications*, Berlin: Springer, 2002.

De Grote Gebeurtenisse van de Geshiedenis [Dutch], Mijn Biblioteek vol. 12, Brussels: Franco-Suisse, c.1965–73.

de Jong, Irene D. F., 'Narrative Unity and Units', in *Companion to Herodotus*, eds E. J. Bakker, Irene J. F. de Jong and Hans van Wees, Leiden: Brill, pp. 245–66.

de Landa, Manuel, *A Thousand Years of Nonlinear History*, Brooklyn, NY: Zone, 1997.

de Larivière, Claire Judde, *The Revolt of Snowballs: Murano Confronts Venice, 1511*, trans Thomas V. Cohen, Abingdon: Routledge, 2018.

Derrida, Jacques, 'A Certain Impossible Possibility of Saying the Event', *Critical Inquiry*, vol. 33(2), 2007, pp. 441–61.

Derrida, Jacques, 'Autoimmunity: Real and Symbolic Suicides', in *Philosophy in a Time of Terror: Dialogues with Jürgen Habermas and Jacques Derrida*, Chicago, IL: University of Chicago Press, 2003, pp. 85–136.

Derrida, Jacques, *The Animal That Therefore I Am*, trans D. Wills, New York: Fordham University Press, 2008.

Desser, D., and Studies, G., 'Never Having to Say You Are Sorry: Rambo's Rewriting of the Vietnam War', *Film Quarterly*, vol. 42(1), 1988, pp. 9–16.

Diamond, Jared, *Collapse: How Societies Choose to Fail or to Succeed*, New York: Viking, 2005.

Diamond, Jared, *Guns, Germs and Steel*, New York: W. W. Norton, 1997a.

Diamond, Jared, *The Third Chimpanzee: The Evolution and Future of the Human Animal*, London: Hutchinson, 1991.

Diamond, Jared, *Why Is Sex Fun?: The Evolution of Human Sexuality*, New York: Basic Books, 1997b.

Dijkstra, Edsger W., 'The Humble Programmer', 1972 ACM Turing Award Lecture, *Communications of the ACM*, vol. 15(10), 1972, pp. 859–66, online at: https://amturing. acm.org/award_winners/dijkstra_1053701.cfm <accessed April 10 2019>.

Diop, Boubacar Boris, *Murambi, The Book of Bones*, trans F. McLaughlin, Bloomington, IN: Indiana University Press, 2006.

Drew, Richard, *The Falling Man [photographic sequence]*, Associated Press, 2001, online at: https://www.esquire.com/news-politics/a48031/the-falling-man-tom-junod/ <accessed January 2021>.

Duedahl, Paul, 'Selling Mankind: UNESCO and the Invention of Global History, 1945–1976', *Journal of World History*, vol. 22(1), 2011, pp. 101–33.

Dull, Jack, 'Marriage and Divorce in Han China: A Glimpse at "Pre-Confucian" Society Divorce in Traditional Chinese Law', in *Chinese Family Law and Social Change in Historical and Comparative Perspective*, ed. David Buxbaum, Seattle: University of Washington Press, 1978, pp. 23–74.

Durant, Will and Durant, Ariel, *The Lessons of History*, New York: Simon and Schuster, 1968.

Dworkin, Ronald, *Sovereign Virtue: The Theory and Practice of Equality*, Cambridge, MA: Harvard University Press, 2000.

Egan, Ronald C., 'The Prose Style of Fan Yeh', *Harvard Journal of Asiatic Studies*, vol. 39(2), 1979, p. 341.

Eigler, Don, 'From the Bottom Up: Building Things with Atoms', in *Nanotechnology*, G. Timp ed, New York: Springer, 1999, pp. 425–36.

el-Showk, Sedeer, 'Neanderthal Clues to Brain Evolution', *Nature*, vol. 571, 2019, pp. S10–S11.

Ellis, Sarah Stickney, *The Mothers of Great Men*, London: Richard Bentley, 1859.

European Science Foundation, *The European Code of Conduct for Research Integrity*, March 2011, online at: http://archives.esf.org/index.php?eID=tx_nawsecuredl&u=0&g=0&t=1614502500&hash=c9c6557043a3b6b869094975466f1a8698036897&file=/fileadmin/be_user/CEO_Unit/MO_FORA/MOFORUM_ResearchIntegrity/Code_Conduct_ResearchIntegrity.pdf <accessed February 27 2021>.

Eusebius, *Ecclesiastical History*, trans K. Lake and J. E. L. Oulton, Cambridge, MA: Harvard University Press, 2 vols, 1926–32.

Evans, Nicholas, *Dying Words: Endangered Languages and What They Have to Tell Us*, New York: Wiley, 2010.

Evans, Richard J., *Lying about Hitler: History, the Holocaust, and the David Irving Trial*, New York: Basic Books, 2001.

Fage, Mary, 'Fame's Rule [1637]', in *The Memory Arts in Renaissance England: A Critical Anthology*, Cambridge: Cambridge University Press, 2016, pp. 309–11.

Fan, Ye, *Hou Han shu* 84/74 2781-2806, as translated in 'Arrayed Traditions of Women (*Lienü zhuan*) from the Book of the Later Han (*Hou Han shu*)', partial translation by Ana Gonzalez, 'Strong Minds, Creative Lives: A Study of the Biographies of Eastern Han Women as Found in *Hou Han shu lienü zhuan*', Master's Thesis, McGill University, 2009.

Fan, Ye, 'Arrayed Traditions of Women (*Lienü zhuan*) from the Book of the Later Han (*Hou Han shu*)', partial translation by Ana Gonzalez, 'Strong Minds, Creative Lives: A Study of the Biographies of Eastern Han Women as Found in *Hou Han shu lienü zhuan*', Master's Thesis, McGill University, 2009, pp. 115–54, online at: http://digitool.library.mcgill.ca/webclient/StreamGate?folder_id=0&dvs=1546819652373~412 <accessed January 7 2019>.

194 Bibliography

Fan, Ye, *Through the Jade Gate: A Study of the Silk Roads 1st to 2nd Centuries CE*, 2 vols, 2/e, trans John E. Hill, Scotts Valley, CA: CreateSpace, 2015.

Fay, Brian (ed), *History and Theory: History and Ethics Theme Issue*, vol. 43(4), 2004.

Findlay, Robert, 'The Refashioning of Martin Guerre', *The American Historical Review*, vol. 93(3), 1988, p. 553–71.

Floridi, Luciano, 'Hyperhistory and the Philosophy of Information Policies', *Philosophy and Technology*, vol. 25(2), 2012, pp. 129–31.

Floridi, Luciano, 'The Method of Levels of Abstraction', *Minds and Machines*, vol. 18(3), 2008, pp. 303–29.

Floridi, Luciano, *The Ethics of Information*, Oxford: Oxford University Press, 2013.

Floridi, Luciano, *The Philosophy of Information*, Oxford: Oxford University Press, 2011.

Foer, John Safran, *Extremely Loud and Incredibly Close*, New York, NY: Houghton Mifflin, 2005.

Fordham, Paddy Wainburranga, *Too Many Captain Cooks [painting]*, c.1989, which can be viewed online at: http://collections.anmm.gov.au/en/objects/details/31547/too-many-captain-cooks;jsessionid=398F9ABB3127794F11B204D6E65878B4 <accessed January 2021>; and *Too Many Captain Cooks* [film], director Penny McDonald, Ronin Films, 1989.

Foucault, Michel, *The Order of Things: An Archaeology of the Human Sciences*, trans A. Sheridan, London: Pantheon, 1970.

Gadsby, Hannah, *Nanette* [recording of a live performance], Netflix, 2018.

Gauthier, David, *Moral Dealing: Contract, Ethics, and Reason*, Ithaca, NJ: Cornell University Press, 1990.

Gauthier, David, *Morals by Agreement*, Oxford: Oxford University Press, 1986.

Gera, D., *Warrior Women: The Anonymous Tractatus de Mulieribus*, Leiden: E. J. Brill, 1997.

Geyer, Michael and Bright, Charles, 'World History in a Global Age', *American Historical Review*, vol. 100(4), 1995, pp. 1034–60.

Ghatasheh, Nazeeh, Faris, Hossam, Aljarah, Ibrahim, and Al-Sayyed, Rizik M. H., 'Optimising Software Effort Estimation Models Using Firefly Algorithm', *Journal of Software Engineering and Applications*, vol. 8(3), 2015, pp. 133–42.

Gibson, Roy, 'Didactic Poetry as "Popular" Form: A Study of Imperatival Expressions in Latin Didactic Verse and Prose', in *Form and Content in Didactic Poetry*, Nottingham Classical Literature Studies, ed. Catherine Atherton, Bari: Levante, 1998, pp. 67–98.

Gilmartin, Kristine, 'A Rhetorical Figure in Latin Historical Style: The Imaginary Second Person Singular', *Transactions of the American Philological Association*, vol. 105, 1975, pp. 99–121.

Ginzburg, Carlo, 'Microhistory: Two or Three Things That I Know about It', *Critical Inquiry*, vol. 20(1), 1993, pp. 10–35.

Ginzburg, Carlo, *The Cheese and the Worms: The Cosmos of a Sixteenth-Century Miller*, trans John and Anne Tedeschi, Harmondsworth: Penguin, 1982.

Ginzburg, Carlo, *The Night Battles: Witchcraft and Agrarian Cults in the Sixteenth and Seventeenth Centuries*, 2/e, Baltimore, MD: John Hopkins University Press, 2013.

Goldberg, David, *Genetic Algorithms in Search, Optimisation and Machine Learning*, Boston, MA: Addison Wesley, 1998.

Goldhagen, Daniel, *Hitler's Willing Executioners: Ordinary Germans and the Holocaust*, New York: Vintage, 1996.

Gombrich, Ernst, *A Little History of the World*, trans. Caroline Mustill, New Haven: Yale University Press, [1936] 2005.

Gourevitch, Philip, *We Wish to Inform You That Tomorrow We Will Be Killed with Our Families*, New York: Farrar, Straus and Giroux, 1998.

Bibliography **195**

Graff, Garrett M., *The Only Plane in the Sky: The Oral History of 9/11*, London: Hatchette, 2019.

Gray, C., *Irving v. Penguin Books Limited, Deborah E. Lipstadt*, EWHC QB 115 (11 April 2000), online at: https://www.bailii.org/ew/cases/EWHC/QB/2000/115.html.

Green, A. and Troup, K. (eds), *The Houses of History: A Critical Reader in Twentieth-Century History and Theory*, New York: New York University Press, 1999.

Green, T. H., 'Faith', in *Works of Thomas Hill Green*, ed. R. L. Nettleship, London: Longmans, Green and Co, vol. 3, 1889, pp. 253–76.

Green, T. H., 'Metaphysic of Ethics, Moral Psychology, Sociology or the Sciences of Sittlichkeit [Late 1860s–1870]', in *Unpublished Manuscripts in British Idealism: Political Philosophy, Theology and Social Thought*, ed. Colin Tyler, vol. 1, Exeter: Imprint Academic, 2/e, 2008, pp. 14–71.

Green, T. H., *Lectures on the Principles of Political Obligation*, eds Paul Harris and John Morrow, Cambridge: Cambridge University Press, 1986.

Green, T. H., *Prolegomena to Ethics*, ed. David O. Brink, Oxford: Oxford University press, 2003.

Greene, Brian, *The Elegant Universe: Superstrings, Hidden Dimensions and the Quest for the Ultimate Theory*, New York: Norton, 1999.

Grosz, E. M., 'Nishida and the Historical World: An Examination of Active Intuition, the Body, and Time', *Comparative and Continental Philosophy*, vol. 6(2), 2014, pp. 143–57.

Groten, F. J., 'Herodotus' Use of Variant Versions', *Phoenix*, vol. 17(2), 1963, pp. 79–87.

Hajime, Tanabe, 'On Kant's Theory of Freedom', trans Takeshi Morisato and Cody Staton in *Comparative and Continental Philosophy*, vol. 5(2), 2013a, pp. 150–6.

Hajime, Tanabe, 'On the Universal', trans Takeshi Morisato and Timothy Burns in *Comparative and Continental Philosophy*, vol. 5(2), 2013b, pp. 124–49.

Hajime, Tanabe, 'Two Essays on Moral Freedom from the Early Works of Tanabe Hajime', *Comparative and Continental Philosophy*, vol. 8(2), 2016, pp. 144–59.

Hajime, Tanabe, *Philosophy as Metanoetics*, trans Takeuchi Yoshinori, Valdo Viglielmo and James W. Heisig, Berkeley, CA: University of California Press, 1987.

Hale, S. J., *Women's Record: Or, Sketches of All Distinguished Women, from "the Beginning" Till AD 1850*, New York: Harper and Brothers, 1853.

Hamilton, Clive and Grinevald, Jacques, 'Was the Anthropocene Anticipated?' *The Anthropocene Review*, vol. 2(1), 2015, pp. 59–72.

Harari, Yuval Noah, *Sapiens: A Brief History of Mankind*, London: Harvill Secker, 2014.

Haraway, Donna J., *Manifestly Haraway*, Minneapolis, MN: University of Minnesota Press, 2016.

Haraway, Donna J., *Modest_Witness@Second_Millennium. FemaleMan© Meets_OncoMouse™: Feminism and Technoscience*, New York: Routledge, 1997.

Hardy, Grant, *Worlds of Bronze and Bamboo: Sima Qian's Conquest of History*, New York: Columbia University Press, 1999.

Hatzfield, Jean, *Life Laid Bare: The Survivors in Rwanda Speak*, trans L. Coverdale, New York: Farrar, Straus and Giroux, 2006.

Hatzfield, Jean, *Machete Season: The Killers in Rwanda Speak*, trans L. Coverdale, New York: Farrar, Straus and Giroux, 2005.

Hatzfield, Jean, *The Antelope's Strategy: Living in Rwanda after the Genocide*, trans L. Coverdale, New York: Farrar, Straus and Giroux, 2009.

Hau, Lisa Irene, *Moral History from Herodotus to Diodorus Siculus*, Edinburgh: Edinburgh University Press, 2016.

Hawking, Stephen, *A Brief History of Time: From the Big Bang to Black Holes*, London: Bantam, 1988.

196 Bibliography

Hays, Mary, *Female Biography; or, Memoirs of Illustrious and Celebrated Women, of All Ages and Countries*, 6 vols, London: Richard Phillips, 1803.

Hegel, Georg Wilhelm Friedrich, *Elements of the Philosophy of Right*, trans H. B. Nisbet, ed. Allen W. Wood, Cambridge: Cambridge University Press, 1991.

Hegel, Georg Wilhelm Friedrich, *Philosophy of Nature*, ed. M. J. Petry, 3 vols, London: Routledge, 1970.

Hegel, Georg Wilhelm Friedrich, *The Philosophy of History*, trans John Sibree, New York: Dover, 2004.

Heidegger, Martin, *Aristotle's Metaphysics Θ 1–3* [1931], trans Walter Brogan and Peter Warnek, Bloomington, IL: Indiana University Press, 1995.

Heidegger, Martin, *Being and Time* [1953], trans Joan Stambaugh, New York, NY: State University of New York Press, 2010.

Heidegger, Martin, *Introduction to Metaphysics*, [1935] trans Gregory Fried and Richard Polt, 2/e, New Haven, CT: Yale University Press, 2014.

Heidegger, Martin, *Off the Beaten Track*, trans Julian Young and Kenneth Haynes, Cambridge: Cambridge University Press, 2002.

Heidegger, Martin, *The Question Concerning Technology and Other Essays*, trans W. Lovitt, New York: Harper, 1977.

Hein, David, and Sankoff, Irene, *Come from Away* [musical], La Jolla Playhouse and Seattle Repertory Company, 2015, official site online at: https://comefromaway.com/about.php <accessed January 2021>.

Heraclitus, *On the Universe*, trans W. H. S. Jones, Harvard: Harvard University Press, 1989.

Heraclitus, *The Cosmic Fragments: A Critical Study*, trans. G. S. Kirk, Cambridge: Cambridge University Press, 1954.

Herodotus, *The Histories*, 4 vols, trans. A. D. Godley, London: Heinemann, 1921–4.

Herrad of Hohenbourg, *Hortus Deliciarum*, eds and trans R. Green, M. Evans, C. Bischoff and M. Curschmann, London: Warbourg Institute, 1979.

Hine, Harry M., '"Discite… Agricolae": Modes of Instruction in Latin Prose Agricultural Writing from Cato to Pliny the Elder', *Classical Quarterly*, vol. 61(2), 2011, pp. 624–52.

Hobsbawm, Eric, *On History*, London: Wiedenfeld and Nicholson, 1997.

Hobsbawm, Eric, *The Age of Extremes: The Short Twentieth Century, 1914–1991*, London: Abacus, 1995.

Horne, Jackie C., *History and the Construction of the Child in Early British Children's Literature*, Abingdon: Routledge, 2011.

Howe, Peter, 'Richard Drew', *The Digital Journalist*, 2001, online at: http://digitaljournalist. org/issue0110/drew.htm <accessed January 2021>.

Hruschka, Joachim, 'The Greatest Happiness Principle and other Early German Anticipations of Utilitarian Theory', *Utilitas*, vol. 3(2), 1991, pp. 165–77.

Hughes-Warrington, Marnie, *'How Good an Historian Shall I Be?': R. G. Collingwood, the Historical Imagination and Education*, Thorverton: Imprint Academic, 2003.

Hughes-Warrington, Marnie, *History as Wonder: Beginning with Historiography*, Abingdon: Routledge, 2019.

Hume, David, *Enquiries Concerning Human Understanding and Concerning the Principles of Morals*, Oxford: Oxford University Press, [1748] 1995.

Hunt, Lynn, *Inventing Human Rights: A History*, New York: W. W. Norton, 2007.

Hutcheson, Francis, *Inquiry into the Original of our Ideas of Beauty and Virtue* [1725], 2/e, London: J. Darby, A. Bettesworth, F. Fayram, J. Permberton, C. Rivington, J. Hooke, F. Clay, J. Batley and E. Symon, 1726.

Huxley, Thomas Henry, *Evidence as to Man's Place in Nature*, London: Williams and Norgate, 1863.

Immerwahr, Henry R., *Form and Thought in Herodotus*, Cleveland: Western Reserve University Press for the American Philological Association, 1966.

Ingersoll, Karin Amimoto, *Waves of Knowing: A Seascape Epistemology*, Durham, NC: Duke University Press, 2016.

International Committee of Historical Sciences Constitution http://www.cish.org/index.php/en/presentation/constitution/ <accessed 20 April 2020>.

Inwood, Brad, and Woolf, Raphael, *Eudemian Ethics*, Cambridge: Cambridge University Press, 2013.

Jackson, Ian, 'Approaches to the History of Readers and Reading in Eighteenth-Century Britain', *The Historical Journal*, vol. 47(4), 2004, pp. 1041–54.

Jacobs, Julia, 'Doctor on Video Screen Told a Man He Was Near Death, Leaving Relatives Aghast', *New York Times*, 9 March 2019 <accessed April 10 2019>.

Jenkins, Keith, *Rethinking History*, London: Routledge, 1991.

Jeremiah, Edward T., *The Emergence of Reflexivity in Greek Language and Thought: From Homer to Plato*, Leiden: Brill, 2012.

Joyce, Patrick, 'The End of Social History?' *Social History*, vol. 20(1), 1995, pp. 73–91.

Jushin, Joshu, *The Recorded Sayings of Zen Master Joshu*, trans and ed. James Green, Walnut Creek, CA: Altamira, 1998.

Juvayni, Atâ-Malek, *Genghis Khan: The History of the World Conqueror*, trans J. A. Boyle, Manchester: Manchester University Press, 1998.

Kahn, Charles, *The Art and Thought of Heraclitus*, Cambridge: Cambridge University Press, 1979, p. 96.

Kamm, Frances M., *The Trolley Problem Mysteries*, Oxford: Oxford University Press, 2016.

Kant, Immanuel, 'Idee zu einer allgemeinen Geschichte in weltbürgerlicher Absicht', *Berlinische Monatsschrift*, 1784, pp. 385–411, online via http://gutenberg.spiegel.de/buch/idee-zu-einer-allgemeinen-geschichte-in-weltburgerlicher-absicht-3506/1 <accessed January 18 2019>.

Kant, Immanuel, *Kant's Idea for a Universal History with a Cosmopolitan Aim: A Critical Guide*, trans and eds Amélie Rorty and James Schmidt, Cambridge: Cambridge University Press, 2009.

Kant, Immanuel, *Practical Philosophy*, Cambridge edition of the works of Immanuel Kant, Cambridge: Cambridge University Press, 1999.

Kant, Immanuel, *Prolegomena to Any Future Metaphysics That Will Be Able to Come Forward as a Science*, trans and ed. Gary Hatfield, Cambridge: Cambridge University Press, 1997.

Keen, Ralph, 'Lucretius and his Reader', *Apeiron*, vol. 19(1), 1985, pp. 1–10.

Keiji, Nishitani, 'My Views on "Overcoming Modernity"', in *Overcoming Modernity: Cultural Identity in Wartime Japan*, trans and ed. Richard Calichman, New York: Columbia University Press, 2008, pp. 51–63.

Keiji, Nishitani, *Religion and Nothingness*, trans Jan Van Bragt, Berkeley, CA: University of California Press, 1982.

Keiji, Nishitani, *The Self-Overcoming of Nihilism*, trans Graham Parkes and Setsuko Aihara, New York: State University of New York Press, 1990.

Kisantal, Tamás, 'Review of *What Is Microhistory?*' *The Hungarian Historical Review*, vol. 4(2), 2015, pp. 512–7.

Kitarō, Nishida, *An Inquiry into the Good*, trans Masao Abe and Christopher Ives, New Haven, CT: Yale University Press, 1990.

198 Bibliography

Kitarō, Nishida, *Place and Dialectic: Two Essays*, trans John W. M. Krummel and Shigenori Nagatomo, Oxford: Oxford University Press, 2012b.

Kleinberg, Ethan, *Haunting History: For a Deconstructive Approach to the Past*, Stanford, CA: Stanford University Press, 2017.

Koza, John, *Genetic Programming: On the Programming of Computers by Means of Natural Selection*, 2 vols, Cambridge, MA: MIT Press, 1992–4.

Kurlansky, Mark, *Cod: A Biography of the Fish That Changed the World* [1997], New York: Vintage, 1999.

Kurlansky, Mark, *Paper: Paging through History*, New York: W. W. Norton, 2016.

Kurlansky, Mark, *Salt: A World History* [2002], London: Vintage, 2003.

Kuukkanen, Jouni-Matti, *Postnarrativist Philosophy of History*, Basingstoke: Palgrave Macmillan, 2015.

La Vita è Bella [*Life Is Beautiful*, film], director Roberto Benigni, Melampo Cinematografica, 1997.

Laertius, Diogenes, *Lives of Eminent Philosophers*, 2 vols, trans R. D. Hicks, Cambridge, MA: Harvard University Press, 1925.

LeCain, Timothy, *The Matter of History: How Things Create the Past*, Cambridge: Cambridge University Press, 2017.

Lehoux, Daryn, 'Seeing and Unseeing, Seen and Unseen', in *Lucretius: Poetry, Philosophy, Science*, eds D. Lehoux and A. D. Morrison, Oxford: Oxford University Press, 2013, pp. 131–52.

Levinas, Emmanuel, 'Humanism and An-Archy', in *Collected Philosophical Papers*. trans A. Lingis. Dordrecht: Martinus Nijhoff, 1987, pp. 127–40.

Levinas, Emmanuel, 'The Name of a Dog, or Natural Rights', in *Difficult Freedom: Essays on Judaism*, Baltimore, MD: Johns Hopkins University Press, 1997, p. 153.

Levinas, Emmanuel, *Basic Philosophical Writings*, eds A. T. Peperzak, S. Critchley and R. Bernasconi, Bloomington, IN: Indiana University Press, 1996.

Levinas, Emmanuel, *Otherwise than Being, or Beyond Essence*. trans A. Lingis, Pittsburgh, NJ: Duquesne University Press, 1998a.

Levinas, Emmanuel, *Totality and Infinity: An Essay on Exteriority*. trans. A. Linguis, Pittsburgh: Duquesnue University Press, 1998b.

Liu, Xiang, *Exemplary Women of Early China*, trans and ed. Anne Behnke Kinney, New York: Columbia University Press, 2014.

Locke, John, *Essays on the Law of Nature and Associated Writings*, ed. Wolfgang von Leyden, Oxford: Oxford University Press, 1954.

Locke, John, *Some Thoughts Concerning Education and of the Conduct of the Understanding*, eds Ruth W. Grant and Nathan Tarcov, Indianopolis, IN: Hackett, 1996.

Longinus, *On Great Writing (On the Sublime)*, trans. G. M. A. Grube, Indianapolis, IN: Hackett, 1991.

Lönnrot, Elias, *The Kalevala*, trans K. Bosley, Oxford: Oxford University Press, 1989.

Lowenthal, David, 'Origins of Anthropocene Awareness', *The Anthropocene Review*, vol. 3(1), 2016, pp. 52–63.

Lucian, 'How to Write History', in *Lucian*, trans K. Kilburn, vol. 6, Cambridge, MA: Harvard University Press, 1959.

Magnússon, Sigurður Gylfi and Szijártó, István M., *What Is Microhistory?: Theory and Practice*, Abingdon: Routledge, 2013.

Magnússon, Sigurður Gylfi, 'The Singularization of History: Social History and Microhistory within the Postmodern State of Knowledge', *Journal of Social History*, vol. 36(3), 2003, pp. 701–35.

Makin, Bathsua, *An Essay to Revive the Ancient Education of Gentlewomen in Religion, Manners, Arts and Tongues with an Answer to the Objections Against this Way of Education*, London: Thomas Pankhurst, 1673, online at: https://digital.library.upenn.edu/women/makin/education/education.html <accessed January 13 2019>.

Malpas, Jeff, *Place and Experience: A Philosophical Topography*, 2/e, Abingdon: Routledge, 2018.

Mandelbrote, Scott, 'The Bible and Didactic Literature in Early Modern England', in *Didactic Literature in England 1500–1800*, eds Natasha Glaisyer and Sara Pennell, Abingdon: Routledge, 2016, pp. 19–39.

Manne, Kate, *Down Girl*, Harmondsworth: Penguin, 2017; id., *Entitled*, Harmondsworth: Penguin, 2020.

Manning, A. G., Khamikov, R. I., Dall, R. G., and Truscott, A. G., 'Wheeler's Delayed-Choice Gedanken Experiment with a Single Atom', *Nature Physics*, vol. 11(7), 2015, pp. 539–42.

Margulis, Lynn and Sagan, Dorion, *Microcosmos*, Berkeley, CA: University of California Press, 1986.

Markovic, Daniel, *The Rhetoric of Explanation in De Rerum Natura*, Leiden: Brill, 2008.

Martin, Rex, 'Collingwood's *Essay on Metaphysics* and the three conclusions to *The Idea of Nature*', *British Journal for the History of Philosophy*, vol. 7(2), 1999, pp. 333–52.

Martineau, Harriet, *The Peasant and the Prince (the Playfellow)*, London: Charles Knight and Co, 1841.

Marx, Karl, 'Economic and Philosophic Manuscripts', in *Selected Writings*, ed. David McLellan, Oxford: Oxford University Press, 2/e, 2000, pp. 104–18.

Mason, Tim, 'Intention and Explanation: A Current Controversy about the Interpretation of National Socialism', in *Nazism, Fascism and the Working Class*, ed. Jane Caplan, Cambridge: Cambridge University Press, 1995, pp. 212–30.

Mazlish, Bruce, 'Global History to World History', *The Journal of Interdisciplinary History*, vol. 28(3), 1998, pp. 385–95.

Mazlish, Bruce, 'Terms', in *Palgrave Advances in World Histories*, ed. Marnie Hughes-Warrington, Basingstoke: Palgrave Macmillan, 2005, pp. 18–43.

McCann, Joy, *Wild Sea: A History of the Southern Ocean*, Kensington: NewSouth, 2018.

McNeill, John R., and McNeill, William H., *The Human Web: A Bird's Eye View of World History*, New York: W. W. Norton, 2004.

McNeill, John R., *Something New Under the Sun: An Environmental History of the Twentieth-Century World*, New York: W. W. Norton, 2000.

McNeill, William H., *The Rise of the West: A History of the Human Community*, Chicago, IL: University of Chicago Press, 1963.

Mill, James, *The History of British India*, London: Baldwin, Cradock and Joy, 1817.

Mill, John Stuart, *Utilitarianism, ed*. Roger Crisp, Oxford: Oxford University Press, 1998.

Miller, Patricia Cox, 'Strategies of Representation in Collective Biography: Constructing the Subject as Holy', in *Greek Biography and Panegyric in Late Antiquity*, eds Thomas Hägg and Philip Rousseau, Berkeley, CA: University of California Press, pp. 209–55.

Mills, Charles W., *The Racial Contract*, Ithaca, NJ: Cornell University Press, 1997.

Mitchell, Melanie, *An Introduction to Genetic Algorithms*, Cambridge, MA: MIT Press, 1996.

Mitsis, Phillip, 'Committing Philosophy on the Reader: Didactic Coercion and Reader Autonomy in De Rerum Natura', *Materiali e discussioni per l'analisi dei testi classici*, vol. 31, 1993, pp. 111–28.

Moffatt, Mark, *The Human Swarm: How Our Societies Arise, Thrive, and Fall*, London: Head of Zeus, 2019.

Monénembo, Tierno, *The Oldest Orphan*, trans M. F. Nagem, Lincoln, NE: University of Nebraska Press, 2004.

Moore, G. E., *Principa Ethica*, Cambridge: Cambridge University Press, 1993.

200 Bibliography

Morazé, Charles and Dumont, Georges-Henri (eds), *History of Humanity*, London: Routledge and UNESCO, 7 vols, 1994–2008.

Morrow, John, 'British Idealism, "German Philosophy" and the First World War', *Australian Journal of Politics and History*, vol. 28(3), 1982, pp. 380–90.

Mukagasana, Yolanda, *Not My Time to Die*, trans Z. Norridge, Kigali: Huza Press, 2019.

Mukasonga, Scholastique, *The Barefoot Woman*, trans J. Stump, Brooklyn, NY: Archipelago Books, 2018.

Myvold, Kristina and Parmenter, Dorina Miller (eds), *Miniature Books: The Format and Function of Tiny Religious Texts*, Sheffield: Equinox, 2019.

National Commission on Terrorist Attacks Upon the United States, *The 9/11 Commission Report*, online at: https://9-11commission.gov/report/ <accessed January 2021>.

Nehru, Jawaharlal, *Glimpses of World History*, 2 vols, Allahabad: Oxford University Press, 1934–5.

Newbery, John, *A Compendious History of the World from the Creation to the Dissolution of the Roman Republic, with a Continuation to the Peace of Amiens 1802*, London: Darton and Harvey, 1804.

Newbery, John, *A Little Pretty Pocket-Book, Intended for the Instruction and Amusement of Little Master Tommy, and Pretty Miss Polly: With Two Letters from Jack the Giant-Killer; as Also a Ball and Pincushion; The Use of which Will Infallibly Make Tommy a Good Boy, and Polly a Good Girl*, 10/e, London: F. Newbery, [1744] 1760.

Newbery, John, *The Holy Bible Abridged; or, the History of the Old and New Testament Illustrated with Notes, and Adorned with Cuts*, London: T. Carnan and F. Newbery, 4/e, [1764] 1775.

Nielson, Michael and Chuang, Isaac, *Quantum Computation and Quantum Information*, Cambridge: Cambridge University Press, 2000.

Nishida, Kitarō, 'Expressive Activity', [1925] and 'The Standpoint of Active Intuition' [1935], in *Ontology of Production: Three Essays*, trans William Haver, Durham, NC: Duke University Press, 2012a, pp. 35–63; and 64–113.

Nishida, Kitarō, 'The Historical Body', [1937] in *Sourcebook for Modern Japanese Philosophy: Selected Documents*, trans and eds David Dilworth, Valdo Viglielmo and Agustin Jacinto Zavala, Westport, CT: Greenwood, 1998, pp. 37–53.

Norton, Claire and Donnelly, Mark, *Liberating Histories*, Abingdon: Routledge, 2019.

Nussbaum, Martha C. *Frontiers of Justice: Disability, Nationality, Species Membership*, Cambridge, MA: Harvard University Press, 2006a.

Nussbaum, Martha C. *Women and Human Development: A Capabilities Approach*, Cambridge: Cambridge University Press, 2001.

Nussbaum, Martha C., 'Beyond Compassion and Humanity: Justice for Nonhuman Animals', in *Frontiers of Justice: Disability, Nationality, Species Membership*, Cambridge, MA: Harvard University Press, 2006b, pp. 325–407.

Nussbaum, Martha C., 'Mill Between Aristotle and Bentham', *Daedalus*, vol. 133(2), 2004, pp. 60–8.

O'Neill, Onora, *Constructions of Reason*, Cambridge: Cambridge University Press, 1989.

O'Neill, Onora, *Autonomy and Trust in Bioethics*, Cambridge: Cambridge University Press, 2002.

O'Neill, Onora, *Bounds of Justice*, Cambridge: Cambridge University Press, 2000.

O'Neill, Onora, *Constructing Authorities: Reason, Politics and Interpretations in Kant's Philosophy*, Cambridge, Cambridge University Press, 2015.

O'Neill, Onora, *Justice Across Boundaries: Whose Obligations?* Cambridge: Cambridge University Press, 2016.

Oldfield, Adrian, 'Moral Judgements in History', *History and Theory*, vol. 20(3), 1981, pp. 260–77.

Orosius, *Seven Books of History against the Pagans*, trans A. T. Fear, Liverpool: Liverpool University Press, 2010.

Osterhammel, Jürgen, *Globalization: A Short History*, Princeton, NJ: Princeton University Press, 2005.

Osterhammel, Jürgen, *The Transformation of the World: A Global History of the Nineteenth Century*, Princeton, NJ: Princeton University Press, 2014.

Osterhammel, Jürgen, *Unfabling the East: The Enlightenment's Encounter with Asia*, Princeton, NJ: Princeton University Press, 2018.

Pascoe, Bruce, *Dark Emu*, Broome: Magabala Books, 2014.

Pateman, Carole and Mills, Charles W., *Contract and Domination*, Cambridge: Polity, 2007.

Pateman, Carole, *The Sexual Contract*, Cambridge: Polity, 1988.

Pelras, Christian, *The Bugis*, Oxford: Blackwell, 1996.

Phillips, Mark Salber, *Society and Sentiment: Genres of Historical Writing in Britain, 1740–1820*, Princeton, NJ: Princeton University Press, 2000.

Philostratus, *Lives of the Sophists*, trans Wilmer C. Wright, Cambridge, MA: Harvard University Press, 1921.

Plato, *Euthydemus*, ed. E. H. Gifford, Cambridge: Cambridge University Press, 2013.

Plato, *Gorgias, Menexenus, Protagoras*, ed. M. Schofield, trans T. Griffith, Cambridge: Cambridge University Press, 2009.

Plato, *The Republic*, trans G. Griffith, Cambridge: Cambridge University Press, 2010.

Plotinus, *Ennead IV*, trans A. H. Armstrong, Loeb Classical Library, Cambridge: Harvard University Press, 1984.

Plutarch, 'On the Fame of the Athenians', in *Moralia*, trans. F. C. Babbitt, Cambridge, MA: Harvard University Press, 1936.

Plutarch, *Lives*, trans Bernadette Perrin, Cambridge, MA: Harvard University Press, 11 vols, 1914–26.

Plutarch, '*Mulierum Virtutes*', in *Moralia*, London: Heinemann, 1927–76.

Polybius, *The Histories*, 2 vols, trans E. S. Shuckburgh, intro. F. W. Walbank, Bloomington, IN: Indiana University Press, 1962.

Povinelli, Elizabeth, *Labor's Lot: The Power, History and Culture of Aboriginal Action*, Chicago, IL: University of Chicago Press, 1993.

Powell, J. E., *The History of Herodotus*, Cambridge: Cambridge University Press, 1939.

Power, Eileen and Power, Rhoda, *Boys and Girls of History*, Cambridge: Cambridge University Press, 1926–8.

Prusinkiewicz, Przemyslaw and Lindenmayer, Aristid, *The Algorithmic Beauty of Plants*, Berlin: Springer, 1990.

Punter, David, 'Arundhati Roy and the House of History', in *Empire and the Gothic*, eds A. Smith and W. Hughes, Basingstoke: Palgrave, 2003, pp. 192–207.

Ratzel, Friedrich, *The History of Mankind*, trans. A. J. Butler, 2/e, New York: Macmillan, 2 vols, 1897.

Rawls, John, *A Theory of Justice*, Cambridge, MA: Harvard University Press, 1971.

Read, Max, 'It Only Took a Day for Microsoft's "Teen" Chatbot to Become a Racist, Misogynist Holocaust Denier', *New York Intelligencer*, 24 March 2016, online at: http://nymag.com/intelligencer/2016/03/microsofts-teen-bot-is-denying-the-holocaust.html <accessed April 10 2019>.

Recanati, François, *Oratio Obliqua, Oratio Recta: An Essay on Metarepresentation*, Cambridge, MA: MIT Press, 2000.

Regele, Lindsay Schakenbach, 'Industrial Manifest Destiny: American Firearms Manufacturing and Antebellum Expansion', *Business History Review*, vol. 92, 2018, pp. 57–83.

Rindos, David, *The Origins of Agriculture: An Evolutionary Perspective*, Orlando, FL: Academic Press, 1984.

202 Bibliography

Robinson, Chase, *Islamic Historiography*, Cambridge: Cambridge University Press, 2002.

Rose, Deborah Bird, 'Jesus and the Dingo', in *Aboriginal Australians and Christian Missions*, eds T. Swain and D. Rose, Bedford Park: Australian Association for the Study of Religions, 1988, pp. 370–1.

Rose, Deborah Bird, 'Ned Kelly Died for Our Sins', *Oceania*, vol. 65(2), 1994, pp. 175–86.

Rose, Deborah Bird, *Wild Dog Dreaming: Love and Extinction*, Charlottesville, VA: University of Virginia Press, 2011.

Royal Historical Society, 'Statement on Ethics', online at: https://royalhistsoc.org/rhs-statement-ethics/ <accessed 20 February 2021>.

Rumelhar, David and McClelland, James, *Parallel Distributed Processing*, Cambridge, MA: MIT Press, 1986.

Sagan, Lynn (née Margulis), 'On the Origin of Mitosing Cells', *Journal of Theoretical Biology*, vol. 14(3), 1967, pp. 225–74.

Salgues, Bruce, *Society 5.0: Industry of the Future, Technologies, Methods and Tools*, New York: Wiley, 2018.

Santayana, George, *The Life of Reason: Reason in Common Sense*, New York: Scribner's, 1905.

Savran, Scott, *Arabs and Iranians in the Islamic Conquest Narrative: Memory and Identity Construction in Islamic Historiography, 750–1050*, Abingdon: Routledge, 2018.

Scott, Joan Wallach, *Gender and the Politics of History*, New York: Columbia University Press, 2/e, 1999.

Semple, Ellen Churchill, *Influences of Geographic Environment, on the Basis of Ratzel's System of Anthropo-Geography*, New York: Henry Holt, 1911.

Sen, Amartya, 'Rights and Agency', *Philosophy and Public Affairs*, vol. 11(1), 1982, pp. 3–39.

Sen, Amartya, *The Idea of Justice*, London: Allen Lane, 2009. September 11 Digital Archive, online at: https://911digitalarchive.org/about <accessed January 2021>.

Sharrock, Alison, '*Haud mollia iussa*', in *Form and Content in Didactic Poetry*, Nottingham Classical Literature Studies, ed. Catherine Atherton, Bari: Levante, 1998, pp. 99–115.

Siculus, Diodorus, *The Library of History*, trans C. H. Oldfather, C. L. Sherman, C. B. Welles, R. M. Geer and F. R. Walton, Cambridge, MA: Harvard University Press, 12 vols, 1933–67.

Silvers, Anita and Francis, Leslie Pickering, 'Justice through Trust: Disability and the "Outlier Problem" in Social Contract Theory', *Ethics*, vol. 116(1), 2005, pp. 40–76.

Sima Qian, *Records of the Grand Historian*, rev. edn, 3 vols, trans B. Watson, New York: Columbia University Press, 1993.

Singer, Peter, *Animal Liberation*, 2/e, New York: New York Review of Books, 1990.

Singer, Peter, *Practical Ethics*, 3/e, Cambridge: Cambridge University Press, 2011.

Sloterdijk, Peter, *Bubbles: Spheres volume 1*, trans. Wieland Hoban, Los Angeles: Semiotext(e), 2011.

Smail, Daniel Lord, *On Deep History and the Brain*, Oakland: University of California Press, 2007.

Small, Audrey, 'The Duty of Memory: A Solidarity of Voices after the Rwandan Genocide', *Paragraph*, vol. 30(1), 2007, pp. 85–100.

Smith, Adam, *The Theory of Moral Sentiments*, ed. Knud Haakonssen, Cambridge: Cambridge University Press, [1759] 2002.

Smith, Linda Tuhiwai, *Decolonizing Methodologies: Research and Indigenous Peoples*, London: Zed, 2012.

Sowenam, Ester and Sharp, Joane (pseuds), *Ester Hath Hang'd Haman, or an Answer to a Lewd Pamphlet, Entitled, The Arraignment of Women* [1617], pamphlet, online at http://www.luminarium.org/renascence-editions/ester.htm, <accessed January 13 2019>.

Specht, Joshua, 'Commodity History and the Nature of Global Connection: Recent Developments', *Journal of Global History*, vol. 14(1), 2019, pp. 145–50.

Speght, Rachel, *Mortalites Memorandum, with a Dream Prefixed, Imaginary in Manner, Real in Matter* [1621], pamphlet, online at http://www.luminarium.org/renascence-editions/ester.htm, <accessed January 13 2019>.

Stanner, W. E. H., 'The Boyer Lectures: After the Dreaming', in *The Dreaming and Other Essays*, Collingwood: Black Inc, 2009, pp. 172–224.

Stavrianos, Leften S., 'A Global Perspective in the Organization of World History', [1964] in *Teaching World History: A Resource Book*, ed. Heidi Roupp, New York: M. E. Sharpe, 1997, pp. 8–9.

Stavrianos, Leften S., Andrews, Loretta Kreider, Blanksten, George, Hackett, Roger F., Leppert, Ella C., Murphy, Paul L. and Smith, Lacey Baldwin, *A Global History of Man*, Boston: Allyn and Bacon, 1962.

Stavrianos, Leften S., *Balkan Federation: A History of the Movement Towards Balkan Unity in Modern Times*, Hamdon, CT: Archon, 1964.

Stavrianos, Leften S., *Lifelines from Our Past: A New World History*, New York: Pantheon, 1989.

Stavrianos, Leften S., *The Balkans 1815–1914*, New York: Rinehart and Winston, 1963.

Stavrianos, Leften S., *The Balkans since 1453*, New York: Reinhart, 1958.

Stavrianos, Leften S., *The Epic of Modern Man: A Collection of Readings*, Englewood Cliffs, NJ: Prentice-Hall, 1966a.

Stavrianos, Leften S., *The Ottoman Empire: Was It the Sick Man of Europe?* New York: Rinehart, 1957.

Stavrianos, Leften S., *The Promise of the Coming Dark Age*, San Francisco, CA: W. H. Freeman, 1976.

Stavrianos, Leften S., *The World Since 1500: A global History*, Englewood Cliffs, NJ: Prentice-Hall, 1966b.

Steffan, Will, Grinevald, J., Crutzen, Paul J., and McNeill, John R. 'The Anthropocene: Conceptual and Historical Perspective', *Philosophical Transactions of The Royal Society A: Mathematical, Physical and Engineering Sciences*, vol. 369, 2011, pp. 842–67.

Steffan, Will J., Crutzen, Paul J., and McNeill, John R. 'The Anthropocene: Are Humans Now Overwhelming the Great Forces of Nature?' *Ambio*, vol. 36(8), 2007, pp. 614–21.

Strickland, Agnes, *Historical Tales of Illustrious British Children*, London: N. Hailes, 1833.

Styres, Sandra D., *Pathways for Remembering and Recognising Indigenous Thought in Education: Philosophies of Iethi'nihsténha Ohwentsia'kékha (Land)*, Toronto: University of Toronto Press, 2017.

Swain, Tony, "The Ghost of Space', Reflections on Walpiri Christian Iconography and Ritual', in *Aboriginal Australians and Christian Missions: Ethnographic and Historical Studies*, eds T. Swain and D. B. Rose, Canberra: Australian Association for the Study of Religions, pp. 452–69.

Sykes, Rebecca Wragg, *Kindred: Neanderthal Life, Love, Death and Art*, London: Bloomsbury Books, 2020.

Ṭabīb, Rashīd al-Dīn, *Compendium of Chronicles: A History of the Mongols*, trans W. M. Thackston, Cambridge, MA: Harvard University Department of Near Eastern Languages and Civilizations, 1998, 2 vols.

Tadjo, Véronique, *The Shadow of Imana: Travels in the Heart of Rwanda*, trans V. Wakerley, Harlow: Heinemann, 2002.

Tagore, Rabindranath, 'Historicality in Literature', [1941] in *History at the Limit of World-History*, trans Ranajit Guha, New York: Columbia University Press, 2002, p. 97.

Taw, Lydia, Gurrapadi, Nishant, Macedo, Mariana, Oliveira, Marcos, Pinheiro, Diego, Bastos-Filho, Carmelo and Menezes, Ronaldo, 'Characterizing the Social Interactions in the Artificial Bee Colony Algorithm', online at https://arxiv.org/abs/1904.04203, <accessed 17 December 2019>.

204 Bibliography

Taylor, Jeffreys, *The Little Historians: A New Chronicle of the Affairs of England in Church and State, by Lewis and Paul: with Explanatory Remarks, and Additional Information upon Various Subjects Connected with the Progress of Civilization; also Some Account of Antiquities*, London: Baldwin, Cradock, and Joy, 1824.

Thomas, Rosalind, *Herodotus in Context: Ethnography, Science and the Art of Persuasion*, Oxford: Oxford University Press, 2000.

Thompson, E. P., 'The Moral Economy of the English Crowd in the Eighteenth Century', *Past and Present*, vol. 50, 1971, pp. 76–136.

Tjin, Thum Ping, Loh, Kah Seng, and Chia, Jack Meng-Tat (eds), *Living with Myths in Singapore*, Singapore: Ethos, 2017.

Tosh, John, *The Pursuit of History*, 5/e, London: Pearson, 2010, p. ix.

Trimmer, Sarah, *An Easy Introduction to the Knowledge of Nature, and Reading the Holy Scriptures. Adapted to the capacities of children*, 9/e, London: T. Longman, G. G. and J. Robinson, 1796.

Troy, Jakelin, *The Sydney Language*, Canberra: Aboriginal Studies Press, 2019.

UK Research Integrity Office, *Code of Practice for Research*, September 2009, online at: http://ukrio.org/wp-content/uploads/UKRIO-Code-of-Practice-for-Research.pdf <accessed February 27 2021>.

van Leeuwen, Jan, 'On Floridi's Method of Levels of Abstraction', *Minds and Machines*, vol. 24(5), 2014, pp. 5–17.

von Ranke, Leopold, 'On Progress in History (from the First Lecture to King Maximilian II of Bavaria, on the Epochs of Modern History)', [1854] in *The Theory and Practice of History*, trans Georg G. Iggers and Konrad von Moltke, Indianapolis, IN: Bobbs Merrill, 1973, p. 53.

Waberi, Abdourahman A., *Harvest of Skulls*, trans D. Thomas, Bloomington, IN: University of Indiana Press, 2016.

Wells, H. G., *The Outline of History*, London: George Newnes, 2 vols, 1920.

White, Hayden, *Metahistory: The Historical Imagination in Nineteenth-Century Europe*, Baltimore, MD: Johns Hopkins University Press, 1975.

White, Hayden, *The Content of the Form: Narrative Discourse and Historical Representation*, Baltimore, MD: Johns Hopkins University Press, 1990.

Wilkinson, Endymion, *Chinese History: A Manual*, 5/e, Harvard-Yenching Monograph Series, Cambridge, MA: Harvard University Asia Center, 2017.

Winchester, Simon, *Exactly: How Precision Engineers Created the Modern World*, London: Harper Collins, 2019.

Wittgenstein, Ludwig, *The Blue and the Brown Books*, Oxford: Blackwell, 1958.

Wong, Sophia Isako, 'Duties of Justice to Citizens with Cognitive Disabilities', *Metaphilosophy*, vol. 40(3–4), 2009, pp. 382–401.

Zeder, Melinda A., 'The Domestication of Animals', *Journal of Anthropological Research*, vol. 68(2), 2012, pp. 161–90.

Zuckoff, Mitchell, *Fall and Rise: The Story of 9/11*, New York: Harper Collins, 2019.

INDEX

Aikin, Lucy 34–7, 39, 137
Al-Farabi 22
Al-Kindī 22
Allerdyce, Gilbert 94
Alonso-Núñez, Jonathan 31
Al-Tabari, Abu Ja'far 12, 25
Al-Tha'alibi 24
American Historical Association 2
angel of history 170
animals, ethics and 89, 105, 127, 133, 154–70, 184
Anthropocene, ethics and 146
Antonova, Kate 2
Appiah, Kwame Anthony 90, 99, 151
Aristotle 4–8, 14–5, 30, 32, 62, 75–6, 81, 147, 184–7; on epics 11, 13; ethics as imprecise 5–8; ethics as practical 5; virtues 6
artificial agents 137; making history and 169, 185–7
Atâ-Malek Juvayni 13, 25–6, 136
Augustine of Hippo 12
Australian Aboriginal peoples 1, 73; history making by 174–82; languages and Countries of 178–9
Australian Historical Association 2
Averroes see Ibn Rushd
Avicenna see Ibn Sīna

bacteria, histories of 161–2
Ban Gu 12
Barad, Karen 156–7
Barclay, Linda 105

Beckert, Sven 155, 159
Beck, Ingrid 16
Beni, Gerardo 156–7
Benigni, Roberto 132
Benjamin, Walter 170, 184
Bentham, Jeremy 33
Bible 70–1; miniature or thumb Bibles 75–6
big history 136–52
biographies, collective 31–2, 34–43, 50
Bode, Katherine 137, 151–2
books: children's 78–9; miniature 67
bots 140
Boucher, David 60
Braudel, Fernand 137, 141–3
Bright, Charles 86
Browning, Christopher 168
Brown, Tom 66
Budiansky, Stephen 156, 160, 163

calculus, moral 33, 38, 47
Canadian First Nations Peoples: ethics of 180–1; histories by 180–1
Carr, David 2
categorical imperative 49
Cato the Elder 74
chatbots 140
Chen Shou 12
Child, Arthur 2
Child, Lydia Maria 38
children, ethics and 66–81
Chitty, Darren 169
Christian, David 136, 139, 146–7, 179, 184
Clarke, Mary Cowden 34, 37–8, 137

206 Index

Clark, George Kitson 2
Codes of conduct, ethics and 154, 186–7
Cohen, Andrew 105, 154
Cohen, Thomas V. 3
Collingwood, R. G. 31, 52–4, 56, 60–1, 81
Come from Away (musical) 123, 131–2
computing: non-classical 157, 167–70;
    object oriented 138–9
Conrad, Sebastian 86, 97–9
Cooper, Anthony Ashley 66; *see also* Third
    Earl of Shaftesbury
cosmopolitan ethics 50, 87–90
Croce, Benedetto 53–4
Crosby, Alfred 143–5, 160
Crossman, Samuel 77
Crouch, Nathaniel 77
Crutzen, Paul 146
cultural history 106–7
Cyborgs, ethics and 163–4

Danayari, Hobbles 176
Davis, Natalie Zemon 110–15
De Baets, Antoon 2
De Jong, Irene 16
De Landa, Manuel 159
deontological ethics or rule-based ethics
    48–9, 61–2
Derrida, Jacques 108, 132, 138
Desser, D. 112
Diamond, Jared 143–5, 179
didacticism, didactic texts 67
diffraction 156–7, 164–6
Diodous Siculus 13, 18–21, 136
Diogenes Laertius 31
Diop, Boubacar Boris 120, 123–5, 129, 132
disability, ethics and 105
distant history 150–2
Djikstra, Edsger 138–9
documentary film, ethics and 123, 130–1
Donnelly, Mark 108
Drew, Richard 123, 130–1, 133
Duedahl, Paul 96
Dumont, Georges-Henri 86
Dworkin, Ronald 90

Eigler, Don 165
Ellis, Sarah Strickney 34, 37–8, 137
empathy 90
entanglement ethics 156–7
entropy, ethics and 140–1, 147–9
environmental history 143, 158–70
Ethos 4–8, 14, 22, 27, 30, 32, 48, 52, 87, 116,
    119, 184–7
eudaimonia 14, 147–8

Eusebius of Caesarea 12, 21
Evans, Richard J. 4

Fage, Mary 39
Fan Ye 12, 39–40, 137
film, historical 112
Findlay, Robert 113–14
Finns Party (*Perussuomalaiset*) 11
Floridi, Luciano 137–40
Foer, John Safran 118
Fordham, Paddy Wainburranga 175
Foucault, Michel 112–13
Francis, Leslie 105
Franco-Suisse Cheese Company 67, 79–80
Frost, Robert 87
Fugan, Nansen 58

Gadsby, Hannah 131
Gandhi, Indira 70–1
Gauthier, David 104
genocide 62, 120
Gentile, Giovanni 53
Geyer, Michael 86
Gibson, Roy 73–4
Ginzburg, Carlo 106, 109–10
global history 86, 97–8, 137, 155
Goldhagen, Daniel 168
Gombrich, Ernst 65–7, 69–71
Gourevitch, Philip 124
Graff, Garrett 123, 129
Green, Thomas Hill 52–3
Grineveld, Jacques 146
Grosz, Elizabeth 57
Groten, F. J. 17

Hajime, Tanabe 52, 58–9
Hale, Sarah Josepha 38
Harari, Yuval 149
Haraway, Donna 156–7, 162–4
Hatzfield, Jean 124
Hau, Lisa 16
Hays, Mary 29, 37–8, 137
health, public, epidemiology 3
Hecateus of Miletus 13
Hegel, Georg Wilhelm Friedrich 50–2, 54,
    60–1, 90–3, 99–100
Heidegger, Martin 58, 118–19
Hein, David 123, 131–2
Heraclitus 15, 163
Herodotus 13, 15–8, 51
Herrad of Hohenbourg 39
Hill, John 39
Hine, Harry 74

histories: aggregation of 29–45, 50; big 136–52; Chinese 12, 38–42; chronological ordering 12; cultural 106–7; cyclical 22–3; distant 150–2; documentary film and 123; environmental 143–52; global 86, 94, 97–8, 155; hate 1; judgement of 2; microhistories 102–4, 137; musical 123; oral 123–4; photographic 123; professional associations 2, 154; responsibility and 2; slice 119–33; social 106–7; universal 12–5, 30; women's 34–5

history: as a discipline 3; film and 112; harm and 119; made by artificial agents 169–70, 185–7; narratives in 4, 114–15; parts and wholes in 30, 82; professional standards in 3

Hobbes, Thomas 104
Hobsbawm, Eric 11
holism 77, 81
Holocaust 168–9; denial of 4; oxgen holocaust and 148, 161–2
Homer 16
Horne, Jackie C. 66, 73
human rights 66, 79
Hume, David 66, 68
Hunt, Lynn 66
Hutcheson, Frances 32–3
Huxley, Thomas Henry 157
hyperhistory 137

Ibn Rushd (Averroes) 22
Ibn Sīna (Avicenna) 22
idealisations, ethics and 90
ignorance, veil of 104
Immerwahr, Henry 16
infinite ethics 120–1
information, ethics of 137–40, 149–51
Ingersoll, Karen Amimoto 181–2
Inwood, Brad 5
Isnāds 12, 23

Jenkins, Keith 108
Jeremiah, Edward 75
Josephus ben Matthias 12
Judde de Larivière, Claire 109–10, 115
Jushin, Joshu 58
Justice: global 87–90; trials and 112–15

Kahn, Charles 15
Kamm, Francis 128
Kanaka Maoli: ethics of 181–2; histories by 181–2
Kankinang, Big Mick 176

Kant, Immanuel 47–9, 52, 54, 57, 60–1, 88, 91–3, 104
Keen, Ralph 74
Keiji, Nishitani 52, 59–60
Kinney, Anne 42
Kitarō, Nishida 48, 52, 55–8
Kleinberg, Ethan 108
Kurlansky, Mark 155, 157–9
Kuukkanen, Jouni-Matti 108
Kyoto school of philosophy 54–5

La Vita è Bella (film) 132
League of Nations 90–1
LeCain, Timothy 155
Lehoux, Daryn 74
Leibniz, Gottfried Wilhelm 32
Levinas, Emmanuel 121–2, 124, 130–3, 169–70
Lewis, Peter 169
Liu Xiang 42–4, 137
Liu Zhiji 39
Locke, John 66, 75–6, 104
Longinus 74–5
Lönnrot, Elias 11–2, 27
Lucian 75
Lucretius 73–4

Magnússon, Sigurður Gylfi 102, 107–9
Makin, Bathsua 39
Makkreel, Rudolf 2
Manne, Kate 47
Māori matauranga or knowledges 65, 73, 180
Margulis, Lynn 148, 156, 161–2
Markovic, Daniel 74
Martineau, Harriet 66
Martin, Rex 60
Marx, Karl 52
Mayor, Frederico 96
Mazlish, Bruce 86
McNeill, John 137, 143–7
McNeill, William H. 137, 143–6
measurement 1, 165
metaphysics, history and 5
microhistories 102–16, 137
Miller, Patricia Cox 31
Mill, James 34
Mill, John Stuart 34
Misrule 102–3
Mitsis, Phillip 74
Moffett, Mark 168
Monénembo, Tierno 123–5, 129, 132
Moore, G. E. 159
Morazé, Charles 86, 96–8

208 Index

Mukagasana, Yolanda 124
Mukasonga, Scholastica 124
Multiscopic histories 103–4
musicals, ethics and 123

Nanette (comedy performance) 131
narrative 4; ring 16–7
naturalistic fallacy 159
nature, ethics and 55, 60–1, 67–8, 80
Neanderthals, human ethics and 140, 155
Nehru, Jawaharlal 70–1
Newbery, John 67, 77–80
Nihilism 60
non-human ethics 67–8, 89, 136–52, 154–70
Norton, Claire 108
novels, ethics and 66
Nussbaum, Martha 34, 89–90, 105, 154–5

objects, ethics and 68, 159
O'Brien, Lewis 182
Oldfield, Adrian 2
O'Neill, Onora 3, 86–9, 99
Oral histories 123–4
Osterhammel, Jürgen 98
Otto of Freising 12
Ovid 73

Parmar, Rakhi 169
Pascoe, Bruce 175
Pateman, Carol 105
patriarchy, ethics and 105–6
Paulus Orosius 13, 21–2, 40, 112, 136
periodisation 99
Phillips, Mark Salber 66, 73
Philostratus 31
photography, ethics and 123, 130–1, 133
Plato 4–5, 14
Plotinus 67
Plutarch 31–2, 39, 75
Polybius 31, 51, 75
post-human ethics *see* non-human ethics
Povinelli, Elizabeth 177
Power, Eileen 71–3
Power, Rhoda 71–3

race, ethics and 105–6
Rashīd al-Dīn Tabīb 13, 23–4, 136
Ratzel, Friedrich 92
Rawls, John 104–6, 115–16
responsibility 2
robots *see* artificial agents
Rose, Deborah Bird 170, 176–7
Rousseau, Jean Jacques 104

Royal Historical Association 2
Rwandan genocide, histories of 120, 123–7, 131

Sachsenmaier, Dominic 160
Sagan, Dorion 156, 161–2
Sankoff, Irene 123, 131–2
Savran, Scott 24
scale shifting 24–5, 48, 61–2, 66–7, 99, 103–4, 108, 113, 129, 132–3, 136, 143–4
Scott, Joan Wallach 108
Sedley, Joseph 70
Semple, Ellen Churchill 92
Sen, Amartya 89
Sentiment ethics 65–9
September 11, 2001, 118–20, 123, 127–32
Sharp, Joane 39
Sharrock, Alison 73
Silvers, Anita 105
Sima Guang 12
Sima Qian 12, 23, 39
Sima Tan 12
Singer, Henry 123, 130–1
Singer, Peter 8–9, 155, 184
slavery, ethics and 105–6
slice histories 119–33
Smail, Daniel Lord 179
Smith, Adam 66, 68, 80
Smith, Linda Tuhiwai 180
social contract ethics 104–6
social history 106–7
Sowernam, Ester 39
Specht, Joshua 155
Speght, Rachel 39
Stanner, William E. H. 175, 177
Stavrianos, Leften Stavros 85–6, 93–6, 98
Steffen, Will 146
Stoermer, Eugene 146
Strickland, Agnes 66
studies, G. 112
Styres, Sandra 181
Swain, Tony 177
Swarms, ethics and 157, 167–70
Sykes, Rebecca Wragg 140, 155
Sympathy 66–9, 74–5
Szijártó, István M. 103–4, 106–8

Tadjo, Veronique 123, 125–6, 129, 132, 154
Tagore, Rabindranath 58
Taylor, Jeffrey 66
Taylor, John 76–7
Thackerey, William 70
Third Earl of Shaftesbury 67, 80; *see also* Cooper, Anthony Ashley

Index **209**

Thomas, Rosalind 16
Thompson, E. P. 2
Thucydides 51, 122–3, 128
Tokens 80
Tosh, John 2
Toys 78–9
Trimmer, Sarah 80
Trolley problem, ethics and 128–31
Troy, Jakelin 174, 179–80

UNESCO history of humanity 86, 95–8
universal histories 12–5
Utilitarianism 32–4

Varro 73
vices 22
violence, histories of mass 122
virtues and virtue ethics 6, 12–5, 26–7, 30
Von Ranke, Leopold 57

Waberi, Abdourahman 123, 125–6, 129, 132, 154
Wang, Jin 156–7
Wanner, Elizabeth 169
Weever, John 76
Wells, H. G. 86, 90–3, 96
Western civilization, histories 92–3
White, Hayden 4, 114–15
Wills, Charles W. 105
Winchester, Simon 29
Wittgenstein, Ludwig 99
Women's history 34–5
Wong, Sophia 105
Woolf, Raphael 5

You, second person address 69–81

Zeder, Melinda 161
Zuckoff, Michael 123, 127–9

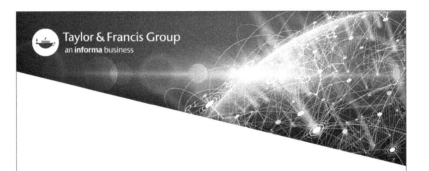